THE SIMPLE & SAVVY WINE GUIDE

THE SIMPLE & SAVVY
WINE GUIDE

BUYING, PAIRING, AND SHARING FOR ALL

LESLIE SBROCCO

wm

WILLIAM MORROW
An Imprint of HarperCollinsPublishers

HarperCollins books may be purchased for educational, business, or sales promotional use. For information please write: Special Markets Department, HarperCollins Publishers, 10 East 53rd Street, New York, NY 10022.

FIRST EDITION

Designed by Fritz Metsch

Title page photograph © Alexshebanov/Dreamstime.com

Library of Congress Cataloging-in-Publication Data

Sbrocco, Leslie, 1963–
   The simple & savvy wine guide: buying, pairing, and sharing for all / Leslie Sbrocco.
      p. cm.
   ISBN-13: 978-0-06-082833-2
   ISBN-10: 0-06-082833-1
   1. Wine and wine making.   I. Title.
TP548.S384 2006
641.2'2—dc22   2006043819

---

08 09 10 WBC/RRD 10 9 8 7 6 5 4 3

To my mother, Beverly, whose limitless strength, remarkable attitude, and selfless dedication to her family inspire me every day. I'm proud to call myself her daughter.

Contents

Acknowledgments

I was told by numerous authors that writing a second book is much easier than the first. Not true. Completing any book—whether it's your first or fiftieth—is a challenging task that requires long hours and laserlike focus. It also takes help.

To the many people who assisted me with this book, I'd like to say a heartfelt thank you.

First, to Cindy Guy. As my research assistant, tasting coordinator, and office manager extraordinaire, Cindy's work ethic is unmatched. Whether immediately answering my two A.M. fact-checking e-mails or thoughtfully bringing me coffee in the morning after a late work night, her loyalty, intelligence, and willingness to tackle any task made this book a reality. I simply call her "Cindy, the Great."

I thank my editor, Harriet Bell, at William Morrow/HarperCollins and my literary agent, Judith Riven, for their neverending support, wisdom, and friendship. Without them both my journey as an author would not have been possible. I am forever indebted.

Thanks to Lucy Baker, Milena Perez, Carrie Bachman, and the entire team at William Morrow for their patience and vision.

To Kate Jessup whose culinary talents are only matched by her effervescent personality and writing prowess. She helped me put together the "Wines with Food" section and I thank her for the brilliant input.

Gail Spangler has been an integral part of my business career since my days at the New York Times Company. Even though we now live a time zone apart, I'm fortunate to continue working with her on brand development, speaking, and marketing projects.

As powerhouse publicist on my first book, Kristen Green impressed me with her tremendous drive and talent. We have become close friends and I'm lucky enough to work with her again on this book.

I raise a glass and toast my wine industry colleagues and friends, including Linda Murphy, Tim McDonald, Terry Wheatley, Steve Burns, Andrew Freeman, Kechia Ley, Evan Goldstein, Anthony Dias Blue, Marco Cappelli, Judith Knudsen, Katrin Naelapaa, Robert Whitley, Tina Salter and Michael Isip of KQED television, the crew at Kimpton Hotel Group, and all the public relations professionals, fellow writers, winemakers, and vintners with whom I've traveled and worked. What a way to make a living. I am one lucky woman.

To Victor Fisher and Holly Seeler, Ani and Mike Larson, Annie and Franz Martins, Susan and Bob Bales, Lyn and Keith Romstad, Paula Lent, and Jack Martens, my friends and neighbors who toiled long hours drinking wine and testing recipes at my house. Tough job, guys.

Thanks to my husband, Leonard Sbrocco, the love of my life. He believes in me and puts up with me—a rare combination. To Rita Sbrocco, my beautiful mother-in-law who always comes to the rescue while I'm traveling. To the fabulous Sbrocco clan (Donald, Dennis, Maureen, and big Len) and the Hartleys (Lisa, Tom, Linde, and especially my warm and giving sister Lauren), I thank you for being there.

Finally, to my precious children, Dominic and Grace, for understanding that Mommy is an author. An award-winning writer herself, my daughter Grace recently jotted in her sixth grade journal, "Mom, when you weren't looking, I noticed how hard you work to finish all your writing projects. From that I have learned the meaning of dedication."

These words give me hope that I will inspire my kids to be their best, just as my mother continues to inspire me.

Introduction

During my first trip to the Mosel-Saar-Ruwer area of Germany, I met with one of the region's wine masters, Wilhelm Haag. As he greeted me in the small tasting room of the Fritz Haag winery, we walked by rows of empty bottles lined up on the floor. I asked enthusiastically if he had just had a large tasting. He said "No, a party." He proceeded to tell me about the food and the great wines his guests had enjoyed as we sat down to begin our formal tasting. Wilhelm was charming and informative. He regaled me with stories as we sampled dozens of awe-inspiring Rieslings, some older vintages, and other rare wines I'd never tasted before. I seriously tasted, spat, took notes, tasted, spat, took notes, and spat again into my small spittoon. When I was nearing the end of the series of wines, I glanced at Wilhelm's spit bucket and noticed it was completely empty. When I innocently asked him, "You're not spitting?" he replied with an impish grin on his face, "Oh yes I am, my dear, but because I love my wine so much I'm spitting backward!"

What I learned from that experience has stayed with me as a wine writer, communicator, and educator. Wine is fun, yet we often take it (and ourselves) too seriously. Wine is an information-intensive subject and takes never-ending study to become an authority, but you don't have to be an expert to buy and drink wine. Are you a computer or car expert when you head out to buy a new laptop or sedan? No, but you are informed. That's what this wine guide is meant to be: an easy-to-use book with suggestions for making informed buying decisions so you can enjoy your purchases to the fullest.

The unique organization and format addresses the questions I always get from regular wine consumers. Which wine goes best with burgers or pizza? Which bottle makes an impressive gift but won't break the bank? What are some great picks for parties or weddings? My most popular advice—whether dispensed in columns or in person—revolves around quick roundups of wine suggestions for various foods and moods.

From beginners to sophisticated buyers this book offers an innovative way to learn about and choose delicious wines, showing how simple it is to be wine-savvy.

How to Use This Book

In most wine-buying guides, entries are organized either alphabetically or by rating, grape variety, or region. This wine guide is arranged differently. Rather than an exhaustive study of wine regions and producers, I recommend lists of wines that work well in the context of everyday life.

Wines by Mood: Feeling adventurous? Kicking back on Saturday with friends? Planning a wedding? Proposing marriage? How about just relaxing in the tub with a glass? In this section you'll find suggestions for hot wine regions, sexy sippers, wedding winners, and much more.

Wines with Food: Wine belongs on the table with food, but that doesn't mean that the fare has to be fancy. Which wines pair well with burgers? Which ones make pizza taste even better (if that's possible)? Here you'll discover fun snack-food wine, dessert sweeties, and pasta-perfect wines, just to name a few.

Wines by Season: We cook with seasonal ingredients and buy clothes to match the weather outside, so why not think about wine the same way? My seasonal "wine wardrobe" is about light-as-air springtime sippers, refreshingly crisp summer wines, cashmere-like fall and winter wines, and favorites to toast the holidays.

Wines for a Reason: If you're seeking out kosher wines, bottles made organically, gift wines that impress for less, or those where the price tag doesn't matter, check out this section. There are star-studded brands made by celebrities, along with quirky wines and those with a story to tell.

Insider Wines: Increase your wine-savvy quotient by imbibing these must-have bottles. Think trendy producers that you might not know about or favorites to search for when dining out. What about a list of wines to try before you die? Uncover wines that overdeliver in quality, and those that have undergone a price makeover. Finally, my secret weapon wines are surefire picks that will introduce anyone to the joys of the grape.

Quick-Pick Guides: In the back pages of the book you can quickly scan all the recommended wines by style, price, region, and producer. Broaden your wine horizons by discovering wines with similar style profiles, new producers of varieties you like, and bargain bottles from unfamiliar regions.

Because this is a different and, I believe, more realistic way of looking at wine, here's a short instruction manual to getting the most from this book:

1. Start by scanning the general sections such as "Wines by Mood" or "Wines with Food," then focus on a list that's of particular interest to you.
2. Pay attention to the reasons I chose the particular wines. While you may or may not find the same wines at your local store, you'll get an idea of type and style to look for. At the beginning of each list I also refer you to other sections in the book that are relevant.
3. It would be impossible for me to list all recommended wines in every list. Therefore, if you find a wine that seems appealing go to the "Quick-Pick Guides" section in the back and scan for similar wines by style, type, or region.
4. All wines listed feature a Web site address and/or the importer name. In many cases, winery Web sites either can sell the wine directly to you, or tell you where you can buy it. The best general resource for locating a particular wine is www.wine-searcher.com. It's free and gives you stores and prices.

5. Feel free to make a tick mark next to interesting suggestions and create a personalized shopping list.

Peppered throughout the book are Cheat Sheets, Myth-busters, Wine ABCs, Design-a-Dinner ideas, and Quick Tips. Drink as deeply as you would like, or take a quick informational sip. Keep the book in your kitchen, your briefcase, or your car's glove compartment and refer to it regularly so you can find wines to enjoy on a daily basis.

WINE ABCS
Vintage

* * *

Vintage most commonly refers to the year that the grapes in a bottle of wine were harvested. However, you might hear terms such as "declaring a vintage" or "making a vintage bottling." These refer to Port and Champagne, which are traditionally made with blends of wines from various years. (On sparkling wine bottles you might notice NV, which stands for nonvintage, *or blends of vintages). However, in exceptionally fine growing years, Port producers will bottle "Vintage Port" from that year and Champagne houses often make special "Vintage-dated Champagne," which is labeled with that harvest year.*

Making the Cut

My job as a wine writer and educator is to taste thousands of wines each year and decide which ones are worthy of recommendation. I judge professional wine competitions, travel constantly to wine regions worldwide, and sample wines nightly in my home. For all the pleasure involved, wine tasting takes commitment and concentration. It's a tough job, but someone has to do it.

For wines to be included in this book, these are my criteria:

Good-to-Great Producers: I focus on wines and wineries that represent various styles, regions, and types well. A producer has to make consistently good wines over a number of years, which is why I don't include vintages. Also included are a number of promising newer labels/producers that I feel have staying power.

Deliver Value for the Price: Whether the price of a bottle is $10 or $100, any wine needs to deliver value. I offer a wide range of price options from bargains (less than $15) to classics ($15 to 30) and luxury wines (more than $30). NOTE: Pricing is one of the most difficult things to peg. Each wine has a suggested retail price, but in actuality pricing is vastly different across the country. I've seen the same wine double or triple in price across state lines! Therefore, I've listed a small price range for each wine—but use it as a general guideline.

Balance of Availability: I try to recommend wines that are generally available (though I offer suggestions on limited production wines, too). There's nothing more frustrating to a wine lover than reading about a bottle and not being able to find it. With that said, availability in every market is impossible to predict; this is why I list winery Web sites, because many of them identify outlets that sell their wines.

The whole point of the book is to share my knowledge and offer guidance so that you learn to trust your own palate. What matters most is not my opinion, but yours.

Your Personal Wine Style

Determining what you like (and dislike) is vital to learning about wine. My style profiles—a central theme in this book—help you do that. Once you identify style profiles of wines you enjoy, the door will open to discovering similar bottles. For example, if you like fresh, crisp whites, you can try New Zealand Sauvignon Blanc, dry Australian Riesling, and Italian Pinot Grigio. Those hankering for a smooth, juicy red can choose among Australian Shiraz, French Merlot, or Malbec from Argentina.

What exactly does it mean to talk about a wine's *style*? There is no one answer. Style can mean many things, from the basic types of wine such as sweet, sparkling, and fortified, to the overall style of a region. Oregon Pinot Noir can be described as "Burgundian" in style or Cabernet Sauvignon from Washington may be "Bordeaux-like." This refers to the notion that even though those wines aren't made in France's Burgundy or Bordeaux regions, they share similar aromas, flavors, and general characteristics. Usually individual producers also strive for a particular style for each wine type. One may craft a lighter, crisper style of white wine while another prides itself on a fuller, richer style.

NAME GAME CHEAT SHEET
What Wine Is Called
* * *

Reading a wine label can be confusing, but think of it in terms of two things: grape and place. In the New World—countries like America, Chile, New Zealand, and Australia—wines are named after their grape varieties, while wines from Old World European countries such as France, Spain, Portugal, and Italy are usually named for their region of origin. For example, Bordeaux and Champagne are regions in France, Rioja is a place in Spain, and Chianti is an Italian wine region.

In the Old World, winemakers discovered through centuries of trial and error that certain grape varieties grow well in certain places. Through a sort of "survival of the fittest," generation after generation of winegrowers honed in on the best grape varieties for their particular soil and climate. Now in most Old World countries only certain grape varieties are legally allowed to be planted in particular regions. Over time the grape has become synonymous with the place. Play the Name Game, and you'll be connecting the label dots in no time.

THE SAME GRAPE VARIETY CAN BE CALLED
BY A DIFFERENT NAME

Pinot Gris	=	Pinot Grigio
Shiraz	=	Syrah
Primitivo	=	Zinfandel

THE NAME GAME

GRAPES	=	PLACE
Chardonnay	=	white wines of Burgundy, France
Pinot Noir	=	red wines of Burgundy, France
Cabernet Sauvignon and Merlot (blended with other varieties such as Cabernet Franc, Malbec, and Petite Verdot)	=	red wines of Bordeaux, France
Sauvignon Blanc + Sémillon	=	white wines of Bordeaux, France
Sauvignon Blanc	=	Sancerre and Pouilly-Fumé regions of France's Loire Valley
Syrah	=	northern Rhône Valley reds
Viognier, Roussanne, and Marsanne	=	Rhône Valley whites from France
Sangiovese	=	the primary grape variety in red wines of Tuscany, Italy, especially those from the Chianti region
Nebbiolo	=	Barolo and Barbaresco wines of northern Italy
Tempranillo	=	red wines of Spain's Rioja, Ribera del Duero, and Toro regions

Start to think of wines not simply in terms of the grape variety they're made from, but also their overall style. Ultimately, that's what defines our preferences. For example, if you usually choose to drink Chardonnay because you are familiar with it, you're selecting wine simply according to grape variety. But there are many different expressions of Chardonnay. Do you prefer lighter, crisper versions, possibly from France? If so, you might enjoy other dry white wines of similar style such as Albariño from Spain, or Moschofilero from Greece. If creamy, buttery Chards are your ideal, you might want to sample wines made from Viognier grapes, as they are fuller-bodied and rich. It's about overall character and style, not just grape variety.

Identifying styles of wine you like helps save money and time in the store aisles, but it's also helpful when uncorking a bottle at mealtime. Don't worry about the outdated guideline of matching red wine with meat and white with fish; instead match lighter-styled wines with delicate dishes (think sleek Pinot Noir with salmon) and rich wines with heavier fare (Alsatian Gewurztraminer with hearty grilled sausages).

The Birth of Style

How does wine come by its style? The overall character of each individual wine is a combination of essentially three things:

What (grape variety) +
Where (place grapes are grown) +
Who (winemaking/producer)

=

STYLE PROFILE

A wine's style is influenced first by the grape variety used to make the wine. Just as varieties of apples look and taste different, so do grape varieties. For example, Chardonnay grapes taste different than Sauvignon Blanc and Cabernet Sauvignon grapes taste and look different than Zinfandel. But because grapes take on unique characteristics depending upon their environment, the final taste is also affected by where those grapes are grown. A region's climate, soil, and topography play crucial roles in determining the character of the grapes and ultimately the finished wine. Warmer climates generally produce fuller, softer, and riper wines, while wines made from grapes grown in cooler climates tend to sport a lighter, brighter quality.

CHEAT SHEET
Crush Me, Squeeze Me, Make Me Wine
* * *

To understand the winemaking process let's start in the vineyard with grapes used for making dry red table wine. During the summer, grape bunches will bask in the sun and develop into sweet, juice-filled berries. In the fall, when berries reach their optimum percentage of sugar (about 22 to 25 percent), they'll be picked, brought to the winery, and then tossed into a crusher/stemmer where the skins of the fruit gently break and the sugary juice inside is released.

ATTACK OF THE KILLER YEAST

All juice, whether from red grapes or white, is pale in color. To make white wine, the juice is immediately separated from the grape skins, thereby retaining the pale color. Red wine, on the other hand, gets its purple color and mouth-puckering tannins from soaking with the deeply-hued grape skins during fermentation. Once the red grapes are crushed, the mixture of juice and skins are put into tanks. The winemaker then adds yeast, which begins to eat the sugar in the juice and convert it to alcohol. When all the sugar is consumed the yeast die in a happy state of intoxication, and the juice is now red wine.

ROLL OUT THE BARREL

At this point, the wine may be put into oak barrels to age. Which kind of oak barrel to use—American or

French—and what percentage of those barrels will be new oak (they impart the most oak flavoring into the wine) is up to each winemaker. Red wine, and some white wines, will undergo a secondary fermentation known as malolactic fermentation. This is when the tangy malic acid in wine (the kind in tart apples) is converted to softer lactic acid (the kind in dairy products—think a big, buttery Chardonnay). After aging, the wine will be bottled and brought to a store or restaurant near you.

Why? Think sun. As grapes ripen they produce sugar, and during the winemaking process that sugar is converted into alcohol through fermentation. Warmer climates tend to produce grapes with loads of sugar, so if there is more sugar, there's more alcohol, which translates into a more full-bodied wine. Conversely, in regions with cooler weather sugar levels generally don't get as high, which means the wine is ultimately lower in alcohol and generally lighter in body. This is not a sign of overall quality, simply style. For example, light yet intensely flavorful German Rieslings from the Mosel-Saar-Ruwer region of Germany come in at a mere 7 to 9 percent alcohol, while huge barrel-chested red Zinfandel from toasty areas of California can top out at nearly 16 percent alcohol. One will be lighter in body, the latter fuller, but both can be world-class wines.

WINE ABCS
Terroir
* * *

The French use the term terroir *(tare-WHA) to refer to the way climate, soil, and grape variety interact in each place to create a unique and specific taste in the wine. Terroir, loosely translated, means the taste of the place in the glass.*

The third piece of the Style Profile after grape variety and growing region has to do with human hands. Nature has done its job, and now it's the winemakers' turn. Their choices on a myriad of issues—from what types of clones, yeasts, or oak barrels to use—heavily influence each wine's ultimate style.

WINE WORDS CHEAT SHEET
In-the-Know Terminology
* * *

Wine is often said to be crisp or soft, light or full, dry or sweet, or tannic. Think of these words, which are used to describe the basic structure of a wine, as you would the elements of a house. Acidity is the foundation of a wine. The tannins and sweetness level are the frame and wood siding, and the alcohol level is the roof. Fruit aromas and flavors from oak barrels can be thought of as decorative touches. Like a house, all these pieces support one another to create a wine's basic shape and style.

BODY: LIGHT-BODIED, MEDIUM-BODIED, FULL-BODIED

Imagine chiffon versus velvet, or skim milk versus whole, and you get the picture. Body *refers to the way the wine feels in your mouth. Primarily, it's a reflection of alcohol levels. Wines with lower alcohol are lighter in style and those with more alcohol give a heavier, more full-bodied impression. Body can also be influenced by sugar levels. Sweeter wines feel thicker and more viscous in your mouth.*

ACIDITY: CRISP OR SOFT

Just as the acidity in a squirt of lemon juice perks up food and drink, the acidity naturally present in grapes is what gives wine life and lift. Acidity is a reflection of grape variety (Sauvignon Blanc and Pinot Noir generally have higher levels of acidity than Viognier or Merlot) as well as where the grapes were grown. Wines made from grapes grown in cooler climates tend to have higher levels of acidity, while those from warmer growing regions generally sport lower acidity. Wines with higher acid are often referred to as crisp, zesty, or bright *while ones with lower levels of acidity are called* soft, or smooth.

SWEETNESS: DRY, OFF-DRY, LIGHTLY SWEET, SWEET

One of the confusing things about wine is the sweetness level. First, sugar is not added back into wine to make it sweeter. Sweetness in wine comes from residual sugar (often referred to as RS). How does it get there? If a winemaker halts fermentation (usually by chilling the tanks) the yeast die and don't have the chance to convert any more sugar in the grape juice to alcohol. What remains is called residual sugar, and it is what gives wine a sweet taste. Just because wine has residual sugar, though, doesn't mean it will taste sweet. Wine is all about balance. Off-dry wines have a touch of residual sugar but are balanced by acidity so you don't get an overly sweet impression. Other wines taste lightly sweet or very sweet because they contain more residual sugar and/or sport lower acid.

TANNINS: LIGHT, SUPPLE, STRONG

Don't know what I'm talking about? Think tea. When you've let the tea bag steep too long, you get a chalky feeling on the insides of your cheeks. That's tannin. This chemical compound is in the skin, seeds, and stems of grapes and is primarily apparent in red wines, since they get their color from the juice steeping with skins during the winemaking process. In finished wine, tannins act as a preservative. In young red wines, they can be very apparent, but over time the tiny tannins bind together, get bigger, and fall to the bottom of the bottle as sediment. That's why wine appears softer and less tannic as it ages. How do you detect the level of tannins in a red wine? We don't taste tannin, but feel it. Light tannins are barely noticeable; medium or supple tannins are balanced by sweet fruit, and strong tannins create a mouth-puckering sensation on the insides of your cheeks.

Finding Your Style

How do you find out what styles of wine you prefer? Note that I said "styles" in plural form. There is no one style that works for every situation. I might crave comforting, hearty reds next to a roaring winter fire, but during a summer heat wave I dream about refreshing rosés. When eating spicy Mexican food I reach for a slightly sweet, racy wine, yet with a huge steak I want a bold, tannic red.

To get a sense of what styles of wine you might prefer, consider the foods you like to eat. I use my sister Linde and my neighbor Ani as benchmarks for figuring out style preferences. Neither one of them are big wine drinkers, but they know immediately what they like. Both crinkle their noses at first sip of high-acid Sauvignon Blanc, preferring instead to drink fruity, soft whites. The same is true of reds. I've never seen either grab a vibrant Italian Chianti; instead they opt for a supple Australian Shiraz or California Merlot. When I ask them about food preferences, high-acid foods are on the bottom of their culinary lists.

What about you? Think of some of the foods you enjoy eating and imagine wine with similar flavors:

• If you hunger for tart apples, mouth-puckering grapefruit juice, and tangy goat cheese, you might like wines with bright levels of acidity and refreshing qualities such as German Riesling, New Zealand Sauvignon Blanc, or Grüner Veltliner from Austria.

- If sweet Fuji apples, milk, and creamy brie cheese are more to your liking, chances are you gravitate toward softer, rounder wines like Torrontes from Argentina, California Merlot, or Australian Shiraz.
- Would you choose lobster over sole? A filet mignon instead of pork? These are fuller, richer foods, so your preference in wine might lean toward buttery California Chardonnay, French Viognier, or Italian Brunello di Montalcino.

If you like all the foods above (as I do), it's a matter of finding a variety of styles that work for you in various situations. In terms of wines you might already drink, look at the list below and see if you spot one you like. Use it as a springboard to explore other types of wines from around the globe. In the pages that follow, you'll discover a world of wine possibilities to fit every mood, every celebration, and every day.

IF YOU LIKE . . .	SUCH AS . . .	THEN TRY . . .
Lighter, crisp whites	New Zealand Sauvignon Blanc, Italian Pinot Grigio	Albariño from Spain; Grüner Veltliner from Austria; other Italian whites like Orvieto and Soave; dry Rieslings from Australia and New York; Chardonnay from the Chablis region of France; or Moschofilero from Greece
Fruity, soft whites	Chardonnay from Australia, California, Chile, and Argentina	Oregon Pinot Gris; California Sauvignon Blanc dubbed Fumé Blanc; French Chardonnay named Pouilly-Fuissé; Italian whites named Gavi; Rueda and white Rioja from Spain; Torrontes from Argentina

IF YOU LIKE . . .	SUCH AS . . .	THEN TRY . . .
Full, rich whites	Pricey California Chardonnay, Viognier from California or France	White Rhône blends from France or California made from grapes like Marsanne, Roussanne, and Viognier; Pinot Gris and Gewurztraminer from Alsace, France; California and Oregon Pinot Blanc, dry rosés
Lightly sweet wines	White Zinfandel and other blush-style wines	Sweeter Rieslings from Germany, New York, or Washington State; Chenin Blanc from Vouvray, France; Italian Moscato d'Asti; Australian Sparkling Shiraz
Lighter, spicy reds	Pinot Noir and Chianti	French Beaujolais; Rioja from Spain; Pinot Noir from Burgundy in France; Oregon and New Zealand Pinot Noir; Chilean Carmenère
Smooth, fruity reds	California Merlot, Australian Shiraz	Washington Merlot; inexpensive Bordeaux; richer styles of Pinot Noir from California; Chilean Cabernet Sauvignon
Powerful, rich reds	Cabernet Sauvignon–based wines, California Zinfandel, Syrah from France	Southern Italian reds such as Nero d'Avola and Primitivo; Malbec from Argentina; Spanish reds from Toro; California Petite Sirah; Italian Brunello di Montalcino
Bubbly	Champagne from France or California sparkling wine	Spanish Cava; Italian Prosecco; French Crémant de Loire or Crémant d' Alsace; rosé Champagne from France; rosé sparkling wines from California

Wines by Mood

⌒

This section focuses on celebrating with wine whether you're getting married, throwing a casual party, or going on a picnic. Toasting an anniversary or heading out on a first date? Take a suggestion from my Sexy Wines roundup. Stressed-out and dreaming of sipping bubbly while soaking in suds? See my recommendations for Bathtub Wines. Feeling like a vinous trip around the world or checking out the hottest spots for new wines? Thumb through my Virtual Vacation Vinos or Hot Spots for ideas. Grab your mood ring and see what you feel like tonight.

QUICK TIP
Win at Wine Trivia
* * *

Impress your friends with these fun tidbits from the Wine Institute:

- *It takes 600 to 800 wine grapes to make one standard-sized (750 ml) bottle of wine.*
- *There are approximately 44 million bubbles in a standard-sized bottle of sparkling wine.*
- *Nearly two of every three bottles of wine consumed in the United States is produced in California.*
- *In a 2005 Gallup Poll, wine edged out beer for the first time as adult Americans' alcoholic beverage of choice.*

Wedding Wines

SELECTIONS TO CELEBRATE THE BIG DAY

It's the big day and everything has to be just right. So whether you, your parents, or your future in-laws are footing the bill, here are wine ideas to help out. My picks range from bargain options to luxury selections that meet the following criteria:

- They overdeliver in the quality department but aren't overexposed
- Are generally available in restaurants, hotels, and retail outlets
- The packaging—from bottle to label—is attractive and appealing

If your wedding reception is to be held at a restaurant or hotel, you can select wine from their list or ask if you can bring in your own. If you choose the latter, you will usually be charged a corkage fee, which ranges from zero to $20-plus per bottle depending upon the venue. It covers staff services and stemware.

Look for . . .

- **Bubbles:** Nothing signals celebration and pleasure like sparkling wine. Bare minimum, you'll need at least one glass per person for cake cutting. Think about serving sparklers throughout the meal, as well as offering white and red wine.
- **Whites:** For crowd-pleasing wine that goes well with a variety of food including appetizers, fish, and chicken, I recommend a fruity Sauvignon Blanc and lighter-styled, crisp Chardonnay.
- **Reds:** My favorite choice is elegant Pinot Noir because it's so food-friendly, but it is often expensive. Another top pick is a juicy Cabernet Sauvignon or smooth Bordeaux-style blend (which includes a varying mix of Cabernet Sauvignon, Merlot, Cabernet Franc, Malbec, and Petite Verdot). This last option satisfies those looking for fuller-bodied reds, but because the hallmark of these blends is suppleness they work well with dishes from chicken to steak.

Want more picks? Check out: Holiday Spirit, Twice-the-Price Wines, Bathtub Wines, Summer Wines, Spring Wines

BUBBLY CHEAT SHEET
Deciphering the Label to
Get What You Want

* * *

Sparkling wine: This is the umbrella category for any wine with bubbles.

Champagne: Champagne is a type of sparkling wine made only in the Champagne region of France. If the wine isn't made in Champagne, it technically should be called sparkling wine.

Cava: Though the word means "cellar," it refers to sparkling wine from Spain.

Spumante: Fully sparkling wines from Italy. Lightly fizzy Italian wines are called frizzante.

Blanc de Blancs: White wine made from white grapes such as Chardonnay. These are usually very crisp.

Blanc de Noirs: White wine made from black (or red) grapes such as Pinot Noir and Pinot Meunier. These often sport a hint of pink and are fuller in body.

Rosé: Pink and usually dry, these great wines are made from red grapes (or have a dash of red wine added to the cuvée for color) and are round and rich.

Natural: Very dry (sometimes called Extra or Ultra Brut).

Brut: Dry. Most sparkling wines are labeled Brut.

Extra-Dry: Funny enough, Extra-Dry bubbly is slightly sweeter than Brut. Nice with lightly sweet desserts.

Demi-Sec: It means "half-dry," so wines labeled Demi-Sec fall on the sweeter side. Great with wedding cake.

NV: Nonvintage. The sparkling wine is made from a blend of vintages to achieve consistency and producer style.

Vintage: If the bubbly carries a year on the label, it is a vintage wine, meaning the grapes were all harvested in one exceptional year. These are generally more expensive.

WEDDING WINES: SPARKLERS

PRODUCER	WINE NAME	FROM	STYLE PROFILE
Zardetto	Brut "Prosecco di Conegliano"	Conegliano, Italy	Light-bodied sparkler, crisp, refreshing
Codorníu	Cava "Reserva Raventós"	Spain	Medium-bodied sparkler, crisp, elegant
Korbel	Chardonnay Champagne	California	Medium-bodied sparkler, smooth, juicy
Gloria Ferrer	Brut "Sonoma"	Sonoma County, California	Medium-bodied sparkler, smooth, juicy
Chandon	"Blanc de Noirs"	Napa Valley, California	Medium-bodied sparkler, crisp, elegant
Segura Viudas	"Reserva Heredad"	Cava, Spain	Medium-bodied sparkler, smooth, juicy
Iron Horse Vineyards	"Wedding Cuvée"	Green Valley, California	Full-bodied sparkler, creamy, rich, toasty
Pommery	Brut "Royal"	Champagne, France	Full-bodied sparkler, creamy, rich, toasty
Perrier-Jouët	Grand Brut	Champagne, France	Full-bodied sparkler, creamy, rich, toasty
G. H. Mumm & Cie	Brut "Cordon Rouge"	Champagne, France	Full-bodied sparkler, creamy, rich, toasty
Veuve Clicquot	"Yellow Label"	Champagne, France	Full-bodied sparkler, creamy, rich, toasty
Cristalino	Extra-Dry Cava	Spain	Light-bodied sparkler, soft, lightly sweet
Chandon	Extra-Dry "Riche"	Napa Valley, California	Light-bodied sparkler, soft, lightly sweet
Schramsberg	Demi-Sec "Crémant"	Napa Valley, California	Light-bodied sparkler, soft, lightly sweet

SPECIAL BECAUSE	PRICE RANGE	MORE INFO . . .
Dry Italian sparkling wine	$10–12	www.bubbly.it
Made from Macabeo and Chardonnay grapes	$12–15	www.Codorniu.com
Korbel's best bubbly	$12–14	www.korbel.com
Good value for the quality	$12–14	www.gloriaferrer.com
Made with Pinot Noir; pour throughout the meal	$15–17	www.chandon.com
Impressive bottle	$18–22	www.seguraviudas.com
The perfect wedding gift wine	$29–34	www.ironhorsevineyards.com
Classicly styled Champagne	$30–35	www.pommery.com
Stylish packaging from top producer	$45–50	www.perrier-jouet.com
Ultra-smooth, crowd-pleasing bubbly	$25–27	www.mumm.com
Familiar wine worth the money	$35–40	www.veuve-clicquot.com
Good for aperitifs and desserts	$8–10	www.civusa.com (importer)
Another option for aperitifs and desserts	$14–18	www.chandon.com
Top California bubbly producer; ideal for drinking with cake	$27–30	www.schramsberg.com

WEDDING WINES: WHITES

PRODUCER	WINE NAME	FROM	STYLE PROFILE
Jacob's Creek	Chardonnay	South Eastern Australia	Medium-bodied, light oak, juicy
Ruffino	Chardonnay "Libaio"	Toscana, Italy	Light-bodied, crisp, refreshing
Castillo de Monjardin	Chardonnay "El Cerezo" Unoaked	Navarra, Spain	Light-bodied, crisp, refreshing
Penfolds	Chardonnay "Thomas Hyland"	South Eastern Australia	Light-bodied, crisp, refreshing
Carmel Road	Chardonnay	Monterey County, California	Medium-full-bodied, crisp, fruity
Veramonte	Sauvignon Blanc	Casablanca Valley, Chile	Medium-bodied, racy, herbal
Kendall-Jackson	Sauvignon Blanc "Vintner's Reserve"	Sonoma County, California	Light-bodied, crisp, refreshing
Baileyana	Sauvignon Blanc "Paragon Vineyard"	Edna Valley, California	Medium-bodied, racy, herbal
St. Supéry	Sauvignon Blanc	Napa Valley, California	Medium-bodied, racy, herbal
Kim Crawford	Sauvignon Blanc	Marlborough, New Zealand	Medium-bodied, racy, herbal
De Loach	Sauvignon Blanc "O.F.S"	Russian River Valley, California	Medium-bodied, light oak, juicy
Robert Mondavi Winery	Fumé Blanc	Napa Valley, California	Medium-full bodied, crisp, fruity
DeLille Cellars	Sauvignon Blanc "Chaleur Estate Blanc"	Columbia Valley, Washington	Medium-full bodied, crisp, fruity

SPECIAL BECAUSE	PRICE RANGE	MORE INFO . . .
Widely available; delivers good value	$6–8	www.jacobscreek.com
Works for cocktails and dinner	$8–10	www.ruffino.com
Hard to find but worth the effort	$10–12	www.winebow.com (importer)
Premier Aussie winery	$11–14	www.penfolds.com
Food-friendly; great with chicken	$13–16	www.carmelroad.com
Overdelivers for the price	$7–10	www.veramonte.com
Widely available; outdoor wedding winner	$7–10	www.kj.com
High quality, family-owned operation	$12–14	www.baileyana.com
Lean New Zealand style from California	$18–20	www.stsupery.com
Popular wine from man named Kim	$15–18	www.kimcrawfordwines.co.nz
Well-known winery's top white selection	$20–22	www.deloachvineyards.com
The original oak-aged style	$17–20	www.robertmondavi.com
Sauvignon Blanc and Sémillon; limited availability	$37–40	www.delillecellars.com

WEDDING WINES: REDS

PRODUCER	WINE NAME	FROM	STYLE PROFILE
Talus Collection	Pinot Noir	California	Medium-bodied, light tannins, fresh, spicy
Five Rivers Winery	Pinot Noir	Santa Barbara County, California	Medium-bodied, light tannins, fresh, spicy
Calera Wine Company	Pinot Noir	Central Coast, California	Medium-bodied, supple tannins, vibrant, earthy
J. Faiveley	Bourgogne	Burgundy, France	Medium-bodied, supple tannins, vibrant, earthy
Louis Jadot	Chambolle-Musigny	Chambolle-Musigny, France	Medium-bodied, supple tannins, vibrant, earthy
Turner Road Vineyards	Cabernet Sauvignon	Paso Robles, California	Medium-bodied, supple tannins, smooth, juicy
Louis M. Martini	Cabernet Sauvignon	Sonoma County, California	Medium-bodied, supple tannins, smooth, juicy
Lyeth Estate Winery	Meritage	Sonoma County, California	Medium-bodied, supple tannins, smooth, juicy
Chappellet	"Mountain Cuvee"	Napa Valley, California	Medium-bodied, supple tannins, smooth, juicy
Franciscan Oakville Estates	"Magnificat" Red Blend	Napa Valley, California	Medium-bodied, supple tannins, smooth, juicy
Clos du Bois	"Marlstone"	Alexander Valley, California	Medium-bodied, supple tannins, smooth, juicy
Rodney Strong Vineyards	"Symmetry" Red Blend	Alexander Valley, California	Medium-bodied, supple tannins, smooth, juicy

SPECIAL BECAUSE	PRICE RANGE	MORE INFO . . .
Overdelivers in quality	$7–8	www.taluscollection.com
Good Pinot character for value price	$10–12	www.fiveriverswinery.com
Owner Josh Jensen is Pinot pioneer	$18–20	www.calerawine.com
Great-looking package from well-known producer	$15–18	www.bourgognes-faiveley.com
Chambolle is my favorite place for Burgundies	$30–35	www.louisjadot.com
Ideal combination of top wine, low price	$11–13	www.turnerroadvineyards.com
Classic Napa producer	$15–17	www.louismartini.com
Mostly Cabernet Sauvignon and Merlot	$15–17	www.boisset.com
Well-priced blend of all five Bordeaux varieties	$25–27	www.chappellet.com
Bordeaux-style blend	$40–45	www.franciscanvineyards.com
A blend of all five Bordeaux varieties	$48–52	www.closdubois.com
Bordeaux-style blend; top gift wine	$55–60	www.rodneystrong.com

WINE ABCS
Meritage

* * *

Ever notice the word Meritage *(rhymes with heritage) on a label of white or red wine? It means that the wine is a blend of classic Bordeaux varieties made outside of France's Bordeaux region. White Meritage wines are generally made from a blend of Sauvignon Blanc and Sémillon; and reds, from traditional Bordeaux grapes such as Cabernet Sauvignon, Merlot, Cabernet Franc, Malbec, and Petite Verdot. But not all Bordeaux-style wines can call themselves Meritage. They must belong to and abide by the regulations set out by the nonprofit Meritage Association. More information: www.meritagewine.org*

QUICK TIP
Smoother Reds in Seconds

* * *

Decanting is most often used to separate the wine from sediment that builds up in older bottles of wine (sediment is simply color pigments and tannin compounds that settle out of the wine over time). My favorite way to use a decanter, however, is to help aerate young, tannic red wines. If you don't have a decanter, simply use a glass pitcher and pour in the wine, then swirl vigorously. No need to be gentle, as you're helping to expose the wine to air and soothe its tannins' youthful exuberance.

Picnic Picks

PORTABLE PICKS FOR AL FRESCO FUN

The great outdoors is calling, and it's asking you to bring wine. Whether you're camping, picnicking, or attending a block party, these fun wines are the ideal beverage to tote along. All of them represent the hottest trend in wine these days: alternative packaging. From jugs to single-serve plastic bottles, tubes, to Tetra Paks, screw caps to Zorks, wine packaging is going hip. Wine-savvy drinkers are embracing these innovations with a passion. My Picnic Picks meet the following criteria:

- First and foremost, they have to taste good. These are all well-made wines.
- They look hip and are portable. Many selections come in traditional bottles as well as single-serves, magnums, or boxes.
- Prices are modest enough to stock up.

Look for . . .

- **Whites:** You'll find mostly familiar varieties such as Chardonnay, Sauvignon Blanc, and Pinot Grigio. A number of brands are going upscale and offering great quality in creative packaging.
- **Pinks:** If you shun pink wine, you're missing a lot. There are sweeter versions and dry versions. Blush wines—often indicated with the word *white* (i.e., White Zinfandel, White Merlot, White Shiraz)—all fall on the lightly sweet side of the scale. When well chilled the sweetness is less apparent. Dry pinks will often say "dry" on the label or be called rosé.
- **Reds:** Think Zinfandel, lighthearted Merlot, and Shiraz.

Want more picks? Check out: Twice-the-Price Wines, Off-the-Grill Wines, Summer Wines, Snack Attack Party Food

PICNIC PICKS: WHITES

PRODUCER	WINE NAME	FROM	STYLE PROFILE
Three Thieves	Pinot Grigio "Bandit"	St. Helena, California	Light-bodied, crisp, refreshing
Wine Cube	Pinot Grigio	California	Light-bodied, racy, off-dry
French Rabbit	Chardonnay	Vin de Pays d'Oc, France	Light-bodied, crisp, refreshing
Stone Cellars by Beringer	Sauvignon Blanc	St. Helena, California	Light-bodied, crisp, refreshing
Lindemans	Sauvignon Blanc "Bin 95"	South Eastern Australia	Light-bodied, crisp, refreshing
Wine Cube	Chardonnay	California	Medium-bodied, light oak, juicy
Dtour Wines	Chardonnay	Mâcon-Villages, France	Medium-bodied, light oak, juicy

CHEAT SHEET
Alternative-Packaging Terms
* * *

Mini or single-serve bottle: 187 milliliters (1 big glass)

Half bottle: 375 milliliters (2 to 3 glasses)

Standard bottle: 750 milliliters (4 to 6 glasses)

Magnum: 1.5 liters (2 bottles, or 10 to 12 glasses)

3-liter box (4 standard bottles, or 20 to 24 glasses)

5-liter box (6.5 standard bottles, or 42 to 50 glasses)

Tetra Pak: Think chic, small cardboard container.

Bag-in-box: Airtight plastic bag holds the wine in the box.

SPECIAL BECAUSE	PRICE RANGE	MORE INFO . . .
A red-hot producer not to miss	$6–7 1-liter Tetra Pak	www.threethieves.com
Only at Target stores	$16–18 3-liter box	www.target.com
Chic, sleek box	$9–10 1-liter box	www.frenchrabbit.com
Shatterproof plastic minis	$6–7 four-pack minis	www.stonecellars.com
Top-notch Sauvignon Blanc	$7–8 four-pack minis	www.lindemans.com
Tastes expensive	$9–11 1.5-liter box	www.target.com
Joint venture of includes chef Daniel Boulud	$37–40 3-liter tube	www.dtourwine.com

MYTH-BUSTER
Screw Caps Mean the Wine Is Cheap
* * *

Screw caps—or twist-offs—are ideal closures for wine. They preserve the freshness of the wine longer than corks, are easy to open, and can be closed again if the bottle isn't finished. Screw caps virtually eliminate the chance that wine will be corked, which makes the wine smell like musty cardboard. Topping wine with the tin roof of progress is a growing trend. Show your wine-savvy quotient is high by proudly proclaiming, "It's hip to be screwed."

PICNIC PICKS: PINKS

PRODUCER	WINE NAME	FROM	STYLE PROFILE
Sutter Home	White Zinfandel	Napa Valley, California	Light-bodied, light tannins, off-dry, juicy
Peter Vella Wines	White Grenache	California	Light-bodied, light tannins, off-dry, juicy
La Vieille Ferme	Rosé	Côtes du Ventoux, Rhône Valley, France	Light-bodied, light tannins, vibrant, fruity
Bonny Doon Vineyards	Ca' del Solo "Big House Pink"	California	Light-bodied, light tannins, vibrant, fruity

PICNIC PICKS: REDS

PRODUCER	WINE NAME	FROM	STYLE PROFILE
Three Thieves	Zinfandel	California	Medium- to full-bodied, supple tannins, vibrant, juicy
Banrock Station	Cabernet Sauvignon	South Eastern Australia	Medium-bodied, supple tannins, vibrant, earthy
Delicato Family Vineyards	Merlot "Bota Box"	California	Medium-bodied, supple tannins, smooth, juicy
Washington Hills	Merlot	Columbia Valley, Washington	Medium-bodied, supple tannins, smooth, juicy
Hardys	Shiraz "Stamp of Australia"	South Eastern Australia	Medium-bodied, supple tannins, smooth, juicy
Black Box Wines	Shiraz	Barossa Valley, Australia	Medium-bodied, supple tannins, smooth, juicy

SPECIAL BECAUSE	PRICE RANGE	MORE INFO . . .
Originator of White Zin; not oversweet.	$3–5 four-pack minis	www.sutterhome.com
Equivalent of six bottles; lightly sweet	$7–10 5-liter box	www.petervella.com
From Perrin brothers of Château de Beaucastel	$7–8 750 ml bottle	www.lavieilleferme.com
From California's master of fun, Randall Grahm	$8–10 750 ml bottle	www.bonnydoonvineyard.com

SPECIAL BECAUSE	PRICE RANGE	MORE INFO . . .
Brand started by three renegade winemakers	$8–10 1-liter glass jug	www.threethieves.com
Sold in standard-sized bottles and minis, too	$10–12 3-liter box	www.banrockstation.com
A value brand not to miss— highly recommended	$15–18 3-liter box	www.delicato.com
Hard to find but fun to drink	$18–20 3-liter box	www.washingtonhills.com
Widely available and tasty	$15–16 3-liter box	www.hardywines.com
Best-quality boxed wine on the market	$23–25 3-liter box	www.blackboxwines.com

Party Wines

TWELVE BOTTLES UNDER $10 TO PLEASE ANY CROWD

∞

When you're having a party, you need to load up on inexpensive wines. Here is a case of top picks that meet the following criteria:

- Are widely available in grocery and wine stores.
- Are focused on the most popular wine types.

Look for . . .

- **Whites:** Despite the ABC movement (anything but Chardonnay), Chardonnay remains the favored white wine in America. Look for wines from South Eastern Australia and California for deals. Fruity, crisp Sauvignon Blanc is also a crowd-pleaser.
- **Reds:** Syrah, also known as Shiraz, is hot these days. Look to Australia for well-priced options. Try soft and juicy Merlot from Washington State and California Zinfandel.

Want more picks? Check out these lists: Holiday Spirit, Twice-the-Price Wines, Summer Wines, Picnic Picks

---

PARTY PLANNING CHEAT SHEET
How Much to Buy?

* * *

- *A standard bottle of wine (750 ml) serves approximately 5 glasses (5 ounces each)*

BRUNCH FOR 8 TO 10

Guests often drink less at brunch, but to be on the safe side I suggest having the following on hand:
- *3 bottles sparkling wine (Italian Prosecco is affordable and my favorite to mix with peach nectar for a bellini;*

California sparkling wine is ideal with orange juice for mimosas or crème de cassis for kir royales)

- *1 bottle vodka and Bloody Mary mix*
- *1 bottle white wine (Pinot Grigio from Italy or Riesling from Germany are my top picks)*
- *1 bottle lighter-style red wine (Beaujolais or Chinon from France or a Rosé)*

DINNER FOR 12

Offer guests sparkling wine when they arrive, then move into white and red with dinner followed by dessert options.

- *3 bottles sparkling wine or Champagne for cocktails*
- *2 to 3 bottles each white and red wine (food-friendly whites include crisp Sauvignon Blanc from New Zealand and Chardonnay from France. Dinner reds to think about are Merlot from Washington State and Pinot Noir from California or Oregon)*
- *1 to 2 bottles dessert wine such as late-harvest Riesling, Sauternes, or tawny Port*

COCKTAIL PARTY FOR 25

Over the course of a two- to three-hour cocktail party, plan on people having at least 3 drinks (some will drink more and others less). Consider buying magnums of wine, which equal 2 standard bottles. These large-format bottles are festive and you get 10 to 12 glasses from each one. With that in mind, stock up on the following:

- *8 to 12 bottles red wine (Both Malbec from Argentina and Australian Shiraz are affordable)*
- *6 to 8 bottles white wine (Chilean Chardonnay or Italian whites are excellent options)*
- *1½ to 2 cases beer*
- *1 bottle each of vodka, gin, rum, and tequila, plus mixers*

PARTY WINES

PRODUCER	WINE NAME	FROM	STYLE PROFILE
Camelot	Sauvignon Blanc	California	Light-bodied, crisp, refreshing
Canyon Road	Sauvignon Blanc	California	Light-bodied, crisp, refreshing
Woodbridge by Robert Mondavi	Sauvignon Blanc	California	Light-bodied, crisp, refreshing
Alice White	Chardonnay	South Eastern Australia	Medium-bodied, light oak, juicy
Fetzer	Chardonnay "Valley Oaks"	California	Medium-bodied, light oak, juicy
Lindemans	Chardonnay "Bin 65"	South Eastern Australia	Full-bodied, creamy, oaky, ripe
Hogue Cellars	Merlot	Columbia Valley, Washington	Medium-bodied, supple tannins, smooth, juicy
Columbia Crest	Shiraz "Two Vines"	Columbia Valley, Washington	Medium-bodied, supple tannins, smooth, juicy
Barefoot Cellars	Cabernet Sauvignon	California	Medium-bodied, supple tannins, smooth, juicy
Yellow Tail	Shiraz-Grenache	South Eastern Australia	Medium-bodied, light tannins, fresh, spicy
Ravenswood	Zinfandel "Vintners Blend"	California	Medium-bodied, light tannins, fresh, spicy
Beaulieu Vineyard	Zinfandel "Coastal"	California	Medium-bodied, light tannins, fresh, spicy

PAIR WITH	PRICE RANGE	MORE INFO . . .
Chips and dips	$6–8	www.camelotwines.com
Tortilla chips and salsa	$8–10	www.canyonroadwinery.com
Vegetable platter	$9–11 1.5 liters	www.woodbridgewines.com
Cheese quesadillas	$6–9	www.alicewhite.com
Cheese platter	$8–10	www.fetzer.com
Turkey sandwiches	$6–8	www.lindemans.com
Chicken wings	$7–9	www.hoguecellars.com
Cheese pizza	$8–10	www.hoguecellars.com
Hamburgers	$6–8	www.barefootwine.com
Meat burritos	$7–9	www.yellowtailwine.com
Grilled Tri-tip	$7–9	www.ravenswood-wine.com
Sausage pizza	$8–10	www.bvwines.com

TASTING CHEAT SHEET
The Four Ss of Wine Tasting
* * *

SEE

Look at the color and clarity of a wine. Wines should generally be clear, not cloudy, with whites ranging in color from pale yellow to gold, and reds from deep purple to light ruby. Color may tell you things about how the wine is made and its age, as well. For example, a white that has been aged in oak barrels (as many Chardonnays are) will be more golden in color than whites aged in steel tanks. Older red wines will usually be lighter in color than youthful ones.

SWIRL

Swirling the wine coats the sides of the glass in order to release the aromas and fruity esters of the wine. In other words, swirling allows the wine to get comfortable in the glass so it can open up and express itself.

SMELL

Smelling a wine is the most important part of wine tasting because you can detect thousands of smells but only four or five tastes. Take a good long sniff and ask yourself what do you smell—fruits, veggies, flowers, butter, spices, herbs?

SIP

Take a sip and swish it around. This coats your mouth with the wine, much like swirling does in the glass, and allows you to assess the wine better. Again, ask yourself questions about the aromas and flavors, then think about the way the wine feels in your mouth: Is it light, medium, or full-bodied? Does it feel smooth or taste tart? Do you taste sweetness?

Is there a pleasant, lingering aftertaste (called the finish)? Most important, do you like the wine? If you can't figure it out, I'm sure you need another sip, then another, then another. . . .

QUICK TIP
Host a Wine Tasting in Five Easy Steps
* * *

1. *Have everyone bring a bottle in a certain price range or that focuses on a particular wine type or region.*

2. *The host should brown-bag the bottles and number each one. This is called* blind tasting, *and it helps you focus on the wine without any preconceived ideas of place, price, or producer.*

3. *Set out glasses, water, spit buckets (anything from paper cups to kids' sand pails), and crackers, olives, or roast beef slices, which help to remove the buildup of tannins from red wine. Make tasting sheets for each wine with a space to note the color, aromas, flavors, and overall impression of each unidentified bottle of wine.*

4. *Swirl, smell, sip, and spit or swallow each wine. Write down tasting notes.*

5. *Once the bag is removed, record the name of the producer, the type of wine, the country and region each one comes from, the year it was made, the cost of a bottle, and the foods you think it would go well with. Talk, sip, and enjoy!*

Girls' Night In

CELEBRATION OF FEMME FATALE WINES

~

Book Club and Bunco nights are often just an excuse for a group of friends to get together to drink wine and talk. Whatever the reason, how about spending a night celebrating the femmes fatales of the wine business? The majority of wine consumers are female, yet women represent a minority in winery boardrooms and cellars. That's changing all across the wine world, though, so let's raise a glass to these amazing women . . . and their wines.

My picks range from bargain options to luxury selections that meet the following criteria:

- They are top-notch examples of region and type.
- Wineries are either owned by women or the wines are made by women winemakers.
- The brand honors a woman in wine.

QUICK TIP
All Bubbles, All the Time

* * *

Bubblies sport moderate alcohol and have higher acidity levels than other wines, which makes them ideal for drinking as a cocktail as well as throughout the entire meal. These are simply wines with sparkle, so enjoy them year-round not just at the holidays. As Lily Bollinger of the famed Bollinger Champagne house once remarked, "I drink Champagne when I'm happy and when I'm sad. Sometimes I drink it when I'm alone. When I have company, I consider it obligatory. I trifle with it if I'm not hungry and drink it when I am. Otherwise, I never touch it unless I'm thirsty."

GIRLS' NIGHT IN: WHITES

PRODUCER	WINE NAME	FROM	STYLE PROFILE
Two Wives	Sauvignon Blanc	Napa Valley, California	Medium-bodied, racy, herbal
Gallo Family Vineyards	Chardonnay	Sonoma County, California	Full-bodied, creamy, oaky, ripe
Meridian Vineyards	Chardonnay	Santa Barbara County, California	Full-bodied, creamy, oaky, ripe
J. Lynne	Chardonnay	Russian River Valley, California	Medium-full bodied, crisp, fruity
Cambria	Chardonnay "Katherine's Vineyard"	Santa Maria Valley, California	Full-bodied, creamy, oaky, ripe
Ceja	Chardonnay	Napa Valley, California	Full-bodied, creamy, oaky, ripe
La Sirena Winery	Moscato "Azul"	Napa Valley, California	Light-bodied, crisp, refreshing
Bodegas Fillaboa	Albariño	Rias Baixas, Spain	Medium-bodied, crisp, minerally
Handley Cellars	Gewürztraminer	Anderson Valley, California	Full-bodied, soft, aromatic
Lungarotti	Pinot Grigio	Umbria, Italy	Light-bodied, crisp, refreshing
Inman Family Wines	Pinot Gris	Russian River Valley, California	Medium-full bodied, crisp, fruity
Westrey Wines	Pinot Gris	Willamette Valley, Oregon	Medium-full bodied, crisp, fruity
MacMurray Ranch	Pinot Gris	Russian River Valley, California	Medium-full-bodied, crisp, fruity
Domaine Weinbach	Tokay Pinot Gris "Cuvée Laurence"	Alsace, France	Full-bodied, soft, aromatic

WOMEN BEHIND THE WINE	PRICE RANGE	MORE INFO . . .
Started by two wives with winemaker husbands	$13–15	www.twowives.net
Great value; made by Gina Gallo	$8–10	www.gallofamily.com
Lee Miyamura makes this widely available winner	$10–12	www.meridianvineyards.com
Limited production; crafted by Jennifer Wall	$22–24	www.jlynnewines.com
Named after Barbara and Jess Jackson's oldest daughter	$15–16	www.cambriawines.com
Amelia Ceja, inspiring woman who started winery from scratch	$25–27	www.cejavineyards.com
Noted winemaking consultant Heidi Barrett's label	$27–30	www.lasirenawine.com
Isabel Salgado de Andrea, hot Spanish winemaker	$16–18	www.bodegasfillaboa.com
One of California's power women of wine Milla Handley	$14–16	www.handleycellars.com
Lungarotti sisters Teresa and Chiara and their mama!	$15–16	www.lungarotti.it
Rising star winemaker Kathleen Inman	$23–25	www.inmanfamilywines.com
Amy Wesselman, a winemaker to watch	$14–17	www.westrey.com
Kate MacMurray, daughter of the late actor Fred	$25–28	www.macmurrayranch.com
Owned by fabulous Faller women: Colette, Catherine, Laurence	$39–40	www.domaineweinbach.com

GIRLS' NIGHT IN: REDS

PRODUCER	WINE NAME	FROM	STYLE PROFILE
Heron	Merlot	California	Medium-bodied, supple tannins, smooth, juicy
Campo Viejo	Tempranillo Crianza	Rioja, Spain	Medium-bodied, light tannins, fresh, spicy
Sokol Blosser	"Meditrina" Red Blend	Willamette Valley, Oregon	Medium-full-bodied, supple tannins, vibrant, juicy
Domaine Parent	Pinot Noir, Bourgogne	Burgundy, France	Medium-bodied, supple tannins, vibrant, earthy
Hanna Winery	Merlot	Alexander Valley, California	Medium-bodied, supple tannins, smooth, juicy
Marimar Torres	Pinot Noir "Don Miguel Vineyard"	Russian River Valley, California	Medium-bodied, supple tannins, vibrant, earthy
Domaine Drouhin	Pinot Noir	Willamette Valley, Oregon	Medium-bodied, supple tannins, vibrant, earthy
Merry Edwards Wines	Pinot Noir	Russian River Valley, California	Full-bodied, supple tannins, smooth, earthy
Dos Victorias	Tempranillo "Elias Mora"	Toro, Spain	Full-bodied, strong tannins, lush, concentrated
Carol Shelton Wines	Zinfandel "Wild Thing," Cox Vineyard	Mendocino County, California	Full-bodied, supple tannins, spicy, ripe
Casa Lapostolle	Cabernet Sauvignon "Cuvée Alexandre"	Colchagua Valley, Chile	Full-bodied, supple tannins, smooth, earthy
Corison	Cabernet Sauvigon	Napa Valley, California	Full-bodied, strong tannins, lush, concentrated

WOMEN BEHIND THE WINE	PRICE RANGE	MORE INFO . . .
Chic, bargain wines from Laely Heron	$9–10	www.heronwines.com
Made by Spanish star Elena Adell	$8–10	www.campoviejo-usa.com
Susan Sokol Blosser, an innovator and leader	$19–21	www.sokolblosser.com
Anne Parent runs venerable family property	$15–18	www.domaine-parent.com
President, Christine Hanna, is a dynamo	$27–29	www.hannawinery.com
Marimar, of the famous Spanish wine family Torres	$30–33	www.marimarestate.com
World-class Pinot made by Véronique Drouhin	$35–40	www.domainedrouhin.com
Merry is Queen of California Pinot; limited availability	$48–55	www.merryedwards.com
Made by two women named Victoria	$22–24	www.dosvictorias.com
Carol Shelton, master of Zin; limited, but worth the search	$28–32	www.carolshelton.com
Alexandra Marnier-Lapostolle, of Grand Marnier family fame	$16–18	www.casalapostolle.com
Cathy Corison, well-known Napa Cabernet specialist	$55–59	www.corison.com

GIRLS' NIGHT IN: PINKS, BUBBLES AND SWEETIES

PRODUCER	WINE NAME	FROM	STYLE PROFILE
Angove's	Rosé "Nine Vines"	South Australia	Light-bodied, light tannins, vibrant, fruity
Olympic Cellars	"Rosé the Riveter"	Columbia Valley, Washington	Light-bodied, light tannins, off-dry, juicy
Fleming-Jenkins	Syrah Rosé	San Francisco Bay, California	Light-bodied, light tannins, vibrant, fruity
Francis Ford Coppola Presents	Rosé "Sofia"	Carneros, California	Light-bodied, light tannins, vibrant, fruity
Domaine Carneros	Brut	Carneros, California	Medium-bodied sparkler, smooth, juicy
Veuve Clicquot	"La Grande Dame"	Champagne, France	Full-bodied sparkler, creamy, rich, toasty
Grgich Hills	"Violetta" white dessert wine	Napa Valley, California	Medium-bodied, sweet, juicy

QUICK TIP
Is This My Glass?
* * *
*To keep glasses from getting mixed up during a party, use a
dry erase or wax-based china marker and write guests'
names on the base of the glasses. Simply wipe off with a dry
paper towel before washing.*

WOMEN BEHIND THE WINE	PRICE RANGE	MORE INFO . . .
Victoria Angove; rosé is Grenache-Shiraz blend	$10–12	www.angoves.com.au
Lemberger-based pink by three fabulous female owners	$13–15	www.workinggirlwines.com
From famous skater and broadcaster Peggy Fleming; limited production	$17–20	www.flemingjenkinswinery .com
Sexy amphora-shaped bottle named for Coppola's daughter, Sofia	$12–15	www.ffcpresents.com
Eileen Crane, winemaker; winery owned by the French firm Taittinger	$20–25	www.domainecarneros.com
Named for the widow (*veuve* in French) who ran the company	$100–110	www.veuve-clicquot.com
Named after owner's daughter, Violet	$44–50 375 ml	www.grgich.com

QUICK TIP
Clean Glasses
* * *

Any residue on a wineglass will make wine taste off. I only use a mild soap every third or fourth washing of my glasses and simply wash with hot water the rest of the time. To get pesky lipstick off, first wipe off with a towel, then put into the suds.

Sexy Wines

BELLY-BUTTON SIPPERS FROM SYRAH TO SAUTERNES

Wine has been the elixir used to lube relaxation gears and induce romance. So whether you're proposing marriage, going on a first date, celebrating an anniversary, or just kicking back on a Saturday night with your sweetie, try uncorking one of my belly-button sippers. My picks range from bargain options to luxury selections that meet the following criteria:

- Have an exotic quality that stimulates your senses.
- Are attractive to admire in the glass and intensely aromatic.
- Sport a sensuous, fleshy, mouth-filling texture.

Look for . . .

- **Whites:** Think of curvaceous, fleshy wines that could star in the vinous version of a Victoria's Secret catalog. Spicy Gewurztraminer and Pinot Gris from the Alsace region of France, floral-scented Viognier and sumptuous Chardonnay. If you think you won't like these wines because they may be sweet, they're not. Many are dry wines with higher alcohol levels, which can mimic sweetness.
- **Reds:** The first thing that comes to mind with sexy reds is supple Syrah, also known as Shiraz. How about a plush Merlot that feels like you're wrapping yourself in cashmere? What about sizzling hot Tempranillo from Spain, Petite Sirah that is anything but small, and juicy Zinfandel that's just bit naughty? I'll stop now before I burn a hole in the page.
- **Sparklers:** Seek out glamorous sparkling wines. My personal favorite is sapphire-pink rosé Champagne, but if you've never been lucky enough to sip a glass of intensely red Australian Sparkling Shiraz, you're in for a sexy treat.

- **Sweeties:** These wines are meant to be sipped slowly. Decadent dessert wines such as Sauternes from France, late harvest Rieslings, and rich Tawny Port from Portugal or Australian dessert wines known as "stickies." Now that's hot.

Want more picks? Check out: Valentine's Day, Winter Wines, Dessert Wines, Thanksgiving Wines

---

WINE ABCS
Syrah, Shiraz, and Petite Sirah
* * *

Syrah is the hearty grape responsible for the great wines of the northern Rhône, such as Hermitage and Côte-Rôtie. From France come intense, earthy wines, while California makes ripe, fruitier styles. Syrah is gaining in popularity thanks in part to Australian Shiraz. Shiraz and Syrah are simply different names for the same grape variety. Inky purple Petite Sirah is a different variety and it's anything but petite. Occasionally called Durif, the small-berried variety is the love child of two grapes, Peloursin and Syrah. The powerhouse red reaches its pinnacle in California, where vines have been planted since the late 1880s.

SEXY WHITES

PRODUCER	WINE NAME	FROM	STYLE PROFILE
Trimbach	Pinot Gris "Reserve"	Alsace, France	Medium-bodied, aromatic, off-dry
Sokol Blosser	Pinot Gris	Dundee Hills, Oregon	Medium-full-bodied, crisp, fruity
Domaines Schlumberger	Gewurztraminer "Fleur"	Alsace, France	Full-bodied, soft, aromatic
Lawson's Dry Hills	Gewürztraminer	Marlborough, New Zealand	Full-bodied, soft, aromatic
Baglio di Pianetto	Viognier Blend "Ficiligno"	Sicily, Italy	Full-bodied, soft, aromatic
Jewel	Viognier	California	Full-bodied, soft, aromatic
E. Guigal	Condrieu	Condrieu, France	Full-bodied, soft, aromatic
Bonterra	Roussanne	Mendocino County, California	Full-bodied, soft, aromatic
Tablas Creek	Roussanne	Paso Robles, California	Full-bodied, soft, aromatic
Virgin Vines	Chardonnay	California	Medium-full-bodied, crisp, fruity
Antinori/Castello della Sala	"Cervaro della Sala"	Umbria, Italy	Full-bodied, creamy, oaky, ripe
Testarossa Vineyards	Chardonnay "Bien Nacido"	Santa Maria Valley, California	Full-bodied, crisp, spicy, elegant

SEXY BECAUSE	PRICE RANGE	MORE INFO . . .
Easy drinking; great beginner wine	$13–15	www.maison-trimbach.fr
Similar to Alsatian versions but fruitier	$21–23	www.sokolblosser.com
So aromatic! Dab it behind your ears like wine perfume	$20–22	www.domaines-schlumberger.com
Limited availability but worth the search	$15–16	www.lawsonsdryhills.co.nz
Blend of Viognier and Insolia from Count Marzotto	$16–18	www.bagliodipianetto.it or www.paternoimports.com (importer)
Overdelivers in value category; try all their wines	$10–12	www.jewelwine.com
Exotic Viognier from world-class producer; cellarworthy	$40–45	www.guigal.com
From organically grown vineyards	$18–20	www.bonterra.com
A Rhône grape akin to Viognier; limited production	$25–27	www.tablascreek.com
Launched by Richard Branson; fun packaging, good wine	$9–12	www.virginvines.com
Complex and classy Chardonnay with dash of Grechetto grapes	$40–45	www.antinori.it
One of my favorite producers; try all their wines	$30–34	www.testarossa.com

SEXY REDS

PRODUCER	WINE NAME	FROM	STYLE PROFILE
Clay Station	Petite Sirah	Lodi California	Medium-full-bodied, supple tannins, vibrant, juicy
Concannon	Petite Sirah	Central Coast, California	Medium-full-bodied, supple tannins, vibrant, juicy
Cosentino	Petite Sirah	Lodi, California	Full-bodied, supple tannins spicy, ripe
Falesco	Merlot "Pesano"	Umbria, Italy	Full-bodied, supple tannins smooth, earthy
Northstar Winery	Merlot	Columbia Valley, Washington	Full-bodied, strong tannins lush, concentrated
Château Gazin	Pomerol	Pomerol, Bordeaux, France	Full-bodied, supple tannins smooth, earthy
Alexander Valley Vineyards	Zinfandel "Sin Zin"	Alexander Valley, California	Full-bodied, supple tannins spicy, ripe
Vall Llach	"Embruix"	Priorat, Spain	Full-bodied, supple tannins smooth, earthy
Chateau Reynella	Shiraz "Basket Press"	McLaren Vale, South Australia	Full-bodied, supple tannins spicy, ripe
Penfolds	Shiraz "Magill Estate"	South Australia	Full-bodied, strong tannins lush, concentrated
Shafer Vineyards	Syrah "Relentless"	Napa Valley, California	Full-bodied, supple tannins spicy, ripe
Bodega Numanthia	Numanthia	Toro, Spain	Full-bodied, strong tannins lush, concentrated

SEXY BECAUSE	PRICE RANGE	MORE INFO . . .
Bargain price, high quality, from the folks at Delicato	$10–13	www.claystationwine.com
Nothing petite about this red from Livermore leader	$10–12	www.concannonvineyard.com
Mitch Cosentino makes concentrated wines worth finding	$26–28	www.cosentinowinery.com
Hot winery with Riccardo Cotarella at the helm; fabulous deal	$12–14	www.falesco.it or www.winebow.com (importer)
One of America's top Merlots, ripe and decadent	$50–55	www.northstarmerlot.com
Amazing Merlot-based wine; drizzle on your date	$80–85	www.gazin.com
The name is sexy, the wine is too	$16–18	www.avvwine.com
Embruix means bewitched— fall under its spell	$25–28	www.vallllach.com
Nearly black in color—not for the faint of heart	$25–28	www.hardywines.com.au
My favorite Australian Shiraz; like drinking velvet	$45–50	www.penfolds.com
Classic Napa producer— hot, hot, hot wine	$58–62	www.shafervineyards.com
Stunning wine from old-vine Tempranillo; limited production	$50–55	www.jorgeordonez.com (importer)

SEXY SPARKLERS

PRODUCER	WINE NAME	FROM	STYLE PROFILE
Yellowglen	"Pink"	Australia	Medium-bodied sparkler, crisp, elegant
Nicolas Feuillatte	Rosé "Premier Cru"	Champagne, France	Medium-bodied sparkler, crisp, elegant
Billecart-Salmon	Brut Rosé	Champagne, France	Medium-bodied sparkler, crisp, elegant
Laurent-Perrier	Rosé "Alexandra"	Champagne, France	Full-bodied sparkler, creamy, rich, toasty
Fox Creek	Sparkling Shiraz "Vixen"	South Australia	Full-bodied sparkler, creamy, lightly sweet

SEXY SWEETIES

PRODUCER	WINE NAME	FROM	STYLE PROFILE
Covey Run	Late-Harvest Riesling	Columbia Valley, Washington	Medium-bodied, sweet, juicy
Bonny Doon Vineyards	Muscat "Vin de Glacière"	California	Light-bodied, crisp, lightly sweet
Château Suduiraut	Sauternes	Sauternes, France	Full-bodied, sweet, supple, rich
Far Niente	"Dolce"	Napa Valley, California	Full-bodied, sweet, supple, rich
Warre's	10-year Tawny Porto "Otima"	Portugal	Medium-bodied, lightly sweet, nutty
Yalumba	Muscat "Museum Reserve" NV	Rutherglen, Australia	Full-bodied, sweet, supple, rich
Royal Tokaji Wine Company	Aszu 5 Puttonyos "Red Label"	Hungary	Full-bodied, sweet, supple, rich

SEXY BECAUSE	PRICE RANGE	MORE INFO . . .
Sleek packaging plus high quality	$12–15	www.yellowglen.com
Available; from well-known producer	$35–40	www.feuillatte.com
Personal favorite, found easily on restaurant wine lists	$50–58	www.champagne-billecart.fr
Antique-styled bottle; worth the price	$85–90	www.laurent-perrier.co.uk
Dark purple and lush; pair with chocolate	$16–19	www.foxcreekwines.com.au

SEXY BECAUSE	PRICE RANGE	MORE INFO . . .
Total value; good for drizzling on ice cream	$12–14	www.coveyrun.com
Even if you don't drink sweet, try this—you'll love it	$15–17 375 ml	www.bonnydoonvineyard .com
Sémillon-based sweetie from world-class producer	$35–45	www.suduiraut.com
Liquid gold; best American dessert wine	$70 375 ml	www.dolcewine.com
Personal favorite; chic bottle, classy wine	$19–22 500 ml	www.warre.com
Like eating caramel— decadent	$16–18 375 ml	www.yalumba.com
Famous dessert wine of Hungary; luscious texture	$28–34 500 ml	www.wilsondaniels.com (importer)

Bathtub Wines
ELEGANT WINES THAT INVITE RELAXATION

◌

I have kids and a husband. I have a job. I have stress. Sound familiar? If so, I'm going to share a secret with you. One of my absolute favorite places to enjoy wine is in the bathtub. My friend who is a stay-at-home mom calls her 5 P.M. glass of wine "Mommy's little helper." I call my end-of-the-day glass my bathtub wine, because I like to soak my stress away in a hot bubble bath. I do it at home, when I'm on the road working, or on vacation. I chose the following wines due to lower alcohol levels and bright levels of acidity, which make them ideal for sipping submerged in bubbles. If the bathtub isn't calling you, these picks are still ideal for a rejuvenating cocktail in or out of the tub.

Look for . . .

- **Whites:** My number one pick is Riesling from the Mosel-Saar-Ruwer region of Germany. These beauties are so thirst-quenching and pack huge flavor into a wine with usually less than nine percent alcohol. Don't miss fun whites with a sense of adventure like zesty Greek Moschofilero or the racy white wine from Spain called Albariño.
- **Reds and Pinks:** Dry rosé is a great tub wine because it's served nice and cool. Another top pick is juicy French Beaujolais. Also, look for wine named Chinon from the Loire Valley in France, made from Cabernet Franc grapes. Both Beaujolais and Chinon are reds that are best enjoyed when slightly chilled.
- **Bubbles:** What about trying bubbly with your bubble bath? It's easy with sparkling wine in single-serve bottles that come complete with a straw. There are top Champagnes and fun sparklers from all over the world now appearing in mini-me sizes . . . perfect for one. No need to waste a whole bottle, just pop, pour, and soak.

Want more picks? Check out: Spring Wines, Summer Wines, Hot Spots, Thanksgiving Wines

BATHTUB WHITES

PRODUCER	WINE NAME	FROM	STYLE PROFILE
Bloom	Riesling	Mosel-Saar-Ruwer, Germany	Light-bodied, racy, off-dry
Snoqualmie	Riesling "Naked"	Columbia Valley, Washington	Medium-bodied, aromatic, off-dry
Selbach-Oster	Riesling Kabinett	Mosel-Saar-Ruwer, Germany	Light-bodied, racy, off-dry
Dr. Loosen/ Chateau Ste. Michelle	Riesling "Eroica"	Columbia Valley, Washington	Medium-bodied, aromatic, off-dry
Boutari	Moschofilero	Mantinia, Greece	Medium-bodied, crisp, minerally
Condes de Albarei	"Salneval" Albariño	Rias Baixas, Spain	Medium-full-bodied, crisp, fruity

BATHTUB PINKS AND REDS

PRODUCER	WINE NAME	FROM	STYLE PROFILE
Marqués de Cáceres	Dry Rosé	Rioja, Spain	Light-bodied, light tannins, vibrant, fruity
Château Routas	"Rouvière" Rosé	Coteaux Varois, France	Light-bodied, light tannins, bright, earthy
SoloRosa	Rosé	California	Light-bodied, light tannins, vibrant, fruity
Georges Duboeuf	Morgon Cru	Beaujolais, France	Medium-bodied, light tannins, fresh, spicy
Marc Bredif	Chinon Rouge	Loire Valley, France	Medium-bodied, supple tannins, vibrant, earthy

SPECIAL BECAUSE	PRICE RANGE	MORE INFO . . .
Easy-open screw cap, lower alcohol	$7–8	www.preceptbrands.com (importer)
Not referring to lack of clothes, but organically grown grapes	$9–11	www.snoqualmie.com
One of my favorite producers in the Mosel	$12–14	www.selbach-oster.de
Joint venture of two world-class wineries; highly recommended	$20–24	www.chateau-ste-michelle.com
Fun, refreshing Greek white	$10–12	www.paternowines.com (importer)
Hot Spanish white similar to Sauvignon Blanc	$9–11	www.civusa.com (importer)

SPECIAL BECAUSE	PRICE RANGE	MORE INFO . . .
Best-buy wine; stock up by the case	$6–8	www.marquesdecaceres.com
Classy dry pink from South of France	$9–12	www.routas.com
Excellent—the pinnacle of pink power	$12–15	www.solorosawines.com
Cru means the top quality wine of Beaujolais	$10–12	www.duboeuf.com
From famous Ladoucette family; made with Cabernet Franc	$16–18	www.mmdusa.net (importer)

BATHTUB SPARKLERS

PRODUCER	WINE NAME	FROM	STYLE PROFILE
Lindauer	Brut Sparkling Wine	New Zealand	Medium-bodied sparkler, smooth, juicy
Francis Ford Coppola Presents	Blanc de Blancs "Sofia"	California	Medium-bodied sparkler, smooth, juicy
Pommery	Brut "POP"	Champagne, France	Medium-bodied sparkler, smooth, juicy
Piper-Heidsieck	Baby Piper	Champagne, France	Medium-bodied sparkler, crisp, elegant
Laurent-Perrier	Brut L-P	Champagne, France	Medium-bodied sparkler, crisp, elegant

CHEAT SHEET
Cellaring/Storing Wine
* * *
RACKING

There's no need to spend a lot of money on wine racks as long as they are sturdy. Use milk crates turned on their sides and lay the wine inside. If you buy specialized racks make sure the individual bottle openings will accommodate curvaceous Pinot Noir or Champagne bottles.

STORING

Laying the bottles on their sides helps keep the corks moist so they won't dry out. Wines bottled with screw caps can be stored upright.

SPECIAL BECAUSE	PRICE RANGE	MORE INFO . . .
Not complex but easy to sip	$8–9 three-pack minis	www.allieddomecqwines.com
Single-serve cans with a ready-made straw	$15–17 four-pack minis	www.ffcpresents.com
Originator of the mini-me bottle with a straw	$8–10 per mini	www.pommery.com
Bottles come swathed in red wrapping—sultry	$8–10 187 ml mini	www.piper-heidsieck.com
One of my favorite Champagne houses	$7–9 per mini	www.laurent-perrier.com

TEMPERATURE

Maintain the wine at a constant, fairly cool temperature, ideally around 50 to 55 degrees. It's more important to keep the wine in a stable temperature than one of perfect coolness. Fluctuation in temperature inflicts the most harm on wine.

DARK

Keep bottles in a darker place as bright light can damage wine. Try in a cool closet, under the bed, in the garage, under the stairs. Heat, dryness, and light are wines' enemies.

Virtual Vacation Vinos

TAKE A VINOUS TRIP AROUND THE WINE WORLD IN ONE
CASE—BARGAIN TO LUXURY OPTIONS

Have an adventure with wine by sipping your way around the world in twelve bottles. Not only is it fun, it's the best way to get a look at the range of wine types and styles available to wine lovers these days. I've selected three mixed cases in various price ranges to satisfy novices as well as those in the know. Many stores offer discounts when you buy a case of twelve bottles. Stash the case and slowly explore the world over a period of months. Pair each wine with a different dish and discover what you like in wine and food pairing. Or, cellar some of the wines and see how they improve with age. Here are my criteria for these case selections:

- A mix of white and red, plus one sparkling wine and one dessert wine.
- Wines that are good examples of their type/style and region.
- Balanced wines that are all drinkable now, but with a number of cellar-worthy selections, indicated by an asterisk:
  *Cellar short term—one to five years
  **Cellar longer—five to ten years

Want more picks? Check out: Gathering of the Greats, 25 to Try Before You Die, Hot Spots, Wines to Watch

BARGAIN CASE: AROUND $100
($8–12 PER BOTTLE)

PRODUCER	WINE NAME	FROM	STYLE PROFILE
Dr. Loosen	Riesling "Dr. L"	Mosel-Saar-Ruwer, Germany	Light-bodied, racy, off-dry
Simonsig	Chenin Blanc	Stellenbosch, South Africa	Light-bodied, crisp, refreshing
Ecco Domani	Pinot Grigio	Delle Venezie, Italy	Light-bodied, crisp, refreshing
Monkey Bay	Sauvignon Blanc	Marlborough, New Zealand	Medium-bodied, racy, herbal
Canyon Road	Chardonnay	California	Medium-bodied, light oak, juicy
Echelon	Pinot Noir	California	Medium-bodied, light tannins, fresh, spicy
Columbia Crest	Merlot "Grand Estates"	Columbia Valley, Washington	Medium-bodied, supple tannins, smooth, juicy
*Cousiño-Macul	Cabernet Sauvignon	Maipo Valley, Chile	Medium-bodied, supple tannins, vibrant, earthy
Catena	Malbec "Alamos"	Mendoza, Argentina	Medium-full-bodied, supple tannins, vibrant, juicy
Rosemount Estate	Shiraz "Diamond Label"	South Eastern Australia	Full-bodied, supple tannins, spicy, ripe
Segura Viudas	Brut Cava "Reserva"	Spain	Medium-bodied sparkler, smooth, juicy
Quady Winery	"Essensia" Orange Muscat dessert wine	California	Light-bodied, crisp, lightly sweet

SPECIAL BECAUSE	PRICE RANGE	MORE INFO . . .
Good introduction to Riesling; leading German producer	$10–12	www.drloosen.com
Complex wine for the price	$10–12	www.simonsig.co.za
Stylish bottle, widely available	$7–10	www.style.com/eccodomani
Wine with sassy personality	$8–10	www.cwine.com (importer)
Well-balanced; good food wine	$10–12	www.canyonroadwinery.com
Good, inexpensive Pinot Noir? You bet	$10–12	www.echelonvineyards.com
Washington is known for Merlot; this is a steal	$8–10	www.columbia-crest.com
Classic Chilean producer crafting high-quality value bottles	$8–10	www.cousinomacul.cl
My top-pick bargain wine from Argentina	$8–10	www.nicolascatena.com
Widely available and delivers the goods; velvety	$9–10	www.rosemountestate.com
Blend of grapes like Macabeo, Parellada, and Xarel·lo	$7–10	www.seguraviudas.com
Crowd-pleasing dessert wine; serve well chilled	$10–12 375 ml	www.quadywinery.com

CLASSIC CASE: AROUND $200
($13–25 PER BOTTLE)

PRODUCER	WINE NAME	FROM	STYLE PROFILE
Dr. Konstantin Frank	"Dry" Johannisberg Riesling	Finger Lakes, New York	Light-bodied, crisp, refreshing
Elk Cove	Pinot Gris	Willamette Valley, Oregon	Medium-full-bodied, crisp, fruity
Leeuwin Estate	"Siblings" Sauvignon Blanc/Sémillon	Margaret River, Western Australia	Medium-bodied, crisp, minerally
Vionta	Albariño	Rias Baixas, Spain	Medium-full-bodied, crisp, fruity
Joseph Drouhin	"Véro" Chardonnay	Bourgogne, France	Full-bodied, crisp, spicy, elegant
Brancott	Pinot Noir "Reserve"	Marlborough, New Zealand	Medium-bodied, light tannins, fresh, spicy
Paul Jaboulet Aîné	"Les Jalets"	Crozes-Hermitage, France	Medium-bodied, supple tannins, vibrant, earthy
*Veramonte	"Primus" red blend	Casablanca Valley, Chile	Full-bodied, supple tannins, smooth, earthy
*Geyser Peak	Cabernet Sauvignon	Alexander Valley, California	Medium-full-bodied, supple tannins, vibrant, juicy
*Prazo de Roriz	Red table wine	Douro, Portugal	Medium-bodied, supple tannins, vibrant, earthy
Schramsberg	"Mirabelle" Brut sparkling wine	North Coast, California	Medium-bodied sparkler, smooth, juicy
*Taylor Fladgate	Late-Bottled Vintage	Portugal	Full-bodied, sweet, supple, rich

SPECIAL BECAUSE	PRICE RANGE	MORE INFO . . .
Discover New York wines with this beauty	$14–16	www.drfrankwines.com
Good example of fleshier Oregon style	$16–18	www.elkcove.com
Label celebrates the family-run business	$19–21	www.leeuwinestate.com.au
Hot Spanish white, perfect with shellfish	$15–18	www.heredadcollection.com
Blended by the talented hands of Véronique Drouhin	$18–20	www.drouhin.com
Available wine showcasing New Zealand style	$18–20	www.brancottvineyards.com
Signature Syrah from the northern Rhône	$15–18	www.jaboulet.com
Blend of Merlot, Cabernet Sauvignon and Carmenère; top quality	$15–18	www.veramonte.com
Consistently good Cabernet from classic Sonoma producer	$13–16	www.geyserpeakwinery.com
Blend of Tinta Roriz and Touriga Nacional grapes	$12–15	www.quintaderoriz.com
Great value, made with Chardonnay and Pinot Noir	$15–18	www.schramsberg.com
A real steal—like a Vintage Port but one-third the price	$20–22	www.taylor.pt

LUXURY CASE: AROUND $400
($25–45+ PER BOTTLE)

PRODUCER	WINE NAME	FROM	STYLE PROFILE
Joh. Jos. Prüm	Riesling Kabinett "Wehlener Sonnenuhr"	Mosel-Saar-Ruwer, Germany	Medium-bodied, crisp, minerally
Jermann	Pinot Grigio	Friuli, Italy	Medium-full-bodied, crisp, fruity
Lynmar	Chardonnay	Russian River Valley, California	Full-bodied, creamy, oaky, ripe
McCrea Cellars	Viognier	Yakima Valley, Washington	Full-bodied, soft, aromatic
*Alvaro Palacios	"Les Terrasses"	Priorat, Spain	Medium-bodied, supple tannins, vibrant, earthy
**M. Chapoutier	"La Bernardine"	Châteauneuf-du-Pape, France	Medium-bodied, supple tannins, vibrant, earthy
*Domaine Serene	Pinot Noir "Evenstad Reserve"	Willamette Valley, Oregon	Medium-full-bodied, supple tannins, vibrant, juicy
**Penfolds	Cabernet-Shiraz "Bin 389"	Southern Australia	Full-bodied, supple tannins, smooth, earthy
**Meerlust	"Rubicon" red blend	Stellenbosch, South Africa	Full-bodied, strong tannins, lush, concentrated
Rancho Zabaco	Zinfandel "Chiotti Vineyard"	Dry Creek Valley, California	Full-bodied, supple tannins, spicy, ripe
Henriot	Blanc de Blancs "Blanc Souverain"	Champagne, France	Medium-bodied sparkler, crisp, elegant
Churchill's	10-Year Tawny Port	Portugal	Medium-bodied, lightly sweet, nutty

SPECIAL BECAUSE	PRICE RANGE	MORE INFO . . .
Known simply as J. J. Prüm, this wine is amazing	$33–35	www.germanwine.net (importer)
One of Italy's best white wine producers	$22–25	www.jermann.it
Well-priced for the quality; limited production	$27–30	www.lynmarwinery.com
One of my favorite Rhône-style producers	$28–30	www.mccreacellars.com
Hottest winemaker in Spain	$28–30	www.rarewineco.com (importer)
Cellarworthy wine; labels are in Braille	$34–38	www.chapoutier.com
Don't know this winery? You should—top-notch	$45–48	www.domaineserene.com
Worth three times the price for its quality	$22–25	www.penfolds.com
Bordeaux-style blend from South African luminary	$28–30	www.meerlust.co.za
Single-vineyard Zinfandel specialists; available	$24–26	www.ranchozabaco.com
Lesser-known Champagne producer but world-class	$35–38	www.champagne-henriot.com
Try even if you don't drink sweet; delicious	$30–35	www.churchills-port.com

MYTH-BUSTER
Older Wine Is Better
* * *

Most wines on the market today are not meant to be aged, but are for immediate consumption. However, there are wines that will improve with age. Powerful reds such as world-class Bordeaux and other Cabernet Sauvignon–based wines, Italian Barolo and Brunello di Montelcino, and Vintage Port will generally improve as the components— such as acid, sweetness, and tannins—preserve the wine. Most whites should be drunk young, though, because you want to capture the freshness of the wine, so buy the latest vintage available on store shelves.

Top whites like Grand Cru white Burgundy, Austrian Grüner Veltliner, sweeter German Rieslings, and French Sauternes can get more complex over time. When you age bottles, however, the fruity quality that is the hallmark of modern wine is usually lost. You gain other interesting characteristics such as earthy and spicy aromas, nutty notes, or hints of leather and dried fruit flavors. To some that's appealing, to others it's not.

Think of aging wine as a bell curve. On the way up and when it hits a plateau, exploring the changes in the wine is great fun. But once the wine is over the hill, it's like a scary roller-coaster ride. That steep downward curve is what you want to avoid. My suggestion is to buy at least three to six bottles of a wine you want to age and drink them over a period of time. When the wine exhibits the character you like, drink up.

Hot Spots

SIZZLING WINES FROM SPAIN TO SICILY AND
CANADA TO TEXAS

CO

You're the first one to buy a new gadget or new fashion. You're cool, hip, and trendy (even if you're not, you like to think you are). Here's a wine litmus test: Do you know these regions? If so, you pass with flying colors. If not, get ready to take a vinous adventure.

SPAIN'S HOT SPOTS

Toro For lovers of bold reds, Toro is for you. Though other varieties such as Garnacha are planted, the celebrated grape of the region is Tinta de Toro. A local name for Spain's trademark red variety Tempranillo, Tinta de Toro has adapted over time to the harsh conditions of Toro. A high-altitude plateau with low rainfall and extreme temperature swings, Toro's continental climate produces grapes with power and concentration. Toro is home to some of the world's most ancient grape vines. It's even said that Toro wines are what Christopher Columbus took with him on his voyages of discovery.

Bierzo Bierzo is situated in the mountainous region of northwestern Spain between the high plateaus of Toro and the lush, green coastline of western Spain. The primary red grape there is one most have never heard of, much less tasted: Mencía. Similarities exist with Cabernet Franc's telltale floral aromas and mineral notes, but wines made from Mencía are also reminiscent of a silky Pinot Noir or a pretty Italian Nebbiolo.

Jumilla Located in southeastern Spain near the Mediterranean, this is a historic winegrowing region dating back to Roman times. Its hearty, full-bodied reds made primarily from the Monastrell grape variety (otherwise known as Mourvèdre) are getting attention lately. Wines under $10 are flooding the market and making a big mark for bargain wine lovers. For more information on all these regions, check out www.winesfromspain.com.

SPAIN'S HOT WINES

PRODUCER	WINE NAME	FROM	STYLE PROFILE
Wrongo Dongo	Monastrell	Jumilla, Spain	Full-bodied, supple tannins, smooth, earthy
Mad Dogs and Englishmen	Monastrell/Cabernet/ Shiraz blend	Jumilla, Spain	Full-bodied, supple tannins, smooth, earthy
Finca Luzón	Castillo de Luzón	Jumilla, Spain	Full-bodied, supple tannins, smooth, earthy
Telmo Rodriguez	"Dehesa Gago"	Toro, Spain	Full-bodied, supple tannins, smooth, earthy
Viñas Cénit	Tinta de Toro	Vino de la Tierra de Zamora, Spain	Full-bodied, strong tannins, lush, concentrated
Bodega Mauro	San Román	Toro, Spain	Full-bodied, strong tannins, lush, concentrated
Dominio de Tares	Mencía "Baltos"	Bierzo, Spain	Medium-bodied, supple tannins, vibrant, earthy
Bodegas Pittacum	Mencía "Aurea"	Bierzo, Spain	Medium-bodied, supple tannins, vibrant, earthy
Bodegas Estefanía	"Tilenus" Mencía Crianza	Bierzo, Spain	Medium-bodied, supple tannins, vibrant, earthy

SPANISH LABEL CHEAT SHEET
Tips for Tastes
* * *

Cosecha/Joven: Fresh and fruity young wines with little or no oak aging.

Crianza: Aged for at least two years with a minimum of six months in barrels. Smooth and approachable.

SPECIAL BECAUSE	PRICE RANGE	MORE INFO . . .
Fun wine, packed with flavor	$6–8	www.jorgeordonez.com (importer)
From Guy Anderson, the brains behind Fat Bastard brand	$10–13	www.clickwinegroup.com (importer)
Blend of Monastrell and Garnacha grapes	$10–13	www.fincaluzon.com
Personal favorite from ultra-hot winemaker, Telmo R.	$12–14	www.jorgeordonez.com (importer)
Amazing wine from sixty-year-old vines	$44–46	www.jorgeordonez.com (importer)
Star-studded owners, including former winemaker of Vega Sicilia	$48–52	www.bodegasmauro.com
Newer winery crafting wines of complexity and value	$16–18	www.dominiodetares.com or www.classicalwines.com (importer)
Reminiscent of Pinot Noir; elegant style	$20–22	www.pittacum.com
A top property in Bierzo; very modern winery	$22–24	www.bodegasestefania.com

Reserva: *Minimum of three years of aging with at least one year in barrel. Reservas are more expensive, but distinctive for their roundness and supple tannins.*

Gran Reserva: *Ages for a minimum of five years with at least twenty-four months in barrel. Gran Reservas are prized for their balance and subtle complexity.*

WINE ABCS
Tempranillo
* * *

Tempranillo is Spain's signature red grape variety. Responsible for the well-known wines of the Rioja region, it's also planted in spots like Ribera del Duero, Toro, and across southern Spain. When aged, Tempranillo exhibits more elegant, spicy notes similar to a Pinot Noir, but when made in a modern style, it sports richness, depth, and loads of cherry/red berry fruit flavors and peppery spice. There are plantings of the variety in other parts of the world, but it still remains Spain's trademark variety.

SOUTHERN ITALY HOT SPOTS

Sicily This island, located off the tip of the boot of Italy, is one of the oldest wine areas in the country. Known in the past primarily for the fortified wine Marsala, Sicily is now home to exciting wines made from white grape varieties like Fiano and Grillo and signature reds such as hearty, bold Nero d'Avola.

Puglia If Italy is shaped like a boot, Puglia (or Apulia, as it's known in Italy) comprises the heel of the boot. Hot and relatively flat, it's one of the largest bulk wine-producing regions in Europe. What's special about the wines of Puglia is the excitement surrounding the local grape Primitivo, which has been shown to be essentially the same variety as Zinfandel. For more information on Italian wine regions, go to www.italianmade.com.

LESSER-KNOWN AMERICAN HOT SPOTS 🖎

When talking about American wine, we're mostly referring to California wine, which makes up nearly 90 percent of domestic production and almost ranks as an entire country by the numbers. Washington and Oregon are also on the map for their world-class bottles. But guess what? Wine is now made in fifty states, so there are interesting examples coming from all over the country. Many of my top-pick selections come from New York State, Texas, Ohio, and Virginia. The hard part is finding these wines if you live in other states. For a listing of state winery associations, check out www.allamericanwineries.com.

CANADA 🖎

Look for stylish bottles from the Okanagan Valley in western British Columbia, located several hours north of Vancouver, or for those from the eastern Niagara Peninsula.

SOUTH AFRICA 🖎

Warm up to the cool wines from South Africa. In what are some of the most dramatically beautiful wine regions in the world, grapes such as Chenin Blanc (or Steen) and Pinotage (a cross of Pinot Noir and Cinsault) grow in the maritime-influenced climate of the Western Cape. Look for wines from the Paarl and Stellenbosch growing regions. To find out more about South African wines, check out www .wosa.co.za.

SOUTHERN ITALIAN HOTTIES

PRODUCER	WINE NAME	FROM	STYLE PROFILE
Feudo Arancio	Grillo	Sicilia, Italy	Medium-full-bodied, crisp, fruity
Mandrarossa	Fiano	Sicilia, Italy	Medium-full-bodied, crisp, fruity
Gabbiano	"Bonello" Primitivo	Puglia, Italy	Medium-bodied, supple tannins, vibrant, earthy
Feudo Monaci	Primitivo	Puglia, Italy	Medium-bodied, supple tannins, vibrant, earthy
A-Mano	Primitivo	Puglia, Italy	Medium-full-bodied, supple tannins, vibrant, juicy
Promessa	Rosso Salento	Puglia, Italy	Medium-full-bodied, supple tannins, vibrant, juicy
Santa Anastasia	Nero d'Avola	Sicilia, Italy	Full-bodied, supple tannins, smooth, earthy
Tenuta Rapitalà	"Nu har" Nero d'Avola Blend	Sicilia, Italy	Full-bodied, supple tannins, smooth, earthy
Mirabile	Nero d'Avola	Sicilia, Italy	Full-bodied, supple tannins, spicy, ripe
Morgante	Nero d'Avola	Sicilia, Italy	Full-bodied, supple tannins, spicy, ripe
Planeta	"Santa Cecilia" Nero d'Avola	Sicilia, Italy	Full-bodied, supple tannins, spicy, ripe

SPECIAL BECAUSE	PRICE RANGE	MORE INFO . . .
Dry white from rare grape variety used in Marsala	$8–10	www.mezzacorona.it
Unique white variety; limited availability	$7–9	www.mandrarossa.it or www.palmbayimports.com (importer)
Famous Tuscan producer's southern Italian offering	$8–9	www.gabbiano.com
Earthier than Zinfandel, great price tag	$7–9	www.frederickwildman.com (importer)
Personal favorite, made by American Mark Shannon	$8–10	www.empson.com (importer)
Another Shannon creation; blend of Negroamaro and Primitivo	$8–10	www.empson.com (importer)
Great value wine from ultra-modern winery; must buy	$12–14	www.empson.com (importer)
Limited availability but serves up value	$10–11	www.rapitala.it
Affordable and easy sipping style; party pick	$11–13	www.casamirabile.it or www.domaineselect.com (importer)
One of Sicily's top producers making stylish bottlings	$14–17	www.winebow.com (importer)
Sicily's premier winery; ageworthy and complex red	$35–37	www.planeta.it

OTHER AMERICAN WINES

PRODUCER	WINE NAME	FROM	STYLE PROFILE
Llano Estacado Winery	Sauvignon Blanc	Texas	Medium-bodied, racy, herbal
Becker Vineyards	Claret	Texas	Medium-bodied, supple tannins, smooth, juicy
Stone Hill	Norton	Missouri	Medium-bodied, supple tannins, smooth, juicy
Horton Cellars	Viognier	Virginia	Full-bodied, soft, aromatic
Barboursville Vineyards	Viognier	Virginia	Full-bodied, soft, aromatic
Kluge Estate	Brut "New World Sparkling Wine"	Virginia	Medium-bodied sparkler, smooth, juicy
Hermann J. Wiemer	Dry Johannisberg Riesling	Finger Lakes, New York	Medium-bodied, crisp, minerally
Dr. Konstantin Frank	Cabernet Franc	Finger Lakes, New York	Medium-bodied, supple tannins, vibrant, earthy
Fox Run Vineyard	Meritage	Finger Lakes, New York	Medium-full-bodied, supple tannins, vibrant, juicy
Bedell Cellars	Merlot	North Fork Long Island, New York	Medium-full-bodied, supple tannins, vibrant, juicy
Wölffer Estate	Merlot "Reserve"	The Hamptons, Long Island, New York	Medium-full-bodied, supple tannins, vibrant, juicy
St. Joseph Vineyard	Pinot Noir "Reserve"	Grand River Valley, Ohio	Medium-bodied, supple tannins, vibrant, earthy
Ste. Chapelle	Riesling Icewine "Reserve"	Idaho	Medium-bodied, sweet, juicy
Gruet Winery	Brut Sparkling Wine	New Mexico	Medium-bodied sparkler, smooth, juicy

SPECIAL BECAUSE	PRICE RANGE	MORE INFO . . .
Most recognizable Texas winery	$12–14	www.llanowine.com
Bordeaux-style blend, mostly Cabernet Sauvignon	$16–18	www.beckervineyards.com
Missouri's best winery; Norton is similar to Zinfandel	$17–18	www.stonehillwinery.com
Specializes in Viognier	$16–18	www.hvwine.com
Winery also makes Italian-style wines	$20–23	www.barboursvillecellar .com
Impressive offering, limited production	$38–40	www.klugeestateonline.com
Specialist of German-style Rieslings	$16–18	www.wiemer.com
Most famous producer in the region; must-try wines	$18–20	www.drfrankwines.com
Blend of Merlot with Cabernet Franc	$35–40	www.foxrunvineyards.com
If you like Merlot, buy this wine	$18–20	www.bedellcellars.com
Classic producer on Long Island; beautiful winery to visit	$20–22	www.wolffer.com
Impressive showing from small, family-run operation	$23–25	www.saintjosephvineyard .com
Idaho icewine? You bet. State's best winery.	$18–21	www.stechapelle.com
Great deal on bubbly; fairly available	$13–15	www.gruetwinery.com

CANADIAN WINES

PRODUCER	WINE NAME	FROM	STYLE PROFILE
Jackson-Triggs	Sauvignon Blanc "Reserve"	Okanagan Valley, British Columbia	Medium-bodied, racy, herbal
Pillitteri Estates	Riesling Ice wine	Niagara, Ontario	Full-bodied, sweet, supple, rich
Mission Hill	"Oculus"	Okanagan Valley, British Columbia	Full-bodied, strong tannins, lush, concentrated
Inniskillin Wines	Ice wine "Vidal" oak-aged	Niagara, Ontario	Full-bodied, sweet, supple, rich

SOUTH AFRICAN WINES

PRODUCER	WINE NAME	FROM	STYLE PROFILE
Mulderbosch	Chenin Blanc	Stellenbosch, South Africa	Medium-bodied, light oak, juicy
Brampton	Sauvignon Blanc	South Africa	Medium-bodied, racy, herbal
Thelema	Sauvignon Blanc	Stellenbosch, South Africa	Medium-bodied, racy, herbal
Fleur du Cap	Sauvignon Blanc "Unfiltered"	South Africa	Medium-bodied, racy, herbal
Fairview	"Goats do Roam"	Western Cape, South Africa	Medium-bodied, supple tannins, vibrant, earthy
Indaba	Pinotage	South Africa	Medium-bodied, light tannins, fresh, spicy
Guardian Peak	"Frontier"	South Africa	Medium-full-bodied, supple tannins, vibrant, juicy
Meerlust	"Rubicon"	Stellenbosch, South Africa	Full bodied, strong tannins, lush, concentrated

SPECIAL BECAUSE	PRICE RANGE	MORE INFO . . .
One of the most widely distributed Canadian wines	$10–12	www.jacksontriggswinery.com
Limited production but worth the effort to find	$28–30 375 ml	www.pillitteri.com
Bordeaux-style blend made by the premier Okanagan winery	$50–55	www.missionhillwinery.com
Worth the cost: Canada's star ice wine producer	$80–85 375 ml	www.inniskillin.com

SPECIAL BECAUSE	PRICE RANGE	MORE INFO . . .
Unique style; dry, touch of oak aging	$10–13	www.capeclassics.com (importer)
Similar in style to New Zealand Sauvignon Blanc	$8–10	www.capeclassics.com (importer)
Classic style with no oak	$16–18	www.thelema.co.za
Available wine from well-known producer	$15–17	www.fleurducap.co.za
Get it? A blend of Rhône varieties	$8–10	www.fairview.co.za
Captures unique earthy quality of Pinotage; available	$8–9	www.capeclassics.com (importer)
Blend of Cabernet, Shiraz, Merlot from Ernie Els Wines	$10–13	www.guardianpeak.com
Cellar-worthy blend of Cabernet Sauvignon and Merlot	$25–30	www.meerlust.co.za

GREECE 🐟

Forget the days of bad retsina and oxidized whites. Greek wines are modern, fruit-driven, and exciting. Grapes are grown on the islands and across the country, but look for those from the Peloponnese peninsula where top wine spots such as Nemea and Mantinia are located. The problem with Greek wines is reading the labels where it all looks, you guessed, Greek, but two key words to remember are Moschofilero and Agiorgitiko. The first is a crisp, fresh white grape variety producing wines similar in style to Sauvignon Blanc, while the second is a red grape that makes smooth, supple reds. For more information, check out www.allaboutgreekwine.com.

PRODUCER	WINE NAME	FROM	STYLE PROFILE
Boutari	Moschofilero	Mantinia, Greece	Medium-bodied, crisp, minerally
Tselepos	Moschofilero	Mantinia, Greece	Medium-bodied, racy, herbal
Spiropoulos	Agiorgitiko "Red Stag"	Peloponnese, Greece	Medium-full-bodied, supple tannins, vibrant, juicy
Palivou Vineyards	Agiorgitiko	Nemea Valley, Greece	Medium-full-bodied, supple tannins, vibrant, juicy
Gaia Estate	"Gaia Estate" Agiorgitiko	Peloponnese, Greece	Medium-full-bodied, supple tannins, vibrant, juicy

WINE ABCS
Retsina
* * *

A unique Greek wine with a rich 3,000-year history, retsina takes its name from the pine pitch, or resin, that once lined wine containers to protect against spoilage. Nowadays you can find high-quality retsina, which is made by adding bits of pine resin during the winemaking process. Uncork a bottle with Greek fare for a virtual trip to the islands.

SPECIAL BECAUSE	PRICE RANGE	MORE INFO . . .
Personal favorite from Greece's best-known producer	$10–12	www.paternowines.com (importer)
Hard to find but worth the effort; try with shellfish	$13–15	www.allaboutgreekwine.com
Ultra-smooth, from organically grown grapes	$15–16	www.domainspiropoulos.com
A wine to seek out; a great deal for quality	$16–18	www.stellarimports.com
Limited production, impressive concentration	$35–38	www.winebow.com

WESTERN AUSTRALIA 🐟

Too often, we think of wines from Down Under as ultra-ripe fruit bombs. It's true that those from warmer-climate growing regions such as the Barossa Valley in South Australia drip with richness, but

PRODUCER	WINE NAME	FROM	STYLE PROFILE
Ferngrove	Sauvignon Blanc/Semillon	Frankland River, Western Australia	Medium-bodied, racy, herbal
Voyager Estate	Chardonnay	Margaret River, Western Australia	Medium-full-bodied, crisp, fruity
Vasse Felix	Chardonnay "Adams Road"	Margaret River, Australia	Medium-full-bodied, crisp, fruity
Evans & Tate	Chardonnay	Margaret River, Australia	Medium-bodied, crisp, minerally
Goundry	Cabernet Sauvignon "Offspring"	Western Australia	Medium-full-bodied, supple tannins, vibrant, juicy
Leeuwin Estate	Cabernet Sauvignon/ Merlot "Prelude Vineyard"	Margaret River, Australia	Medium-full-bodied, supple tannins, vibrant, juicy
Cullen	Cabernet Sauvignon/ Merlot "Diana Madeline"	Margaret River, Australia	Full-bodied, supple tannins, spicy, ripe

Australia is a big country. One of the hippest spots for wine is the remote western side of the continent, where the sun meets the surf. This ocean-influenced climate moderates temperatures and lends elegance to the wines of the region, particularily those from Margaret River. For more information, check out www.wawine.com.au.

SPECIAL BECAUSE	PRICE RANGE	MORE INFO . . .
Up-and-coming region and producer	$19–22	www.ferngrove.com/au
Must-buy. Chablis-like elegance at stellar price	$21–23	www.voyagerestate.com/au
Captures Western Aussie style—fresh	$12–15	www.vassefelix.com.au
Similar to Chablis in its minerality. Top producer	$15–17	www.evansandtate.com.au
Affordable second label of Goundry; available	$13–16	www.goundry.com
Personal favorite; preeminent winery of the region	$19–23	www.leeuwinestate.com.au
World-class wine at a price tag to match	$58–62	www.cullenwines.com.au

Wines to Watch

EXCITING SIGNATURE VARIETALS MAKING A SPLASH
IN THE WINE WORLD

∞

Don't let your wine world get boring. Reach out past Chardonnay and Cabernet. Put Pinot Grigio and Pinot Noir aside for the night and seek out some wines that may be unfamiliar. Just like herbal-scented Sauvignon Blanc from Marlborough, New Zealand, has created buzz for its singular style, the following wine types are ideal combinations of the right grape variety planted in the right place.

WINE ABCS
Appellations

* * *

Winegrowing areas can also be called appellations, *a French term now used throughout the world. Whether large or small, appellations are officially recognized and regulated geographic winegrowing areas. Depending upon the size of the appellation or region, wines develop similar style characteristics—the smaller the region, the more definitive the taste. In the United States we call these American Viticultural Areas (AVA). The wine must contain 85 to 100 percent of grapes from the AVA listed on the label, and if it is a varietal wine, such as Merlot or Chardonnay, at least 75 percent of wine must come from that grape variety. Other countries, however, are even more highly regulated in terms of the kinds of grapes planted, how the grapes are grown, and techniques of making the wine. For more information check out www.appellationamerica.com.*

ALBARIÑO FROM RIAS BAIXAS, SPAIN 🍷

The region of Rias Baixas is located across the border from Portugal
along the Atlantic coastline of Spain. The larger area is called Galicia,
with its own language—Gallego—and it's a world away from what
most people imagine Spain to be. Lush, green mountains are a back-
drop for sandy beaches and dramatic rias (fjordlike inlets) rising

PRODUCER	WINE NAME	FROM	STYLE PROFILE
Condes de Albarei	Albariño	Rias Baixas, Spain	Medium-bodied, crisp, minerally
Martin Codax	"Burgans" Albariño	Rias Baixas, Spain	Medium-bodied, crisp, minerally
Mar de Frades	Albariño	Rias Baixas, Spain	Medium-bodied, crisp, minerally
Bodegas Fillaboa	Albariño	Rias Baixas, Spain	Medium-bodied, crisp, minerally
Pazo de Barrantes	Albariño	Rias Baixas, Spain	Medium-full-bodied, crisp, fruity
Morgadio	Albariño	Rias Baixas, Spain	Medium-bodied, crisp, minerally
Vionta	Albariño	Rias Baixas, Spain	Medium-full-bodied, crisp, fruity
Lusco	Albariño	Rias Baixas, Spain	Medium-full-bodied, crisp, fruity
Santiago de Ruiz	O Rosal	Rias Baixas, Spain	Medium-bodied, crisp, minerally
Terras Gauda	O Rosal	Rias Baixas, Spain	Medium-full-bodied, crisp, fruity

from the sea. The star white grape in Rias Baixas is Albariño. Though other white grapes such as Treixadura may be part of the blend, Albariño has a unique citrusy freshness wrapped around a strong backbone of acidity. There are a few plantings of Albariño elsewhere around the world, but it's really only in this area that the grape shines.

SPECIAL BECAUSE	PRICE RANGE	MORE INFO . . .
One of the most available versions	$12–13	www.condesdealbarei.com
Hint of sweetness; crowd-pleasing style	$13–15	www.martincodax.com
Sleek blue bottle—ideal gift wine	$15–17	www.grantusa.com
Limited availability but one of the best	$14–16	www.bodegasfillaboa.com
A darling of wine lists; watch for in restaurants	$16–18	www.marquesdemurrieta.com
Complex white comparable to wines twice the price	$18–20	www.morgadio.com
Fuller style; available	$15–18	www.heredadcollection.com
Personal favorite for its intensity	$20–23	www.classicalwine.com
Albariño blended with Loureiro, Treixadura	$17–18	www.bodegasantiagoruiz.com
Blend of Albariño with Loureiro and Caino Blañco	$18–20	www.terrasgauda.com

GRÜNER VELTLINER FROM AUSTRIA 🦜

Grüner Veltliner is Austria's most planted variety and makes white
wines that are not only some of the most food-friendly on the planet,
but also some of the longest-lived. Bone dry with lemony freshness
and laden with mineral notes, it's a top option with fish or spicy fare.

PRODUCER	WINE NAME	FROM	STYLE PROFILE
Erich Berger	Grüner Veltliner	Kremstal, Austria	Medium-bodied, crisp, minerally
Schloss Gobelsburg	"Gobelsburger" Grüner Veltliner	Kamptal, Austria	Medium-bodied, crisp, minerally
Ott	Grüner Veltliner "Am Berg"	Wagram-Donauland, Austria	Medium-bodied, crisp, minerally
Dr. Unger	Grüner Veltliner "Ried Gottschelle"	Kremstal, Austria	Medium-bodied, crisp, minerally
Leth	Grüner Veltliner	Donauland, Austria	Medium-bodied, crisp, minerally
Weingut Pfaffl	Grüner Veltliner	Weinviertel, Austria	Medium-bodied, crisp, minerally
Schloss Gobelsburg	Grüner Veltliner "Lamm"	Kamptal, Austria	Medium-bodied, crisp, minerally
Bründlmayer	Grüner Veltliner "Alte Reben"	Kamptal, Austria	Medium-bodied, crisp, minerally

SPECIAL BECAUSE	PRICE RANGE	MORE INFO . . .
This wine is a steal!	$10 for 1 liter	www.skurnikwines.com (importer)
Second label of Schloss, so great value	$11–13	www.gobelsburg.at
Young star Bernard Ott is one to watch	$14–16	www.winzerhaus-ott.at www.skurnikwines.com (importer)
Petra Unger is a rising-star woman of wine	$15–17	www.drunger.at
Family-owned winery specializing in local varieties	$15–17	www.domaineselect.com (importer)
Limited production, but worth search	$17–18	www.bluedanubewine.com (importer)
Classic style, world-class producer	$40–43	www.gobelsburg.at
Personal favorite; Willi Bründlmayer is a genius	$44	www.bruendlmayer.com

Malbec from Argentina

Malbec is a brawny, thick-skinned, and deeply hued grape used to add a bit of muscle in Bordeaux blends. Planted around the world from France to California, the grape has found its true home in

PRODUCER	WINE NAME	FROM	STYLE PROFILE
San Telmo	Malbec	Mendoza, Argentina	Medium-bodied, supple tannins, smooth, juicy
Bodega Norton	Malbec	Mendoza, Argentina	Medium-bodied, supple tannins, smooth, juicy
Rutini	Malbec "Trumpeter"	Tupungato, Argentina	Medium-full-bodied, supple tannins, vibrant, juicy
Altos	Malbec "Las Hormigas"	Mendoza, Argentina	Medium-full-bodied, supple tannins, vibrant, juicy
Valentin Bianchi	Malbec "Elsa"	Mendoza, Argentina	Medium-full-bodied, supple tannins, vibrant, juicy
Andeluna	Malbec "Winemaker's Selection"	Mendoza, Argentina	Medium-full-bodied, supple tannins, vibrant, juicy
Trapiche	Malbec "Broquel"	Mendoza, Argentina	Medium-full-bodied, supple tannins, vibrant, juicy
Salentein	Malbec	Mendoza, Argentina	Medium-full-bodied, supple tannins, vibrant, juicy
Susana Balbo	Malbec "Dominio del Plata"	Mendoza Argentina	Full-bodied, strong tannins, lush, concentrated
Catena	Malbec "Alta"	Mendoza, Argentina	Full-bodied, strong tannins, lush, concentrated

Argentina. When the variety is planted on the sunny slopes of Argentina's Andes Mountains, where nighttime temperatures plunge, the grapes retain their zesty acidity and produce reds with a unique marriage of power and elegance.

SPECIAL BECAUSE	PRICE RANGE	MORE INFO . . .
Not complex but good party wine	$7–8	www.palmbayimports.com
Classic restaurant brand	$7–9	www.norton.com
Good value wine, high-quality producer	$7–9	www.billingtonwines.com
Dream team of winemaker Alberto Antonini and importer Marco DeGrazia	$8–10	www.altoslashormigas.com
Top-notch producer—Elsa is great value brand	$8–10	www.vbianchi.com
Affordable yet complex	$12–14	www.andeluna.com
Fairly available; serves up complexity and value	$15–17	www.trapiche.com.ar
Famous consultant Michel Rolland helps make the wine	$15–17	www.bodegasalentein.com
Hard to find but worth effort; top female winemaker	$25–27	www.vineconnections.com
Ranks among best of Argentina; cellar-worthy	$50–55	www.nicolascatena.com

CARMENÈRE FROM CHILE ✍

An obscure red Bordeaux grape, Carmenère was planted in Chile in the late 1800s and until fairly recently was confused with Merlot. It can have the velvety, sometimes herbal quality of Merlot, but serves up a spicy edge like Zinfandel. Now that the vines have been correctly identified, Chile is embracing Carmenère as their signature grape.

PRODUCER	WINE NAME	FROM	STYLE PROFILE
Calina	Carmenère	Maule Valley, Chile	Medium-bodied, light tannins, fresh, spicy
Tarapaca	Carmenère	Maipo Valley, Chile	Medium-bodied, light tannins, fresh, spicy
OOPS	Carmenère	Central Valley, Chile	Medium-bodied, light tannins, fresh, spicy
Santa Rita	Carmenère	Rapel Valley, Chile	Medium-bodied, light tannins, fresh, spicy
Baron Philippe de Rothschild	Carmenère "Reserva"	Rapel Valley, Chile	Full-bodied, supple tannins, spicy, ripe
Viña Chocalán	Carmenère	Maipo Valley, Chile	Full-bodied, supple tannins, smooth, earthy
Montes	Cabernet Sauvignon/ Carmenère	Colchagua Valley, Chile	Full-bodied, supple tannins, smooth, earthy

DESIGN-A-DINNER
Spicy Sausage Sandwich
* * *

To highlight the herbal spiciness of Carmenère, serve it with a sausage sandwich. Cook sausages (the spicier the better) and slice in half lengthwise. Cut warm, crusty bread into sandwich-size pieces, then spread bread with mustard. Add sausages and layer with caramelized onions and grilled red peppers.

SPECIAL BECAUSE	PRICE RANGE	MORE INFO . . .
Best-buy bottle; part of the Kendall-Jackson portfolio	$8–9	www.calina.com
Available wine, good introduction to variety	$8–9	www.tarapaca.cl
Brand specializing in Carmenère	$11–13	www.oopswines.com
Personal favorite, complex and affordable	$10–12	www.santarita.com
Pedigree is French, taste is Chilean	$10–12	www.bpdr.com
Hip packaging—classy gift idea	$11–13	www.chocalanwines.com or www.domaineselect.com (importer)
High-quality producer with great prices	$12–15	www.monteswines.com

Wines with Food

The only rule when pairing food and wine is that there are no rules. Drink what you like and eat what you like. I've had steak with Chardonnay and fish with Cabernet and though neither were my favorite combinations, at the end of the meal my glass was empty. There are, however, guidelines that help make the combination of food and wine reach new heights.

Match the Texture or Feel of the Food and Wine Delicate foods with delicate wines and big foods with big wines. It's not the outdated mantra of red wine with meat and white with fish; it's about the weight of the food and wine in your mouth. A rich hearty stew goes best with a robust red and a refreshing white pairs perfectly with light vegetable pasta.

Highlight Complementary Aromas and Flavors in the Wine and Food An earthy Pinot Noir complements pork in a mushroom sauce, while a zesty red wine like Chianti works well with an acidic tomato sauce.

Go for Contrast Serve a tangy wine like Sauvignon Blanc or Pinot Grigio to slice through the richness of dishes from scallops to pizza.

Consider the Concentration or Intensity of the Aromas and Flavors Asian food goes beautifully with a highly aromatic white wine like Gewürztraminer. Both have intense aromas and strong flavors.

Protein Softens Tannins If you have a tannic red wine, think a big steak or hunk of rich cheese. The wine will seem softer and smoother.

Focus on Sauces Don't worry too much about the type of meat, as many are interchangeable when pairing wine. Chicken in a cream sauce calls for the same wine as pork or veal in the identical sauce.

In the following pages you'll find wine suggestions for everything from barbeque to dessert. Scan this quick guide to pairing general characteristics of food and wine to whet your appetite.

WINE AND FOOD PAIRING CHEAT SHEET

MAIN CHARACTER	DISHES/CUISINE TYPES	WINE TYPE	REASON
Spicy	Chinese Kung Pao chicken, Indian curry sauces, fiery Mexican fare	**Whites:** Riesling, Chenin Blanc, Gewürztraminer, Sauvignon Blanc **Pink and Bubbly:** dry rosé, sweeter blush wines, all types of sparkling wine **Reds:** Beaujolais, Pinot Noir, Rioja	Lightly sweet or fruit-driven, crisp, and refreshing wines offer a counterpoint to the piquant character of many dishes. Look for wines with spicy aromas, no oak or light oak, high acid, and restrained alcohol.
Tangy	Fresh goat cheese, pesto sauces, zesty salad dressings and vinaigrettes, tomato-based sauces and salsas, bruschetta	**Whites:** Sauvignon Blanc–based wines, including Sancerre and white Bordeaux, Orvieto, Albariño **Reds:** Sangiovese-based wines like Chianti, dry Portugese reds	Higher-acid wines stand up to the tangy character of many sauces and dishes. If the wine doesn't have enough zesty character, it will be overpowered by the food.
Earthy	Cassoulet, stews, braised meats, mushroom risotto	**Whites:** white Rhône wines from France; Marsanne, Roussanne, Pinot Blancs from Alsace **Reds:** Pinot Noir from Burgundy, Spanish Rioja, Chilean Carmenère	Echo the earthiness of the food with the wine. If the wine is simply fruity with little underlying complexity, it will get lost with deep flavors of the dishes.

MAIN CHARACTER	DISHES/CUISINE TYPES	WINE TYPE	REASON
Rich	Lobster with drawn butter, fleshy fishes, creamy soups, grilled meats	**Whites:** creamy, full-bodied styles of Chardonnay, aromatic Viognier **Reds:** Cabernet Sauvignon, Malbec from Argentina, Brunello di Montalcino from Italy	Matching the texture of the food and wine is paramount. If the dish is full and fleshy in your mouth, you need a wine that can match that lush texture.
Salty	Chips, salted almonds, smoked salmon, cured olives, harder salty cheeses	**Bubbly:** Champagne, California sparkling wine, Spanish Cava, dry Sherry, tawny Port	Higher-acid sparkling wine tempers saltiness while acting as a foil to smoked foods. Dry styles of Sherry and tawny Ports sport a nutty quality that complements nuts.
Sweet	Fruity salsas, dishes with teriyaki sauce, desserts	**Lightly sweet:** Moscato d'Asti, Spätlese and Auslese Rieslings from Germany, Gewürztraminer **Sweet:** Sauternes, Port	If the food has a touch of sweetness, the wine needs to as well or both will taste flat. Ideally, the wine needs to be at least as sweet as the dish or dessert.

What about cooking with wine? There's only one rule: Avoid cooking with wine you wouldn't drink. Though the alcohol burns off, the flavor still remains and will be reflected in the dish. Here are tips for cooking with wine:

Color Match: White wine with white meats, red wine with red meats.

Echo Flavors: If you're serving Chardonnay, for example, add a dash of the wine to the sauce. If the wine you're serving is pricey, buy a less expensive version of the same wine type to use in cooking.

Add Complexity: Using a sweeter wine such as Madeira, tawny Port, or late-harvest Riesling adds layer of complexity to sauces, soups, and stews. For my money, the best all-purpose cooking wine is a dry Fino Sherry.

Freeze It: If you have wine left over in a bottle, don't throw it away. Pour it into ice cube trays and freeze it, then pop out a cube or two when needed for a bit of sauce or another dish. Freezing sparkling wine in ice cube trays works, too. Not only do they make a flavorful addition to sauces, bubbly cubes perk up Sunday morning mimosas.

WINE ABCS
Food-Friendly
* * *

Food-friendly refers to the ability of certain wines to pair well with food because they fall on the elegant side of the style scale. Alcohol and oak levels are in check, since it's hard to pair high-alcohol or very oaky wines with food. Wines with higher levels of crisp acidity are ideal dinner companions as they refresh your palate and get it ready for the next bite.

QUICK TIP
Magic Pairing Moments
* * *

You never know when it will happen, but then it does; a magical food-and-wine moment where the sum of the two parts becomes exponentially greater. Here are a few of my favorite combinations:

- *Grilled romaine lettuce salad topped with crunchy bacon, pungent blue cheese, and sweet vinaigrette paired with Fritz Haag Riesling (page 168). Why it worked? The dressing and wine were both high acid and lightly sweet, but the Riesling also provided a foil for the salty bacon and warm wilted greens. Opposites do attract in love and food.*

- *Warm goat cheese round rolled in crushed pistachios then fried and drizzled with honey. The cheese topped a bed of caramelized onions and was served with Alvaro Palacios "Les Terrasses" Priorat (page 66). Why it worked? The dish had almost too much going on with the sweet/savory battle, but the elegant red complemented the tangy brightness of the cheese while echoing the earthy quality of the dish.*

- *New Zealand grilled lamb with rosemary alongside Penfolds "Bin 389" Cabernet/Shiraz (page 66). Why it worked? The richness of the wine matched the texture of the lamb and a hint of herbal notes in the wine were underscored by the rosemary.*

- *A simple plate of roasted almonds, a hunk of Parmigiano-Reggiano cheese, and a glass of Delaforce "Colheita" tawny Port (page 162). Why it worked? The sweetness of the wine acted as a counterpart for the cheese while the almonds augmented the Port's beautiful nutty notes.*

Pizza Picks

While beer and pizza go well together, cheese, bread, and tomato sauce is perfect with vino. Give these pairings a try.

WITH VEGETABLE PIZZA

White wines work surprisingly well with pizza topped with peppers, mushrooms, fresh herbs, and tangy tomato sauce. One of my favorite combinations is feta cheese and spinach pizza, accompanied by zesty Sauvignon Blanc.

PRODUCER	WINE NAME	FROM	STYLE PROFILE
Yelcho	Sauvignon Blanc "Reserva"	Chile	Light-bodied, crisp, refreshing
Mirassou	Sauvignon Blanc	California	Light-bodied, crisp, refreshing
Chateau Souverain	Sauvignon Blanc	Alexander Valley, California	Medium-full-bodied, crisp, fruity
Valentin Bianchi	Sauvignon Blanc	San Rafael, Mendoza, Argentina	Medium-full-bodied, crisp, fruity
Nepenthe	Sauvignon Blanc	Adelaide Hills, South Australia	Medium-full-bodied, crisp, fruity
Honig	Sauvignon Blanc	Napa Valley, California	Medium-full-bodied, crisp, fruity
Simi Winery	Sauvignon Blanc	Sonoma County, California	Medium-full-bodied, crisp, fruity
St. Supéry	Sauvignon Blanc	Napa Valley, California	Medium-bodied, racy, herbal
Groth	Sauvignon Blanc	Napa Valley, California	Medium-full-bodied, crisp, fruity

Want more picks? Check out these lists: Summer Wines, Snack
Attack Party Food, Party Wines

DESIGN-A-DINNER

Goat Cheese and Wild Mushroom Pizza

* * *

*Top ready-made pizza crust with olive oil, wild mushrooms,
fresh basil, and goat cheese. Bake until the cheese is bubbly,
and serve with a crisp, earthy white such as Soave or Orvieto.*

SPECIAL BECAUSE	PRICE RANGE	MORE INFO . . .
Chile's cool, coastal Casablanca Valley is ideal for Sauvignon	$7–10	www.ventisquero.com
Family has been making wine for 150 years	$8–10	www.mirassou.com
Classic California style—juicy	$11–13	www.chateausouverain.com
Dash of Chardonnay adds richness	$14–16	www.vbianchi.com
Limited availability but worth the search	$14–17	www.nepenthe.com.au
Popular restaurant wine	$14–17	www.honigwine.com
A touch of Sémillon adds depth	$15–17	www.simiwinery.com
Complex yet quaffable	$18–20	www.stsupery.com
One of California's best versions	$16–18	www.grothwines.com

WITH CHEESE PIZZA ⋙

Whites complement plain cheese pizza nicely. Try a toasty, medium-to-full-bodied Chardonnay, especially if the topping is a smoky cheese such as provolone. For red wine lovers a higher-acid, lighter-bodied Sangiovese-based wine is ideal.

PRODUCER	WINE NAME	FROM	STYLE PROFILE
Gallo Family Vineyards	Chardonnay "Twin Valley"	California	Medium-bodied, light oak, juicy
Woodbridge Winery	Chardonnay "Ghost Oak Select Vineyard Series"	Lodi, California	Medium-bodied, light oak, juicy
Beringer Vineyards	Chardonnay "Founders' Estate"	California	Medium-bodied, light oak, juicy
Columbia Crest	Chardonnay "Grand Estates"	Columbia Valley, Washington	Medium-bodied, light oak, juicy
Toasted Head Vineyards	Chardonnay	Dunnigan Hills, California	Full-bodied, creamy, oaky, ripe
Monte Antico	Rosso	Toscana, Italy	Light-bodied, light tannins, bright and earthy
Banfi	"Centine"	Toscana, Italy	Light-bodied, light tannins, bright and earthy
Frescobaldi	Chianti "Castiglioni"	Toscana, Italy	Light-bodied, light tannins, bright and earthy
Rocca delle Macìe	Chianti Classico	Chianti Classico, Italy	Medium-bodied, supple tannins, vibrant, earthy

Want more picks? Check out these lists: Party Wines, Cheese-Friendly Wines, Winter Wines

SPECIAL BECAUSE	PRICE RANGE	MORE INFO . . .
Super deal, party pick	$4–6	www.gallofamily.com
Woodbridge's Vineyard series is good value	$7–9	www.woodbridgewines.com
Bargain brand from big name	$7–10	www.beringer.com
Personal favorite; overdelivers in quality	$8–10	www.columbia-crest.com
Affordable example of a big, bold Chardonnay	$8–10	www.rhphillips.com
Sangiovese from importer Empson; best-buy brand	$7–10	www.empson.com
Blend of Sangiovese, Merlot, and Cabernet Sauvignon	$7–9	www.banfi.com
Top Tuscan producer's value label; great deal	$12–14	www.frescobaldi.it
Classically styled but with modern twist	$16–18	www.roccadellemacie.com

Pizza with Meat Toppings ✑

When a steaming pepperoni-sausage special arrives at your door, what should you reach for? Powerful, spicy reds with enough oomph to match the hearty texture of the pie. Look for peppery Shiraz-based reds or juicy California Zinfandel.

PRODUCER	WINE NAME	FROM	STYLE PROFILE
Talus Collection	Zinfandel	Lodi, California	Medium-bodied, supple tannins, smooth, juicy
Estancia	Zinfandel "Keys Canyon Ranches"	Paso Robles, California	Full-bodied, supple tannins, spicy, ripe
Cline Cellars	Zinfandel "Ancient Vines"	California	Full-bodied, supple tannins, spicy, ripe
Ridge Vineyards	Zinfandel "Lytton Springs"	Dry Creek Valley, California	Full-bodied, supple tannins, spicy, ripe
Osborne	Tempranillo/Shiraz "Solaz"	Tierra de Castilla, Spain	Medium-bodied, supple tannins, smooth, juicy
Cycles Gladiator	Syrah	Central Coast, California	Medium-bodied, supple tannins, smooth, juicy
Caracol Serrano	Tinto	Jumilla, Spain	Full-bodied, supple tannins, smooth, earthy
Bulletin Place	Shiraz	South Eastern Australia	Medium-bodied, supple tannins, smooth, juicy
McDowell Valley Vineyards	Syrah	Mendocino, California	Medium-bodied, supple tannins, smooth, juicy

Want more picks? Check out these lists: Winter Wines, Sexy
Wines, Meat-Lover Wines

SPECIAL BECAUSE	PRICE RANGE	MORE INFO . . .
Hot bargain brand—try all their wines	$7–9	www.taluscellars.com
True Zin character at good price	$10–12	www.estanciaestates.com
Made from 100-year-old vines; intense	$16–19	www.clinecellars.com
Must-have wine—Ridge makes classic Zinfandel	$30–35	www.ridgewine.com
Historic company; look for the label with the bull	$8–10	www.osbornesolaz.com
Adorned with drawing of antique bicycle	$9–11	www.cyclesgladiator.com
Powerful blend of Monastrell, Syrah, and Cabernet	$8–10	www.vinosandgourmet.com (importer)
From Aussie wine icon Len Evans; widely available	$7–9	www.vineyardbrands.com (importer)
A leader of California-style Rhône wines	$13–15	www.mcdowellsyrah.com

Meat-Lover Wines

Meat has been the natural partner for wine since people discovered how to ferment grapes. Things haven't changed much in a few thousand years. The sizzling sound of steak on the grill is still a cue to pour a glass. When pairing meat, though, think about the preparation. Are you barbequing, roasting, or braising? Are you serving a sauce with the meat? These make a difference in the ultimate flavor and ideal wine match. Try the following suggestions and unveil wine beauty and the beef.

DESIGN-A-DINNER
Simple Barbequed Pork Ribs

* * *

Boil ribs for thirty minutes in a large pot of water sprinkled with a handful of jerk seasoning or salt. This not only cooks the meat, but removes most of the extra fat while leaving it very moist. Coat ribs in barbeque sauce of your choice and grill them until hot. It's easy to doctor up store-bought sauce to make it special.

SWEET BARBEQUE SAUCE

Take standard hickory barbeque sauce and pour one cup of it into a bowl. Add one tablespoon of dark molasses and one tablespoon Jack Daniels whiskey.

SPICY BARBEQUE SAUCE

Take standard hickory barbeque sauce and pour one cup of it into a bowl. Add two cloves pressed garlic and a quarter teaspoon ground cayenne pepper.

DESIGN-A-DINNER
Plum Roasted Pork Loin

* * *

Wash a pork loin in cool water, then pat dry. Place in a heavy-bottomed casserole dish drizzled with a tablespoon of olive oil. If in season, slice up two peaches and three or four plums and lay them around the pork loin. If fresh stone fruits are not in season, use one handful each dried apricots and prunes. Peel one white onion and slice thinly. Add the onion around and beneath the meat. Sprinkle the dish with a quarter cup of brown sugar, a quarter cup of cider vinegar, sea salt, and one bunch culinary lavender.

Roast at 400°F for about one hour or until meat is cooked through and the onions and fruit are tender. Strain the pan juices and thicken them in a small pan with a bit of cornstarch. Season the sauce with salt, lemon juice, and black pepper to taste. Slice the loin into rounds and top each serving with some of the onions, fruit, and a spoonful of the thickened sauce.

Serve with Pinot Noir or dry rosé.

OFF THE GRILL: RIBS AND BURGERS 🐟

There's nothing like a pile of grilled ribs slathered with barbeque sauce or a juicy burger. Consider matching the sweetness or tanginess of the sauce with the wine. Both sweet and spicy sauces work beautifully with pink wines (they are made from red grapes). For red

PRODUCER	WINE NAME	FROM	STYLE PROFILE
Shenandoah Vineyards	White Zinfandel	Amador County, California	Light-bodied, light tannins, off-dry, juicy
Eberle	Syrah Rosé	Paso Robles, California	Light-bodied, light tannins, vibrant, fruity
Langlois-Château	Rosé "La Bretonnière" Sec	Cabernet de Saumur, Loire Valley, France	Light-bodied, light tannins, vibrant, fruity
Pedroncelli	Zinfandel "Mother Clone"	Dry Creek Valley, California	Medium-bodied, supple tannins, smooth, juicy
Benson Ferry Vineyards	Zinfandel "Old Vines"	Lodi, California	Full-bodied, supple tannins, spicy, ripe
St. Francis Winery	Zinfandel "Old Vines"	Sonoma County, California	Full-bodied, supple tannins, spicy, ripe
L'Uvaggio di Giacomo	Barbera "Il Gufo"	Lodi, California	Medium-bodied, supple tannins, vibrant, earthy
Santo Tomas	Barbera	Baja, Mexico	Medium-bodied, supple tannins, vibrant, earthy
Michele Chiarlo	Barbera "Le Orme"	Barbera d'Asti, Italy	Medium-bodied, supple tannins, vibrant, earthy
Pio Cesare	Barbera	Barbera d'Alba, Italy	Medium-bodied, supple tannins, vibrant, earthy

lovers, seek out powerful wines with a kick of spice such as Barbera and Zinfandel.

Want more picks? Check out these lists: Overlooked Surprises, Summer Wines, Winter Wines

SPECIAL BECAUSE	PRICE RANGE	MORE INFO . . .
A savvy version of White Zin; chill well	$5–7	www.sobonwine.com
Dry, full pink from Syrah specialist	$14–16	www.eberlewinery.com
Dry pink wine from Cabernet Franc grapes	$14–16	www.langlois-chateau.fr www.paternowines.com (importer)
Vines cloned from original 100-year-old Zinfandel	$14–16	www.pedroncelli.com
Lodi is lesser-known hot spot for Zin	$12–14	www.bensonferry.com
Widely available, top Sonoma producer	$13–15	www.stfranciswine.com
Gufo means "owl" in Italian; fun label	$10–12	www.uvaggio.com
Limited availability, but worth the search	$12–14	www.santotomas.com.mx
Personal favorite; a show-stopping value	$12–14	www.chiarlo.it
Classic producer, classic style	$20–25	www.piocesare.it

WINE ABCS

The *B*s of Piedmont: Barolo, Barbaresco, and Barbera

* * *

Piedmont, a region in northern Italy, means "foot of the mountains." The towering, snow-capped Alps, cupping the region like a gentle giant hand, make this a unique environment to grow grapes. Often referred to as the Burgundy of Italy, Piedmont is a patchwork of small vineyards planted mostly on sloping hillsides. The three big names in red wine from this region are Barolo, Barbaresco, and Barbera.

Barolo and Barbaresco are both made from the Nebbiolo grape variety. Fog shrouds many of the vineyards in the Barolo area, and it is there that a red grape named Nebbiolo—nebbia is "fog" in Italian—thrives and produces Barolo. Nebbiolo is also the grape responsible for the great reds of Barbaresco, a nearby Piedmontese region of the same name. Though expensive themselves, Barbarescos are often more approachable when young than Barolos.

While Nebbiolo is Piedmont's star grape, Barbera is the region's workhorse. Widely planted around the towns of Alba and Asti, the prolific grape variety produces affordable, juicy, smoky reds simply called Barbera.

SLOW-COOKED MEATS 🦚

Whether you're serving beef bourguignon, lamb and vegetable stew, or braised veal shanks, slow-cooked dishes require reds with an earthy yet tender touch. Think Grenache-based wines from Spain or Châteauneuf-du-Pape from the sun-baked south of France. How about spicy Carmenère from Chile or aged Barolos from northern Italy? Underscore the earthy flavors and smooth textures with similarly styled wines.

Want more picks? Check out these lists: Fall Wines, Wines to Watch, Take-Out Favorites

---

DESIGN-A-DINNER
Burgundian-Style Beef Stew
* * *

In a Dutch oven, heat a bit of butter and olive oil and add approximately two pounds of cubed beef stew meat. Quickly sear the meat over high heat and remove. Brown one diced onion and one carrot, several minced garlic cloves and one tablespoon of Herbes de Provence. Return the meat to the pot and add two cups each of Pinot Noir (or other red wine) and beef broth. Cover the pot, and let it simmer for several hours. Uncover pot and add one cup of quartered mushroom caps and one-half cup of brandy or Cognac. Cook for another hour or so to reduce the liquid. Season with salt and pepper and serve over white rice or noodles.

SLOW-COOKED MEAT WINES

PRODUCER	WINE NAME	FROM	STYLE PROFILE
Yellow Tail	Shiraz/Grenache	South Eastern Australia	Medium-bodied, light tannins, fresh, spicy
Rosemount Estate	Shiraz/Grenache	South Eastern Australia	Medium-bodied, supple tannins, vibrant, earthy
Calina	Carmenère	Maule Valley, Chile	Medium-bodied, light tannins, fresh, spicy
Paul Jaboulet Aîné	"Parallele 45"	Côtes-du-Rhône, France	Medium-bodied, light tannins, fresh, spicy
Pont d'Avignon	Côtes-du-Rhône	Côtes-du-Rhône, France	Medium-bodied, light tannins, fresh, spicy
Morgan	"Côtes du Crow's"	Monterey County, California	Medium-bodied, light tannins, fresh, spicy
Perrin & Fils	"La Gille"	Gigondas, France	Medium-bodied, supple tannins, vibrant, earthy
Morlanda	Crianza	Priorat, Spain	Medium-bodied, supple tannins, vibrant, earthy
Château Mont-Redon	Châteauneuf-du-Pape Rouge	Châteauneuf-du-Pape, France	Medium-bodied, supple tannins, vibrant, earthy
Château la Nerthe	Châteauneuf-du-Pape Rouge	Châteauneuf-du-Pape, France	Full-bodied, supple tannins, smooth, earthy
Fratelli Revello	Barolo	Barolo, Italy	Full-bodied, supple tannins smooth, earthy
Marchesi di Barolo	Barolo	Barolo, Italy	Full-bodied, supple tannin smooth, earthy
Fontanafredda	Barolo	Serralunga d'Alba, Barolo, Italy	Full-bodied, supple tannin smooth, earthy

SPECIAL BECAUSE	PRICE RANGE	MORE INFO . . .
Best wine of the popular brand	$7–9	www.yellowtailwine.com
Great value from well-known producer	$11-13	www.rosemountestate.com
Great value from the folks at Kendall-Jackson	$8–9	www.calina.com
Widely available, easy-drinking style	$9–11	www.jaboulet.com
Honors the famous bridge in French city, Avignon	$13–15	www.gallofamily.com
Light-hearted Grenache/Syrah combination	$17–19	www.morganwinery.com
Grenache/Syrah like a "baby" Châteauneuf	$26–28	www.perrin-fils.com
Grenache-based red made by duo of women	$45–48	www.heredadcollection.com
Relatively affordable version; rustic	$30–35	www.chateaumontredon.fr
Personal favorite; ageworthy	$45–50	www.chateaulanerthe.fr
Young producer, New World, modern style	$44–48	www.revellofratelli.com
Classic producer, classic style; available	$46–50	www.marchesibarolo.com
Ultra-smooth, classic style; limited production	$48–53	www.domaineselect.com (importer)

Three Classic Meat Matches

Like the culinary version of Sonny and Cher, Lucy and Ricky, or Fred and Ginger, these meat-and-wine match-ups are favorites.

STEAK AND CABERNET SAUVIGNON

Also try: Argentine Malbec for its powerful yet elegant character

PRODUCER	WINE NAME	FROM	STYLE PROFILE
Carmen	Cabernet Sauvignon "Reserve"	Valle Central, Chile	Medium-bodied, supple tannins, vibrant, earthy
Wente Vineyards	Cabernet Sauvignon "Vineyard Selection"	Livermore Valley, California	Medium-full-bodied, supple tannins, vibrant, juicy
Clos du Bois	Cabernet Sauvignon	Sonoma County, California	Medium-bodied, supple tannins, smooth, juicy
Wynn's Coonawarra	Cabernet Sauvignon	Coonawarra, Australia	Medium-full-bodied, supple tannins, vibrant, juicy
Arrowood Vineyards	Cabernet Sauvignon	Glen Ellen, California	Full-bodied, strong tannin, lush, concentrated
Stag's Leap Wine Cellars	Cabernet Sauvignon "Artemis"	Stags Leap District, Napa Valley, California	Full-bodied, strong tannin, lush, concentrated
Long Meadow Ranch	Cabernet Sauvignon	Napa Valley, California	Full-bodied, strong tannin, lush, concentrated
Inca	Cabernet/Malbec	Calchaqui Valley, Argentina	Medium-full-bodied, supple tannins, vibrant, juicy
Amancaya	Malbec/Cabernet Sauvignon	Mendoza, Argentina	Medium-full-bodied, supple tannins, vibrant, juicy

Want more picks? Check out these lists: Hot Spots, Winter Wines, Twice-the-Price Wines, Glamorous Gift Wines

SPECIAL BECAUSE	PRICE RANGE	MORE INFO . . .
Not complex, but smooth style	$6–8	www.carmen.com
Highly regarded winery from historic Livermore	$10–13	www.wentevineyards.com
Widely available; crowd-pleasing style	$11–14	www.closdubois.com
Great deal from Down Under; must-buy wine	$15–17	www.wynns.com.au
Richard Arrowood crafts legendary Cabs	$45–48	www.arrowoodvineyards.com
Personal favorite; complex and classy	$45–50	www.cask23.com
Limited production, but worth the effort to find; ageworthy	$58–62	www.longmeadowranch.com
Elegant blend of both varieties	$9–11	www.appellationimports.com (importer)
Joint venture of Rothschild and Catena	$18–20	www.pasternakwine.com (importer)

Pork and Pinot

Also try: Chardonnay, especially if the pork is prepared with a mustard sauce

Want more picks? Check out these lists: Wedding Wines, Bathtub Wines, Holiday Spirit

PRODUCER	WINE NAME	FROM	STYLE PROFILE
King Estate	Pinot Noir	Oregon	Medium-bodied, supple tannins, vibrant, earthy
Palliser Estates	Pinot Noir	Martinborough, New Zealand	Medium-bodied, supple tannins, vibrant, earthy
Au Bon Climat	Pinot Noir "Estate"	Santa Maria Valley, California	Medium-bodied, supple tannins, vibrant, earthy
Villa Mt. Eden	Pinot Noir "Grand Reserve-Bien Nacido Vineyard"	Santa Maria Valley, California	Medium-full-bodied, supple tannins, vibrant, juicy
MacMurray Ranch	Pinot Noir	Russian River Valley, California	Medium-full-bodied, supple tannins, vibrant, juicy
Etude	Pinot Noir	Carneros, California	Medium-full-bodied, supple tannins, vibrant, juicy
J. Lohr	Chardonnay "Riverstone"	Arroyo Seco, California	Medium-bodied, light oak, juicy
Sterling	Chardonnay	Napa County, California	Medium-bodied, light oak, juicy
Chateau St. Jean	Chardonnay "Belle Terre Vineyard"	Alexander Valley, California	Full-bodied, creamy, oaky, ripe

DESIGN-A-DINNER

* * *

See page 107 for a pork and Pinot pairing idea.

SPECIAL BECAUSE	PRICE RANGE	MORE INFO . . .
Widely available; delivers consistent quality	$20–24	www.kingestate.com
Leading producer, limited availability	$25–28	www.palliser.co.nz
Owner Jim Clendenen is a Pinot Noir specialist	$25–28	www.aubonclimat.com
Great deal from world-class Pinot vineyard	$17–20	www.villamteden.com
Named after late actor Fred MacMurray	$27–32	www.macmurrayranch.com
From uber-talented winemaker Tony Soter	$40	www.etudewines.com
Value not to miss	$13–15	www.jlohr.com
A step up in complexity from Vintners Collection	$16–18	www.sterlingvineyards.com
Well-known wine that delivers	$20–23	www.chateaustjean.com

LAMB AND SHIRAZ/SYRAH 🐑

Also try: red Bordeaux or other Cabernet Sauvignon-based blends

PRODUCER	WINE NAME	FROM	STYLE PROFILE
E. Guigal	Côte-Rôtie "Brune et Blonde"	Côte-Rôtie, France	Medium-bodied, supple tannins, vibrant, earthy
Geyser Peak Winery	Shiraz	Sonoma County, California	Medium-bodied, supple tannins, smooth, juicy
Wattle Creek	Shiraz	Alexander Valley, California	Full-bodied, supple tannins, spicy, ripe
Rosemount	Shiraz "Balmoral"	McLaren Vale, South Australia	Full-bodied, supple tannins, spicy, ripe
Dunham	Syrah	Columbia Valley, Washington	Full-bodied, supple tannins, spicy, ripe
Penfolds	Cabernet/Shiraz "Bin 389"	South Australia	Full-bodied, supple tannins, smooth, earthy
Jackson-Triggs	Cabernet/Shiraz "Grand Reserve"	Okanagan Valley, Canada	Full-bodied, supple tannins, smooth, earthy
Devil's Lair Winery	"Fifth Leg"	Western Australia	Medium-full-bodied, supple tannins, vibrant, juicy
Château les Ormes de Pez	Cru Bourgeois	Saint-Estèphe, France	Full-bodied, supple tannins, smooth, earthy
Château La Louvière	Pessac-Léognan	Pessac-Léognan, Graves, France	Full-bodied, supple tannins, smooth, earthy
Château D'Issan	Margaux	Margaux, Bordeaux, France	Full-bodied, supple tannins, smooth, earthy
Château Ducru-Beaucaillou	St. Julien	St. Julien, Bordeaux, France	Full-bodied, supple tannins, smooth, earthy

Want more picks? Check out these lists: Sexy Wines, Wedding Wines, Holiday Spirit, 25 to Try Before You Die

SPECIAL BECAUSE	PRICE RANGE	MORE INFO . . .
Classic producer, classic wine; ageworthy	$55–58	www.guigal.com
Widely available, easy-drinking wine	$18–20	www.geyserpeakwinery.com
Australian style from California; sexy	$25–27	www.wattlecreek.com
Huge and complex—historic Aussie wine	$30–35	www.rosemountestate.com
Limited production but worth the search	$45–48	www.dunhamcellars.com
Personal favorite, worth twice the price	$22–25	www.penfolds.com
Impressive effort, seamless integration	$20–24	www.jacksontriggswinery.com
Blend of Cabernet Merlot and Shiraz	$12–15	www.devils-lair.com or www.fifthleg.com.au
Velvety texture; good value for the quality	$22–25	www.ormesdepez.com
Cabernet Sauvignon with a dash of Merlot, Cabernet Franc	$35–38	www.andrelurton.com
Classic producer; Cabernet Sauvignon/Merlot	$55–60	www.chateau-issan.com
Ageworthy—plush style	$58–62	www.chateau-ducru-beau caillou.com

Pasta-Perfect Wines

∞

Just about every country has a form of pasta—from Asian noodles to German spaetzle—but it is Italian-style specialties that come to mind when pasta is mentioned. Since noodles are simply a canvas for sauce and other ingredients, the toppings are really what you consider when choosing wine for pasta dishes. Is the sauce buttery, creamy, or a tangy tomato-based sauce? Overflowing with vegetables or laden with meat? While it's true that what grows together goes together when it comes to the affinity of Italian wines with pasta, that's not the only answer.

DESIGN-A-DINNER
Peppery Pesto Pasta

* * *

In a food processor or blender purée two bunches of basil leaves, one peeled, sliced garlic clove, and a sprig of parsley. Add a handful of pine nuts and grated parmesan, then drizzle with olive oil and purée until smooth. Add more olive oil if the mixture is too thick. Slice and sauté thin strips of red, yellow, and green bell peppers. Cook and drain shaped pasta such as penne. In a bowl combine the warm pasta, peppers, and pesto, then top with freshly grated Parmigian-Reggiano or asiago cheese.

PASTA WITH PESTO SAUCES OR VEGETABLES SUCH AS PASTA PRIMAVERA 🐟

When pesto and vegetables meet pasta, you can't go wrong drinking a tangy, herbal white such as Sauvignon Blanc from New Zealand. Also try Pinot Grigio from northern Italy or a bright Pinot Gris (both the

PRODUCER	WINE NAME	FROM	STYLE PROFILE
Michel Lynch	Sauvignon Blanc	Bordeaux, France	Medium-bodied, racy, herbal
Wairau River	Sauvignon Blanc	Marlborough, New Zealand	Medium-bodied, racy, herbal
Novelty Hill	Sauvignon Blanc "Klipsun Vineyard"	Columbia Valley, Washington	Medium-full-bodied, crisp, fruity
Bella Sera	Pinot Grigio	Delle Venezie, Italy	Light-bodied, crisp, refreshing
Tiefenbrunner	Pinot Grigio	Delle Venezie, Italy	Light-bodied, crisp, refreshing
Attems	Pinot Grigio	Collio, Italy	Medium-full-bodied, crisp, fruity
Alois Lageder	Pinot Grigio	Vigneti delle Dolomiti, Italy	Medium-full-bodied, crisp, fruity
Estancia	Pinot Grigio	California	Light-bodied, crisp, refreshing
Chehalem	Pinot Gris	Willamette Valley, Oregon	Medium-full-bodied, crisp, fruity
Masi	"Masianco"	Delle Venezie, Italy	Light-bodied, crisp, refreshing

same grape variety) from Oregon. These wines echo the fresh crunchiness of the vegetables and the herbal notes of the basil-based pesto.

Want more picks? Check out these lists: Pizza Picks, Summer
Wines, Snack Attack Party Food

SPECIAL BECAUSE	PRICE RANGE	MORE INFO . . .
Project from Jean-Michel Cazes from Lynch-Bages	$8–10	www.michellynch.com
Owners Phil and Chris Rose— special people, special wine	$15–18	www.wairauriverwines.com
Dash of Sémillon adds richness	$14–16	www.noveltyhillwines.com
Widely available brand; easy-drinking quaffer	$5–7	www.bellaserawine.com
Classic producer, classy wine	$14–16	www.tiefenbrunner.com
Joint venture of Conti Attems and famous Frescobaldi family	$18–24	www.attems.it
Highly-regarded producer, complex wine	$18–20	www.lageder.com or www .dallaterra.com (importer)
Very Italian in style	$10–13	www.estanciaestates.com
One of the pioneers of Oregon wine industry	$13–15	www.chehalemwines.com
A blend of Pinot Grigio and Verduzzo	$11–13	www.masi.it

PASTA WITH CREAMY BECHAMEL OR BUTTERY SAUCES SUCH AS FETTUCINE ALFREDO ⤳

The richness of a creamy sauce needs a similarly styled wine such as buttery, oaky Chardonnay. Also try Italian whites made with the

PRODUCER	WINE NAME	FROM	STYLE PROFILE
Dezzani	Il Gavi	Gavi, Italy	Medium-full-bodied, crisp, fruity
Fontanafredda	Gavi	Gavi, Italy	Medium-full-bodied, crisp, fruity
Michele Chiarlo	Gavi	Gavi, Italy	Medium-full-bodied, crisp, fruity
Lungarotti	Bianco Di Torgiano "Terre Di Giano"	Umbria, Italy	Medium-full-bodied, crisp, fruity
Podere il Caio	Grechetto	Umbria, Italy	Light-bodied, crisp, refreshing
Arnaldo Caprai	Grechetto	Umbria, Italy	Medium-full-bodied, crisp, fruity
Black Swan	Chardonnay/Semillon	South Eastern Australia	Medium-full-bodied, crisp, fruity
Hamilton Russell Vineyards	Chardonnay	Walker Bay, South Africa	Full-bodied, creamy, oaky, ripe
Landmark	Chardonnay "Overlook"	California	Full-bodied, creamy, oaky, ripe
Argyle	Chardonnay "Nuthouse"	Oregon	Full-bodied, creamy, oaky, ripe

grape named Grechetto, which is slightly nutty and full. Instead of matching the richness, try using a refreshingly zesty wine such as Gavi as a foil.

Want more picks? Check out these lists: Pizza Picks, Fall Wines

SPECIAL BECAUSE	PRICE RANGE	MORE INFO . . .
Made from Cortese grapes	$18–20	www.dezzani.it
Classic producer, limited production	$20–22	www.domaineselect.com (importer)
Classic producer, great gift wine	$17–19	www.michelechiarlo.it
Grechetto and Trebbiano blend	$14–16	www.lungarotti.it
Hip, modern label, ideal for gift giving	$12–15	www.vineyardbrands.com (importer)
Hot producer in Umbria; must try	$13–17	www.arnaldocaprai.it
Great value for complexity	$7–9	www.blackswanwines.com
South African luminary; rich wine	$28–30	www.martinscottwines.com (importer)
Personal favorite—big style but balanced	$20–24	www.landmarkwine.com
Winemaker Rollin Soles is Oregon star	$26–30	www.argylewinery.com

PASTA WITH TOMATO-BASED SAUCES 🐟

Certainly Italian reds, especially those made from the Sangiovese grape, complement the high acidity of tomato-based sauces. But don't limit yourself just to Italy. Jump to Spain or Portugal and experience their racy reds, too.

Want more picks? Check out these lists: Pizza Picks, Twice-the-Price Wines, Meat-Lover Wines

PRODUCER	WINE NAME	FROM	STYLE PROFILE
Vino Noceto	Sangiovese	Amador County, California	Medium-bodied, supple tannins, vibrant, earthy
Baroncini	Morellino di Scansano	Morellino de Scansano, Italy	Medium-bodied, supple tannins, vibrant, earthy
Badia a Coltibuono	Chianti Classico	Chianti Classico, Italy	Medium-bodied, supple tannins, vibrant, earthy
Castello di Volpaia	Chianti Classico Riserva	Chianti Classico, Italy	Medium-bodied, supple tannins, vibrant, earthy
Valdubon	Cosecha	Ribera del Duero, Spain	Medium-bodied, supple tannins, vibrant, earthy
Quinta do Carmo	Dry Red wine	Alentejo, Portugal	Medium-bodied, supple tannins, vibrant, earthy
Prazo de Roriz	Dry Red wine	Duoro, Portugal	Medium-bodied, supple tannins, vibrant, earthy

DESIGN-A-DINNER IDEAS
Mama Rita's Meatballs

* * *

My Italian mother-in-law makes the best (and easiest) meat-balls. Mix a pound each of ground veal and pork in a bowl. With your hands, work in two eggs, half a cup each of bread crumbs and grated Romano or Parmesan cheese. Add a quar-ter cup each fresh parsley and oregano and a dash of ground fennel seed, salt, and pepper. Shape into golf-ball-sized meat-balls and lightly brown in a pan with olive oil. Drop into your simmering tomato sauce and cook them for a half hour or so. Toss with spaghetti, and grab a bottle of zesty red.

SPECIAL BECAUSE	PRICE RANGE	MORE INFO . . .
One of California's best Sangioveses	$15–18	www.noceto.com
Hot area in Tuscany for affordable Sangiovese	$9–11	www.baroncini.it
Historic winery dates to the eleventh century	$15–18	www.coltibuono.com
One of Tuscany's most beautiful properties	$23–27	www.volpaia.com
Modern winery producing classic Tempranillos	$14–16	www.valdubon.com
Grapes Aragonez and Periquita make this rustic red	$20–23	www.pasternakwine.com (importer) or www.lafite.com
Outstanding value; primarily Tinta Roriz and Touriga Franca	$14–16	www.quintaderoriz.com

Take-out Favorites

∽

Take-out choices usually include ethnic food favorites such as Chinese, Mexican, Indian, Thai, or Japanese. Dishes range from mild sushi rolls to piquant lamb vindaloo or fiery Kung Pao chicken. Though these cuisines vary greatly, wines with common stylistic threads can be ideal partners. My take-out-friendly wines all share the following characteristics:

- Sport bright levels of acidity, making them refreshing.
- Many have a touch of sweetness, which balances the heat of the food. Even if you don't think you like sweet wines, give these suggestions a try. You just might be converted.
- Have intensity of flavor to match the intensity of the dishes.
- Alcohol levels are moderate with no overtly oaky flavors.

TAKE-OUT CHEAT SHEET
It's All About the Sauces

* * *

Curry: *With classic yellow curry, look for aromatic and spicy Gewürztraminer.*

Tomato-based Salsa: *Match the acid and herbal notes with an herbal Sauvignon Blanc.*

Soy Sauce: *Tough because of the saltiness, so balance it with lightly sweet bubbly.*

Peanut Sauce: *Sauce is nutty and often sweet, so try creamy Viognier or rosé.*

Teriyaki Sauce: *Sweeter than soy sauce, so works best with off-dry Riesling.*

Look for . . .

- **Bubbly:** Sparkling wine has acid and often a hint of sweetness that tempers spice and saltiness of these dishes. Pop the cork on Italian Prosecco and Spanish Cava or pick up bottles labeled Extra Dry, which ironically means the bubbly is a tad sweet.
- **Whites:** High acid or intensely aromatic options are racy Riesling, sassy Sauvignon Blanc, lemony Chenin Blanc, floral Viognier, and spicy Gewürztraminer, all of which have the aromatic intensity to stand up to the food.
- **Pinks:** One of my favorites with just about any ethnic food is rosé. With a really spicy dish, try blush wine with a dash of sweetness, otherwise dry rosé works great. It has the power to match the dishes yet is refreshing.
- **Reds:** You need reds with lighter tannins, good acid, and hint of spiciness. Drink elegant Pinot Noir, fruity Beaujolais, or lighter-styled Sangiovese-based wines.

Want more picks? Check out these lists: Snack Attack Party Food, Spring Wines, Summer Wines, Overlooked Surprises

WINE ABCS
Umami

* * *

Umami (add "ooh" to "mommy" for the correct pronunciation) is the controversial fifth taste after sweet, sour, salty, and bitter. Umami was discovered by a Japanese scientist in the early 1900s and refers to the savory taste of food caused by glutamate. Think MSG in Chinese food and you get the picture. You will notice its mouth-filling character in common foods such as mushrooms, tomatoes, Parmesan cheese, and of course many Japanese and Chinese dishes. For more information on umami, check out www.umamiinfo.com.

DESIGN-A-DINNER
Exotic Chicken Platter
* * *

Fill small serving dishes with a selection of store-bought dipping sauces such as tomato or mango salsa, teriyaki, curry, and peanut sauce. Arrange in the center of a large serving platter. Cut chicken breasts into medium-sized chunks and sauté in butter or olive oil until fully cooked. Skewer each chicken piece with a toothpick and arrange on the platter around the sauces. Garnish with fresh parsley, mint leaves, or sliced cucumbers.

QUICK TIP
What's a Good Wine to Drink with Sushi?
* * *

High-quality sake is excellent with most sushi, but so is wine. For more delicately-textured sushi such as vegetarian maki, sip refreshingly light Riesling or crisp sparkling wine. For slightly richer versions like a California sushi roll, try fruity Sauvignon Blanc or Pinot Gris. For rich tuna Maguro and Toro nigiri sushi, seek out Viognier or even stylish, low-tannin reds like Pinot Noir and Beaujolais. If you want to add spicy wasabi, make sure you're armed with a full-bodied Alsatian Gewurztraminer. Sushi aficionados should look for the lightly sweet wine named Oroyā. Crafted by a Japanese winemaker in Spain from a blend of aromatic Spanish white grapes, it is made specifically for sushi.

TAKE-OUT FAVORITES: WHITES

PRODUCER	WINE NAME	FROM	STYLE PROFILE
Oroyă	White Blend "Oroyă"	Tierra de Castilla, Spain	Light-bodied, racy, off-dry
Beringer Vineyards	Chenin Blanc	California	Light-bodied, racy, off-dry
Barton & Guestier	Vouvray	Vouvray, Loire Valley France	Light-bodied, racy, off-dry
Rémy Pannier	Vouvray	Vouvray, Loire Valley, France	Light-bodied, racy, off-dry
Chateau Ste. Michelle	Johannisberg Riesling	Columbia Valley, Washington	Light-bodied, racy, off-dry
Columbia Winery	"Cellarmaster's Riesling"	Columbia Valley, Washington	Light-bodied, crisp, lightly sweet
S.A. Prüm	Riesling "Essence"	Mosel-Saar-Ruwer, Germany	Light-bodied, racy, off-dry
Villa Wolf	Riesling "Saint M"	Pfalz, Germany	Medium-bodied, crisp, minerally
Avery Lane	Gewürztraminer	Columbia Valley, Washington	Medium-bodied, aromatic, off-dry
Fetzer	Gewürztraminer "Valley Oaks"	California	Medium-bodied, aromatic, off-dry
Villa Maria	Gewürztraminer "Private Bin"	Marlborough, New Zealand	Medium-full-bodied, crisp, fruity
Thomas Fogarty	Gewürztraminer	Monterey County, California	Medium-bodied, aromatic, off-dry
Fazi Battaglia	Verdicchio	Castelli di Jesi Classico, Italy	Light-bodied, crisp, refreshing
Sokol Blosser	"Evolution"	Willamette Valley, Oregon	Medium-bodied, aromatic, off-dry

SPECIAL BECAUSE	PRICE RANGE	MORE INFO . . .
Blend of Airen, Macabeo, and Muscat	$7–9	www.freixenet.com
Classic Napa winery; a crowd-pleaser	$6–8	www.beringervineyards.com
Widely available, made from Chenin Blanc	$7–10	www.barton-guestier.com
Chenin Blanc from Loire's largest producer	$10–12	www.palmbayimports.com (importer)
Top pick from Washington's founding winery	$7–9	www.ste-michelle.com
Personal favorite; unique style, low alcohol, fairly sweet	$10–15	www.columbiawinery.com
Available wine from two-hundred-year-old family winery	$8–10	www.sapruem.com or www.palmbayimports.com
Owned by Ernst Loosen, one of Germany's famous names	$10–12	www.jlwolf.com
Washington is a hot spot for Gewürz	$7–10	www.averylanewine.com
Great value, easy to find	$8–10	www.fetzer.com
Top winery; limited production	$13–16	www.villamaria.co.nz
California's Gewürztraminer leader	$14–16	www.fogartywinery.com
Bottle shaped like amphora; seriously fun	$8–10	www.fazibattaglia.com or www.palmbayimports.com
Personal favorite; blend of nine aromatic varieties	$12–14	www.sokolblosser.com

TAKE-OUT FAVORITES: REDS

PRODUCER	WINE NAME	FROM	STYLE PROFILE
Castello di Gabbiano	Chianti Classico	Chianti Classico, Italy	Medium-bodied, light tannins, fresh, spicy
Antinori	Sangiovese "Santa Cristina"	Toscana, Italy	Light-bodied, light tannins, bright, earthy
Bodegas Montecillo	Crianza	Rioja, Spain	Light-bodied, light tannins, bright, earthy
J. Lohr	Valdiguie "Wildflower"	Monterey, California	Light-bodied, light tannins, vibrant, fruity
Château de Varennes	Beaujolais-Villages	Beaujolais, France	Light-bodied, light tannins, vibrant, fruity
Jean Descombes	Morgon Cru	Beaujolais, France	Medium-bodied, light tannins, fresh, spicy
Georges Duboeuf	Morgon Cru	Beaujolais, France	Medium-bodied, light tannins, fresh, spicy
Camelot	Pinot Noir	California	Medium-bodied, light tannins, fresh, spicy
Talus Collection	Pinot Noir	Lodi, California	Medium-bodied, light tannins, fresh, spicy
Echelon	Pinot Noir	California	Medium-bodied, light tannins, fresh, spicy
Turning Leaf	Pinot Noir "Coastal Reserve"	North Coast, California	Medium-bodied, light tannins, fresh, spicy
Estancia	Pinot Noir "Pinnacles Ranches"	Monterey County, California	Medium-bodied, light tannins, fresh, spicy

SPECIAL BECAUSE	PRICE RANGE	MORE INFO . . .
Classic brand, widely available	$12–14	www.gabbiano.com
Good deal from top Tuscan winery	$10–12	www.antinori.it
Historic property making high-quality wines	$8–10	www.wjdeutsch.com (importer)
Unique grape variety Valdiguie; similar to Gamay	$8–10	www.jlohr.com
Made from Gamay grapes; higher quality than Beaujolais	$9–12	www.duboeuf.com
Personal favorite; top-quality producer serving up great value	$10–13	www.duboeuf.com
Most famous wine name in Beajolais	$10–12	www.duboeuf.com
Unbelievable price for solid Pinot—try it	$7–9	www.camelotwines.com
Hot bargain brand—makes affordable gift	$6–8	www.taluscellars.com
Fruit is primarily from the Santa Lucia Highlands; great deal	$8–10	www.echelonvineyards.com
Widely available Pinot with character	$10–12	www.turningleaf.com
Impressive value; founded by wine luminary Augustin Huneeus	$15–18	www.estanciaestates.com

TAKE-OUT FAVORITES: ROSÉS

PRODUCER	WINE NAME	FROM	STYLE PROFILE
Pedroncelli	Zinfandel Rosé	Sonoma County, California	Light-bodied, light tannin, off-dry, juicy
Monmousseau	Rosé d'Anjou	Anjou, Loire Valley, France	Light-bodied, light tannin, off-dry, juicy
Bonny Doon Vineyards	"Vin Gris De Cigare" Rosé	California	Light-bodied, light tannin, vibrant, fruity
Rutherford Hill	Rosé of Merlot	California	Light-bodied, light tannin, vibrant, fruity

TAKE-OUT FAVORITES: BUBBLES

PRODUCER	WINE NAME	FROM	STYLE PROFILE
Freixenet	Extra Dry Cava "Cordon Negro"	Spain	Light-bodied sparkler, soft, lightly sweet
Casalnova	Prosecco	Veneto, Italy	Light-bodied sparkler, soft, lightly sweet
Domaine Ste. Michelle	Extra Dry Sparkling Wine	Columbia Valley, Washington	Light-bodied sparkler, soft, lightly sweet
Willm	Crémant d'Alsace	Alsace, France	Medium-bodied sparkler, smooth, juicy
Langlois-Château	Crémant de Loire Brut	Loire Valley, France	Medium-bodied sparkler, smooth, juicy
Caves de Bailly	Crémant de Bourgogne Rosé	Burgundy, France	Medium-bodied sparkler, smooth, juicy
Rotari	Blanc de Noir	Trento, Italy	Medium-bodied sparkler, crisp, elegant
Korbel	Brut Rosé	California	Medium-bodied sparkler, crisp, elegant

SPECIAL BECAUSE	PRICE RANGE	MORE INFO . . .
Less sweet than White Zinfandel	$7–9	www.pedroncelli.com
Made from Cabernet Franc and Grolleau	$8–10	www.monmousseau.com
Personal favorite; one of California's top pinks	$10–13	www.bonnydoonvineyard.com
Dry style—pair it with meat dishes	$9–11	www.rutherfordhill.com

SPECIAL BECAUSE	PRICE RANGE	MORE INFO . . .
Popular wine in black bottle with a touch of sweetness	$8–10	www.freixenetusa.com
Available in single-serve bottles, too	$9–14	www.grantusa.com (importer)
Ideal with extra-spicy dishes	$10–12	www.domaine-ste-michelle.com
First Alsatian producer to export to United States	$11–15	www.alsace-willm.com
Good-value alternative to Champagne	$12–14	www.langlois-chateau.fr
Limited production but worth the effort to find	$13–16	www.caves-bailly.com
Primarily made with Pinot Noir; great deal	$10–12	www.mezzacorona.it
Delicate and dry, a well-priced pink bubbly	$11–13	www.korbel.com

Snack Attack Party Food

∽

Whether the gathering is Super Bowl Sunday, a graduation party, movie night, or birthday bash, when there's a crowd there is snack food. Many people set up a cooler filled with beer, but try wine, which goes just as well with party fare.

DESIGN-A-DINNER
Crudité Platter

* * *

To make a fresh-from-the-garden appetizer platter, choose a selection of vegetables such as carrots, celery, red and yellow bell peppers, cherry tomatoes, jicama, sugar snap peas, broccoli, and asparagus. Note on blanching: Certain veggies, like asparagus, green beans, snap peas, and broccoli, taste better when they're parboiled. Put the cut-up vegetables in a large pot of boiling water for around three to five minutes, until just tender. Drain them immediately into an ice bath—a bowl of ice cubes and cold water—for several minutes. Remove and pat dry before putting on the platter. They will remain crunchy and colorful. Serve with:

ZIPPY VINAIGRETTE

Combine one heaping tablespoon of smooth Dijon mustard with a quarter cup of balsamic vinegar and three tablespoons cider vinegar. Whisk in one-half cup olive oil until creamy. Season with sea salt and freshly ground black pepper.

VEGETABLE PLATTERS/CHIPS AND SALSA 🐟

Think zesty, high-acid wines such as New Zealand and South African Sauvignon Blanc, Austrian Grüner Veltliner, and Spanish Albariño. These refreshing whites complement the herbal crunchiness of vegetables as well as chips and salsa, because they echo the herbal, tangy salsa and act as a foil for the fatty saltiness of chips.

Want more picks? Check out these lists: Holiday Spirit, Twice-the-Price Wines, Bathtub Wines

PRODUCER	WINE NAME	FROM	STYLE PROFILE
Brancott	Sauvignon Blanc	Marlborough, New Zealand	Medium-bodied, racy, herbal
RedCliffe	Sauvignon Blanc	Marlborough, New Zealand	Medium-bodied, racy, herbal
Matua Valley	Sauvignon Blanc	Marlborough, New Zealand	Medium-bodied, racy, herbal
The Crossings	Sauvignon Blanc	Marlborough, New Zealand	Medium-bodied, racy, herbal
Rancho Zabaco	Sauvignon Blanc "Dancing Bull"	California	Medium-bodied, racy, herbal
Brampton	Sauvignon Blanc	South Africa	Medium-bodied, racy, herbal
Fat Bastard	Sauvignon Blanc	Vin de Pays D'Oc, France	Medium-bodied, crisp, minerally
Erich Berger	Grüner Veltliner	Kremstal, Austria	Medium-bodied, crisp, minerally
Martin Codax	"Burgans" Albariño	Rias Baixas, Spain	Medium-bodied, crisp, minerally

SPECIAL BECAUSE	PRICE RANGE	MORE INFO . . .
Top-selling New Zealand wine internationally	$9–12	www.brancottvineyards.com
Great value wine	$10–12	www.palmbayimports.com (importer)
Partner of Beringer Blass, so easy to find	$8–10	www.matua.co.nz
Intense and complex wine; must try	$15–18	www.thecrossings.co.nz
Personal favorite; widely available value wine	$8–10	www.ranchozabaco.com
Lean, green style	$8–10	www.capeclassics.com (importer)
Popular brand named for slang expression meaning great wine	$9–10	www.fatbastardwine.com
This wine is a steal! Imported by Terry Theise	$10 for 1 liter	www.skurnikwines.com (importer)
Hint of sweetness, crowd-pleasing style	$13–15	www.martincodax.com

CHICKEN WINGS

For mildly spicy wings served with creamy ranch or blue cheese dressing, try vibrant, fruity Merlot. When there's bite-me hot sauce, go for slightly sweet pink wine. Many versions are now being made from Merlot or Shiraz.

PRODUCER	WINE NAME	FROM	STYLE PROFILE
Beringer Vineyards	White Merlot	California	Light-bodied, light tannins, off-dry, juicy
Trinity Oaks	White Merlot	California	Light-bodied, light tannins, off-dry, juicy
The Little Penguin	White Shiraz	South Eastern Australia	Light-bodied, light tannins, off-dry, juicy
Christian Moueix	Merlot	Bordeaux, France	Light-bodied, light tannins, bright, earthy
Marquis de Chasse	Bordeaux	Bordeaux, France	Light-bodied, light tannins, bright, earthy
Turning Leaf	Merlot	California	Medium-bodied, supple tannins, smooth, juicy
Blackstone	Merlot	California	Medium-bodied, supple tannins, smooth, juicy
Buena Vista	Merlot	Carneros, California	Medium-bodied, supple tannins, smooth, juicy

Want more picks? Check out these lists: Spring Wines, Summer Wines, Take-Out Favorites

SPECIAL BECAUSE	PRICE RANGE	MORE INFO . . .
Popular alternative to White Zinfandel	$5–7	www.beringer.com
Not too sweet, nice balance	$5–6	www.trinityoaks.com
Spicy side of Shiraz shows through	$7–8	www.thelittlepenguin.com
Affordable red from superstar of Bordeaux	$8–10	www.kobrandwine.com (importer)
Mostly Merlot with Cabernet Sauvigon; good deal for complexity	$9–10	www.vineyardbrands.com (importer)
High-volume but high-quality, value producer	$8–10	www.turningleaf.com
Widely available wine, especially in restaurants	$10–12	www.blackstonewinery.com
Zesty bottlings from cool Carneros	$15–19	www.buenavistacarneros .com

Nuts/Popcorn/Potato Chips

Two of my favorite culinary combinations are salty potato chips with bubbly, and almonds and olives with dry Sherry. Zesty sparkling wine and ice-cold Sherry offset the salty richness of the food while offering palate-cleansing freshness.

Want more picks? Check out these lists: Holiday Spirit, Overlooked Surprises, Bathtub Wines

PRODUCER	WINE NAME	FROM	STYLE PROFILE
Osborne	Amontillado "Rare Sherry Solera Primera"	Jerez de la Frontera, Spain	Light-bodied, crisp, refreshing
Domecq	Manzanilla Sherry	Jerez de la Frontera, Spain	Light-bodied, crisp, refreshing
Cristalino	Cava Brut	Spain	Light-bodied sparkler, crisp, refreshing
Folonari	Prosecco "Brio"	Veneto, Italy	Light-bodied sparkler, crisp, refreshing
Bodegas Naveran	Blanc de Blancs Brut "Reserva" Cava	Spain	Light-bodied sparkler, soft, lightly sweet
Mumm Napa	Blanc de Blancs Vintage	Napa Valley, California	Medium-bodied sparkler, crisp, elegant
Domaine Chandon	Brut Classic	California	Medium-bodied sparkler, smooth, juicy

QUICK TIP
Gourmet Popcorn in a Flash
* * *
Pop regular corn and while warm toss with truffle oil,
finely diced culinary lavender, cracked pepper, or sea salt.
Pair with bubbly.

SPECIAL BECAUSE	PRICE RANGE	MORE INFO . . .
Personal favorite; nutty, dry, elegant	$11–14	www.osborne.es
Dry style with hint of salty tang	$12–15	www.domecq-usa.com
Great deal, widely available	$5–7	www.civusa.com (importer)
Bottled with a pop-top; bone dry	$10–12	www.folonariwines.com
Traditional Cava blend of Macabeo, Xarel-lo, Parellada	$15–17	www.oleimports.com (importer)
Unique marriage of Chardonnay and Pinot Gris	$19–22	www.mummnapa.com
Classic producer, classy wine	$19–23	www.chandon.com

Cheese-Friendly Wines

∞

Pairing cheese and wine is a no-brainer for many people: grab a glass of red and go. Not so fast. I often serve white and/or sweet wines with cheeses. As with general food and wine pairing there is no right or wrong, only better and worse. My advice is simple: The whiter and fresher the cheese, the lighter and more crisp the wine and the darker, aged, and more pungent the cheese, the richer and stronger the wine.

DESIGN-A-DESSERT
The Perfect Cheese Platter

* * *

Variety is key. Offer fresh and dried fruits such as grapes, sliced apples and pears, and dates, apricots, or quince paste. Sprinkle a selection of nuts including almonds, hazelnuts, and pecans along with a range of cheeses from tangy chevre to creamy brie and rich blue. Instead of crackers, slice a loaf of nutty whole wheat bread for a textural contrast.

WITH SOFT, CREAMY CHEESES SUCH AS BRIE, CAMEMBERT, AND EPOISSES

Texture, texture, texture works here. Avoid heavy oak, loads of tannins, and huge power, which will overwhelm the cheeses. Look for mild, creamy white wines with a core of racy acidity such as cool-climate Chardonnay and Alsatian Pinot Gris. If reds are your choice, focus on bright and earthy Pinot Noir from New Zealand, Oregon, or the cool Carneros area between Napa and Sonoma Valleys in California.

Want more picks? Check out these lists: Fall Wines, Girls' Night In, Holiday Spirit

WITH SOFT, CREAMY CHEESES

PRODUCER	WINE NAME	FROM	STYLE PROFILE
Red Bicyclette	Chardonnay	Vin de Pays D'Oc, France	Medium-bodied, light oak, juicy
Stag's Leap Wine Cellars	Chardonnay "Hawk Crest"	California	Medium-bodied, light oak, juicy
Raymond Estates	Chardonnay	Monterey, California	Medium-bodied, light oak, juicy
Beaulieu Vineyards	Chardonnay "Carneros"	Carneros, California	Medium-bodied, light oak, juicy
The Hess Collection	Chardonnay	Napa Valley, California	Medium-bodied, light oak, juicy
Louis Jadot	Pouilly-Fuissé	Burgundy, France	Medium-full-bodied, crisp, fruity
Domaine Louis Moreau	Chablis "1er Cru Vaillons"	Chablis, France	Full-bodied, crisp, spicy, elegant
Domaine Schlumberger	Pinot Gris "Les Princes Abbes"	Alsace, France	Full-bodied, soft, aromatic
Erath	Pinot Noir	Dundee, Oregon	Medium-bodied, supple tannins, vibrant, earthy
Saintsbury	Pinot Noir "Garnet"	Carneros, California	Light-bodied, light tannins, bright and earthy
Brancott	Pinot Noir	Marlborough, New Zealand	Medium-bodied, supple tannins, vibrant, earthy
Felton Road	Pinot Noir	Central Otago, New Zealand	Full-bodied, supple tannins, smooth, earthy

SPECIAL BECAUSE	PRICE RANGE	MORE INFO . . .
Light-hearted wine—fun label	$8–10	www.redbicyclette.com
Second label of legendary Napa winery; great value	$9–11	www.cask23.com
Family-owned for five generations	$10–12	www.raymondwine.com
Showcases crisp character of Carneros wines	$16–18	www.bvwines.com
Must-visit winery—art collection and stunning architecture	$20–25	www.hesscollection.com
Chardonnay made by venerable negociant house	$18–20	www.louisjadot.com
Complex Chardonnay from top producer	$39–42	www.louismoreau.com
Must-try wine from one of Alsace's best	$12–14	www.domaines-schlumberger.com
Dick Erath was one of Oregon's pioneers	$15–18	www.erath.com
Popular-priced, Burgundian style from Pinot specialist	$16–18	www.saintsbury.com
Great value from New Zealand leader	$10–13	www.brancottvineyards.com
Personal favorite; world-class Pinot from exciting region	$42–46	www.feltonroad.com

WITH FRESH, TANGY CHEESES SUCH AS CHEVRE, BOURSIN, AND FETA 🖅

Focus on crisp, bright whites with a touch of minerality such as dry Riesling, Spanish Albariño, and Sauvignon Blanc–based wines from the Sancerre, Pouilly-Fumé, and Bordeaux regions of France.

PRODUCER	WINE NAME	FROM	STYLE PROFILE
Vionta	Albariño	Rias Baixas, Spain	Medium-full-bodied, crisp, fruity
Boutari	Moschofilero	Mantinia, Greece	Medium-bodied, crisp, minerally
Annie's Lane	Riesling	Clare Valley, Australia	Medium-bodied, crisp, minerally
Smith-Madrone	Riesling	Napa Valley, California	Medium-bodied, crisp, minerally
Concha y Toro	Sauvignon Blanc "Terrunyo"	Casablanca Valley, Chile	Medium-bodied, crisp, minerally
Whitehaven	Sauvignon Blanc	Marlborough, New Zealand	Medium-bodied, racy, herbal
Pascal Jolivet	Sancerre	Sancerre, France	Medium-bodied, crisp, minerally
De Ladoucette	Pouilly-Fumé	Pouilly-Fumé, France	Medium-bodied, crisp, minerally
Château Couhins Lurton	Blanc	Pessac-Léognan, Graves, France	Medium-bodied, crisp, minerally
Château Lynch-Bages	Blanc	Pauillac, Bordeaux, France	Full-bodied, crisp, spicy, elegant

Want more picks? Check out these lists: Hot Spots, Overlooked
Surprises, Summer Wines

SPECIAL BECAUSE	PRICE RANGE	MORE INFO . . .
Hot Spanish white, perfect with shellfish	$15–18	www.heredadcollection.com
Fun, refreshing Greek white	$10–12	www.paternowines.com (importer) or www.boutari.gr
Like drinking key lime pie	$12–15	www.annieslane.com.au
Award-winning, dry styled Riesling	$17–19	www.smithmadrone.com
Classic Chilean producer; limited availability	$20–22	www.conchaytoro.com
Personal favorite, intense and complex	$18–20	www.whitehaven.co.nz
Made from Sauvignon Blanc by top producer	$20–25	www.pascal-jolivet.com
Smoky and exotic—world-class Sauvignon Blanc	$38–42	www.mmdusa.net
Sauvignon Blanc from historic property; oak-aged	$20–23	www.andrelurton.com
Limited production; gorgeous Sauvignon Blanc plus Sémillon	$35–37	www.lynchbages.com

WITH HARDER, NUTTY CHEESES SUCH AS AGED PARMIGIANO-REGGIANO, ASIAGO, AND MANCHEGO

These cheeses take on earthy, vibrant Italian reds with ease, but also shine when paired with amber-colored sweeties like tawny Port. For Spanish manchego, look to an earthy dry Portugese red or Spanish Rioja.

PRODUCER	WINE NAME	FROM	STYLE PROFILE
Atlas Peak	Sangiovese	Napa Valley, California	Medium-bodied, supple tannins, vibrant, earthy
Marchesi De' Frescobaldi	"Remole"	Tuscany, Italy	Light-bodied, light tannins, bright, earthy
Castello di Bossi	Chianti Classico "Berardo"	Chianti Classico, Italy	Medium-bodied, supple tannins, vibrant, earthy
Barone Ricasoli	Chianti Classico "Castello di Brolio"	Chianti Classico, Italy	Full-bodied, supple tannins, smooth, earthy
Marqués de Cáceres	Crianza	Rioja, Spain	Light-bodied, light tannins, bright, earthy
Quinta de Crasto	Dry red wine	Duoro, Portugal	Medium-bodied, supple tannins, vibrant, earthy
Col d'Orcia	Rosso di Montalcino	Rosso di Montalcino, Italy	Medium-bodied, supple tannins, vibrant, earthy
Cockburn's	Fine Tawny Porto	Portugal	Medium-bodied, lightly sweet, nutty
Ramos Pinto	Tawny Porto	Portugal	Medium-bodied, lightly sweet, nutty
Churchill's	20-Year Old Tawny Porto	Portugal	Full-bodied, sweet, supple, rich

Want more picks? Check out these lists: Dessert Wines, Spring Wines, Pasta-Perfect Wines

SPECIAL BECAUSE	PRICE RANGE	MORE INFO . . .
Best California Sangiovese from vines brought by Piero Antinori	$12–15	www.atlaspeak.com
Great value from family with seven-hundred-year wine history	$8–10	www.frescobaldi.it
Old property that has undergone quality renaissance	$30–33	www.castellodibossi.it or www.winebow.com (importer)
Barone Ricasoli developed the original formula for Chianti	$55–60	www.ricasoli.it
Classic producer, widely available	$10–12	www.marquesdecaceres.com
Limited production but worth effort to find	$19–21	www.broadbent-wines.com
"Baby Brunello" made from Sangiovese grosso	$18–20	www.coldorcia.it
Good beginner Tawny, soft and smooth	$10–12	www.cockburns-usa.com
Not overly sweet; light style	$15–18	www.ramospinto.pt
Personal favorite, decadently rich; pour with Parmigiano-Reggiano	$50–55	www.churchills-port.com

WITH SEMI-HARD CHEESES SUCH AS CHEDDAR, GOUDA, PROVOLONE, OR GRUYÈRE ⧽ Fruity, supple reds sporting smoky undertones and moderate tannins are the ticket. Think cooler-climate Merlot and Syrah from California or Western Australia.

PRODUCER	WINE NAME	FROM	STYLE PROFILE
Havens	Merlot "Reserve"	Carneros, California	Medium-full-bodied, supple tannins, vibrant, juicy
Robert Keenan	Merlot	Carneros, California	Medium-full-bodied, supple tannins, vibrant, juicy
Cline	Syrah "Cool Climate"	Sonoma Coast, California	Medium-full-bodied, supple tannins, vibrant, juicy
Cape Mentelle	Shiraz	Margaret River, Western Australia	Medium-bodied, supple tannins, vibrant, earthy

WITH PUNGENT, AGED BLUE CHEESES SUCH AS ROQUEFORT, STILTON, AND GORGONZOLA ⧽ Bottle-aged Ports offer richness to contrast the salty intensity of these cheeses.

PRODUCER	WINE NAME	FROM	STYLE PROFILE
Dow's	Reserve Porto	Portugal	Full-bodied, lightly sweet, smooth
W. & J. Graham's	"Six Grapes" Reserve Porto	Portugal	Full-bodied, lightly sweet, smooth
Taylor Fladgate	Late Bottled Vintage (LBV)	Portugal	Full-bodied, sweet, supple, rich
Offley	Late Bottled Vintage (LBV)	Portugal	Full-bodied, sweet, supple, rich
Quinta do Vesuvio	Vintage Port	Portugal	Full-bodied, sweet, supple, rich

Want more picks? Check out these lists: Snack Attack Party Food, Sexy Wines

SPECIAL BECAUSE	PRICE RANGE	MORE INFO . . .
Michael Havens is a Carneros master—try his Syrah	$23–25	www.havenswine.com
Lesser-known but elegantly styled Merlot	$25–28	www.keenanwinery.com
Known for Zinfandel, don't miss Cline's spicy Syrah	$15–17	www.clinecellars.com
Famous sister company of Cloudy Bay	$19–22	www.capementelle.com.au

Want more picks? Check out these lists: Winter Wines, Dessert Wines

SPECIAL BECAUSE	PRICE RANGE	MORE INFO . . .
Dow's makes drier styles of ports	$17–19	www.dows-port.com
Popular port from classic producer	$21–23	www.grahams-port.com
A steal—similar to vintage but for half the price	$20–22	www.taylor.pt
Less available than others, but ultra-smooth style	$20–22	www.portugal-info.net
Highly recommended ageworthy port from single estate	$60–65	www.quintadovesuvio.com

Dessert Wines

You can have your cake and eat it too . . . by drinking dessert. Not only does it satisfy a sweet tooth, a glass of dessert wine has fewer calories (around 125) than a piece of chocolate cake. Whether indulging in Vin Santo with biscotti, ice wine with ice cream, or port with chocolate, if you haven't yet been introduced to the joys of dessert wine, get ready. My picks will take you on a voyage of discovery to the sweet side of life.

QUICK TIP
Pairing Wine and Dessert
* * *

MATCH SWEETNESS

The wine should be at least as sweet as the dessert so delicately sweet treats call for a lightly sweet wine. Conversely, rich, decadent desserts need a no-holds-barred sweetie.

MATCH COLOR

Match the color of the wine with the food. Golden-colored sweet wines and amber-hued Tawny Ports sing with softer cheeses, nuts, dried apricots, fruit tarts with pears, apples or peaches, and sugar cookies, or caramels. Ruby and dark purple wines are ideal with bittersweet chocolate and intense blue cheese, dark nuts, and brownies.

DESSERT WINES: LIGHTLY SWEET

PRODUCER	WINE NAME	FROM	STYLE PROFILE
Martin and Weyrich	Allegro Moscato	Paso Robles, California	Light-bodied, crisp, lightly sweet
Fontanafredda	Moscato d'Asti	Asti, Italy	Light-bodied, crisp, lightly sweet
Bonny Doon	Muscat Vin de Glacière	California	Light-bodied, crisp, lightly sweet
Quady	Orange Muscat "Essensia"	California	Light-bodied, crisp, lightly sweet
Washington Hills	Late-Harvest Riesling	Columbia Valley, Washington	Light-bodied, crisp, lightly sweet
G. H. Mumm & Cie	"Joyesse" Demi-Sec Champagne	Champagne, France	Full-bodied sparkler, creamy, lightly sweet
Schramsberg	Crémant Demi-Sec Sparkling Wine	Napa Valley, California	Full-bodied sparkler, creamy, lightly sweet
Hardys	Sparkling Shiraz	Southern Australia	Full-bodied sparkler, creamy, lightly sweet

DESIGN-A-DESSERT

Fast, Faux Fondue

* * *

Melt two to three quality bittersweet chocolate bars or a bag of dark chocolate chips. Dip store-bought pecan shortbread cookies, dried apricots, and fresh large strawberries

SPECIAL BECAUSE	PRICE RANGE	MORE INFO . . .
Made in the style of Italian Asti; try with cookies	$10–12	www.martinweyrich.com
Sexy, tall bottle; lightly fizzy—good gift	$14–16	www.domaineselect.com
Must-try wine made with frozen Muscat grapes	$15–17 half bottle	www.bonnydoonvineyard.com
Delicious beginner dessert wine, floral and fresh	$22–25	www.quadywinery.com
Limited production but great value	$8	www.washingtonhills.com
Demi-sec means "half dry" so look for that on the label of bubbly	$26–30	www.mumm.com
Top California bubbly producer, ideal with pound cake	$30–35	www.schramsberg.com
Purple bubbles—uncork with chocolate	$20–22	www.hardys.com.au

halfway into the chocolate. Set on wax paper to harden and serve as a complement to a selection of dessert wines.

DESSERT WINES: MEDIUM SWEET

PRODUCER	WINE NAME	FROM	STYLE PROFILE
Beaulieu Vineyards	Muscat de Beaulieu	Napa Valley, California	Medium-bodied, sweet, juicy
Peter Lehmann	Botrytis Semillon	Barossa Valley, Australia	Medium-bodied, sweet, juicy
King Estate	Pinot Gris "Vin Glacé"	Oregon	Medium-bodied, sweet, juicy
Vigne Regali	"Rosa Regale" Brachetto d'Acqui	Piedmont, Italy	Light-bodied sparkler, soft, lightly sweet
Kracher	Cuvée Auslese	Austria	Medium-bodied, sweet, juicy
Fèlsina	Vin Santo "Berardenga"	Chianti Classico, Italy	Medium-bodied, sweet, juicy
Broadbent	Madeira "Rainwater"	Madeira, Portugal	Medium-bodied, lightly sweet, nutty
Churchill's	10-Year Tawny Port	Portugal	Medium-bodied, lightly sweet, nutty
Dow's	Vintage Porto	Oporto, Portugal	Full-bodied, lightly sweet, smooth
M. Chapoutier	Banyuls	Banyuls, France	Full-bodied, lightly sweet, smooth

SPECIAL BECAUSE	PRICE RANGE	MORE INFO . . .
Great value for elegant-styled sweetie	$10–12 half bottle	www.bvwines.com
Personal favorite; try it for brunch . . . alone	$16–18 half bottle	www.peterlehmannwines .com
Serve well chilled over fruit	$24–26 half bottle	www.kingestate.com
Personal favorite; pale red, strawberry-scented sparkling wine	$16–18	www.vigneregali.com or www.castellobanfi.com
Blend of Chardonnay and Welschriesling from Austrian master	$25–30 half bottle	www.kracher.net
Famous Tuscan wine made from dried Malvasia and Trebbiano	$30–35 500 ml	www.felsina.it
Famous fortified wine made on the island of Madeira	$7–10 half bottle	www.broadbent-wines.com
Try even if you don't like dessert wines	$30–35	www.churchills-port.com
Serve with bittersweet chocolate	$10–12	www.dows-port.com
Chocolate-lovers watch out! Fortified Grenache-based red	$20–25 500 ml	www.chapoutier.com

DESSERT WINES: DECADENTLY SWEET

PRODUCER	WINE NAME	FROM	STYLE PROFILE
Castoro Cellars	Late-Harvest Zinfandel	Paso Robles, California	Full-bodied, sweet, supple and rich
Campbells	Muscat	Rutherglen, Victoria, Australia	Full-bodied, sweet, supple and rich
Argiolas	"Angialis"	Sardinia, Italy	Full-bodied, sweet, supple and rich
Quinta de Crasto	Vintage Porto	Portugal	Full-bodied, sweet, supple and rich
Château Coutet	Sauternes	Sauternes, France	Full-bodied, sweet, supple and rich
Château Rieussec	Sauternes	Sauternes, France	Full-bodied, sweet, supple and rich
Delaforce	Tawny "Colheita"	Portugal	Medium-bodied, sweet, nutty
Blandy's	Madeira "Alvada" 5-Year-Old Rich	Madeira, Portugal	Full-bodied, sweet, supple and rich
Osborne	Pedro Xímenez "1827" Sweet Sherry	Spain	Full-bodied, sweet, supple and rich

WINE ABCS
Sauternes

* * *

Sauternes is part of the larger Graves region of Bordeaux and within its boundaries lays Barsac. As the cold waters of the nearby Ciron River spill into Bordeaux's warmer Garonne River, they create a cooling steam bath. Misty autumn

SPECIAL BECAUSE	PRICE RANGE	MORE INFO . . .
Similar to Port, this is a chocolate-lovers wine	$20–22	www.castorocellars.com
Rutherglen is a special place for sweet wine	$16–19 half bottle	www.campbellswines.com.au
Rare Nasco/Malvasia blend from superstar Giacomo Tachis	$35–42 500 ml	www.winebow.com (importer)
Limited production but worth it for value	$38–35	www.broadbent-wines.com/ wines.cfm
One of Bordeaux's oldest wine estates	$40–45	www.chateaucoutet.com
Classic, ageworthy wine; highly recommended	$50–55	www.lafite.com
Personal favorite; rare single-vintage Tawny	$60–70	www.kobrandwine.com (importer)
Ideal with caramel and nut desserts	$15–18 500 ml	www.blandys.com
Made from Pedro Xímenez grapes. Like drinking chocolate!	$17–20	www.wjdeutsch.com (importer)

mornings give way to sunny harvest afternoons creating optimum conditions for the development of botrytis cinerea, or noble rot. Because the grape varieties that make Sauternes—Sémillon and Sauvignon Blanc—are particularly susceptible to noble rot, which concentrates the grape's flavors and imparts a honeyed richness to the wine, Sauternes is the ideal place to produce world-class dessert wines.

Wines by Season

W̲e eat by the seasons and dress for the seasons so why not drink with the seasons? You most likely do it already. On a warm summer day, what do you crave? A weighty red or a crisp, refreshing white? Conversely, when the cold days of January hit, are you sipping a zesty light wine or soul-soothing, full-bodied red? Just as you stock your refrigerator with seasonal produce or fill your closet with light fabrics in spring and heavier ones in winter, building a wine wardrobe is about stocking your shelves with wines that follow the seasons.

SEASONAL CHEAT SHEET

SEASON	LOOKING FOR	WINE TYPES
Spring: Refreshingly light, these wines are the "spring dresses" of wine	Bright and juicy wines with spicy complexity	Riesling, Chenin Blanc, Chablis, Pinot Noir, Rioja, Chianti
Summer: Thirst-quenching, outdoor party winners akin to beachwear	Sassy sippers that offer refreshment and fun	Sauvignon Blanc, Grüner Veltliner, Albarino, Rosé, inexpensive Zinfandel, and Shiraz
Fall: Stylish wines with a streak of richness. Think sleek cashmere sweaters in a bottle	Earthy yet elegant wines to transition from warm weather to cool	Sémillon, Rueda, Grenache-based wine like Châteauneuf-du-Pape and Priorat, Carmenère
Winter: Like leather keeps you toasty in winter, these hearty comfort wines will warm the soul	Rich, mouth-filling wines with smooth textures and lush flavors	Chardonnay, Rhône whites such as Viognier, Gewürztraminer, Syrah, Cabernet Sauvignon, Amarone, Port

WINE ABCS
Chianti

* * *

Chianti is a famous wine-producing district in Italy's Tus-
cany region, planted primarily with the red grape variety
Sangiovese. Wines labeled simply Chianti are affordable
reds sporting a medium-bodied, zesty character. For more
depth and character, seek out wines from Chianti Classico
(look for the stamp of quality—a black rooster on the label).
Chianti Classicos tend to be more expensive and complex
than regular Chiantis due to extended aging and higher-
quality grapes. There are seven subzones in Chianti, includ-
ing not only well-known Chianti Classico (the filet mignon
of the entire region) but also Chianti Rufina, Colli Senesi,
Colli Fiorentini, and Colline Pisane, which are named for
hillside areas that surround the region's main cities of
Siena, Florence, and Pisa.

Pinot Noir

* * *

Pinot Noir is a red grape variety producing sexy, seductive
reds that are the equivalent of drinking silk. (I always say
that if wines could show emotion, they would surely all
have Pinot envy.) A member of the Pinot family, along with
Pinot Blanc and Pinot Gris, Pinot Noir is often dubbed the
heartbreak grape. Part of the grape's demanding nature is
that it thrives only in select wine-growing regions, which
push the climate envelope. Pinot prefers cool places and
needs every ray of sunshine to ripen fully. France is the
spiritual home of Pinot, but California, Oregon, and New
Zealand are making wines to rival the best of Burgundy.

Spring Wines

Spring is all about renewal and rejuvenation. When giving your closet a spring cleaning, heavy winter sweaters and wool pants are out while linen shirts and light suits are in. Give your wine stash the same attention as your wardrobe. Replace comfort wines of winter with light-as-air springtime sippers.

Look for . . .

- **Whites:** Rieslings from Washington state, New York, and Germany capture a minerally freshness but still sport a bit of heft. Fruity and zesty Chardonnay from places such as Chablis in Burgundy, France, or versions from New Zealand hit the spot as do Chenin Blanc-based wines. One of my favorites not to miss is northern Italian Gavi, made from the Cortese grape.
- **Reds:** Pinot Noir works all year round because of its elegance, but I crave it in springtime. Spanish wines based on the Tempranillo grape, hailing from regions such as Rioja and Ribera del Duero, are seasonal stars. And, Italian Sangiovese-based wines from Tuscany and the neighboring region of Umbria, warm up chilly spring evenings.

Want more picks? Check out these lists: Thanksgiving Wines, Overlooked Surprises, Hot Spots

SPRING WHITES

PRODUCER	WINE NAME	FROM	STYLE PROFILE
Lagaria	Chardonnay	Delle Venezia, Italy	Light-bodied, crisp, refreshing
Murphy-Goode	Chardonnay "Tin Roof"	Sonoma County, California	Light-bodied, crisp, refreshing
Kumeu River	Chardonnay "Village"	New Zealand	Medium-full-bodied, crisp, fruity
Domaine Louis Moreau	Chablis	Chablis, France	Medium-full-bodied, crisp, fruity
Hermann J. Wiemer	Dry Johannisberg Riesling	Finger Lakes, New York	Medium-bodied, crisp, minerally
Dr. H. Thanisch	Riesling Classic	Mosel-Saar-Ruwer, Germany	Medium-bodied, crisp, minerally
Fritz Haag	Riesling Kabinett	Mosel-Saar-Ruwer, Germany	Medium-bodied, crisp, minerally
Indaba	Chenin Blanc	Stellenbosch, South Africa	Medium-bodied, aromatic, off-dry
Pine Ridge Winery	Chenin Blanc/Viognier	California	Medium-bodied, aromatic, off-dry
Chappellet	Dry Chenin Blanc	Napa Valley, California	Medium-bodied, crisp, minerally
Domaine du Closel	"Le Clos du Papillon"	Savennières, Loire Valley, France	Medium-bodied, crisp, minerally
Michele Chiarlo	Gavi	Gavi, Italy	Medium-full-bodied, crisp, fruity

SPECIAL BECAUSE	PRICE RANGE	MORE INFO . . .
Great value, named after northeastern Italian valley, Vallagarina	$8–10	www.empson.com (importer)
Top Sonoma producer's bargain brand	$9–11	www.tinroofwines.com
New Zealand's Chardonnay specialist; leader in screw caps	$19–22	www.kumeuriver.co.nz
Highly regarded family winery; well-priced classic Chablis	$26	www.louismoreau.com
German-born Hermann Wiemer is Riesling specialist	$16	www.wiemer.com
Dry wine from historic property	$13–15	www.chapincellars.com
Personal favorite; one of Germany's best estates	$25–27	www.germanwine.net (importer) or www.fritz-haag.de
Good value and generally available	$7–9	www.capeclassics.com
Limited production but worth the effort to find	$13–15	www.pineridgewinery.com
California's best Chenin from pioneering Napa winery	$13–15	www.chappellet.com
Chenin Blanc–based wine; ageworthy	$20–25	www.savennieres-closel.com
Must-try wine; impressive quality, chic packaging	$17–19	www.michelechiarlo.it

SPRING REDS

PRODUCER	WINE NAME	FROM	STYLE PROFILE
Louis Latour	Pinot Noir, Bourgogne	Burgundy, France	Light-bodied, light tannins, bright and earthy
Rex Hill	Pinot Noir	Oregon	Medium-bodied, supple tannins, vibrant, earthy
Carmel Road	Pinot Noir	Monterey County, California	Medium-bodied, supple tannins, vibrant, earthy
Charles Krug	Pinot Noir	Carneros, California	Medium-bodied, supple tannins, vibrant, earthy
Skewis	"Demuth Vineyard" Pinot Noir	Anderson Valley, California	Medium-bodied, supple tannins, vibrant, earthy
Navarro Vineyards	"Méthode à L'Ancienne" Pinot Noir	Anderson Valley, California	Medium-bodied, supple tannins, vibrant, earthy
Torremoron	Tempranillo	Ribera del Duero, Spain	Medium-bodied, light tannins, fresh, spicy
Legaris	Crianza	Ribera del Duero, Spain	Medium-bodied, light tannins, fresh, spicy
Valdubón	Reserva	Ribera del Duero, Spain	Medium-bodied, light tannins, fresh, spicy
Marchese de' Frescobaldi	Chianti "Castiglioni"	Chianti, Italy	Medium-bodied, light tannins, fresh, spicy
Castello di Gabbiano	Chianti Classico	Chianti Classico, Italy	Medium-bodied, light tannins, fresh, spicy
Silverado Vineyards	Sangiovese	Napa Valley, California	Medium-bodied, supple tannins, smooth, juicy

SPECIAL BECAUSE	PRICE RANGE	MORE INFO . . .
Good deal from one of Burgundy's top negociants	$8–12	www.louislatour.com
Affordable introduction to Oregon Pinot	$19–23	www.rexhill.com
Part of the Kendall-Jackson family of wines; elegant	$16–18	www.carmelroad.com
Historic Napa winery undergoing a renaissance of quality	$18–20	www.charleskrug.com
Personal favorite; family-owned winery focusing on Pinot	$35–37	www.skewiswines.com
Boutique California winery; classy wines	$23–25	www.navarrowine.com
Real deal for Tempranillo from Ribera	$9–12	www.torremoron.com
Part of the Codorníu group; elegant packaging	$18–20	www.legaris.com
Aged longer than Crianza; smooth	$24–26	www.valdubon.com
Mostly Sangiovese with touch of Merlot	$12–14	www.frescobaldi.it
One of the most beautiful Tuscan properties to visit	$12–14	www.gabbiano.com
Limited-production Sangiovese from top Napa winery	$15–20	www.silveradovineyards.com

Summer Wines

THIRST-QUENCHING, OUTDOOR PARTY WINNERS
AKIN TO BEACHWEAR

∞

The sun's out, the surf's up, so it's time to head to the beach or hang out by the pool. Grilling out is a given, salads and fresh vegetables fill your refrigerator, and relaxing in a hammock is the order of the day. Just like you favor wearing shorts and T-shirts, summertime sipping is about casual fun.

Look for . . .

- **Whites:** Refreshment with a capital R. A host of crisp, sassy whites line store shelves to choose from during the summer months: fruity Sauvignon Blanc, steely Austrian Grüner Veltliner, zesty Spanish Albariño, and snappy Italian and California Pinot Grigio.

- **Pinks and Reds:** Dry-styled rosés are perfect on warm summer days and nights. For reds, try inexpensive versions of California Zinfandel, Argentine Malbec, Spanish wines from Jumilla, and Aussie Shiraz. All go great with burgers and steaks.

- **Sweet Treats:** Moscato d'Astis are light, lemony fizzies ideal for summer drinking. Made from aromatic muscat grapes in northern Italy near the town of Asti, they ring in at a delicate 6 to 7 percent alcohol. Another fun and casual northern Italian sparkler is Prosecco.

Want more picks? Check out these lists: Meat-Lover Wines, Snack Attack Party Foods, Take-Out Favorites, Overlooked Surprises

SUMMER WHITES

PRODUCER	WINE NAME	FROM	STYLE PROFILE
Redcliffe	Sauvignon Blanc	Marlborough, New Zealand	Medium-bodied, racy, herbal
Villa Maria	"Private Bin" Sauvignon Blanc	Marlborough, New Zealand	Medium-bodied, racy, herbal
Spy Valley	Sauvignon Blanc	Marlborough, New Zealand	Medium-bodied, racy, herbal
Sauvignon Republic Cellars	Sauvignon Blanc	Russian River Valley, California	Medium-bodied, racy, herbal
Geyser Peak	Sauvignon Blanc	California	Medium-full-bodied, crisp, fruity
Simi Winery	Sauvignon Blanc	Sonoma County, California	Medium-full-bodied, crisp, fruity
Cavit	Pinot Grigio	Delle Venezie, Italy	Light-bodied, crisp, refreshing
Tiefenbrunner	Pinot Grigio	Delle Venezie, Italy	Light-bodied, crisp, refreshing
Adelsheim Vineyard	Pinot Gris	Willamette Valley, Oregon	Medium-full-bodied, crisp, fruity
Ruffino	Orvieto	Orvieto, Italy	Light-bodied, crisp, refreshing
Erich Berger	Grüner Veltliner	Kremstal, Austria	Medium-bodied, crisp, minerally
Santiago de Ruiz	O Rosal	Rias Baixas, Spain	Medium-bodied, crisp, minerally

SPECIAL BECAUSE	PRICE RANGE	MORE INFO . . .
Personal favorite, full of personality, great price	$10–12	www.palmbayimports.com
Staple winery of Marlborough; excellent-value wines	$10–12	www.villamaria.co.nz
Named after a satellite communications base in the valley	$15–17	www.spyvalleywine.co.nz
All-star team of owners focusing on Sauvignon Blanc	$16–18	www.sauvignonrepublic.com
Classic California style	$7–10	www.geyserpeakwinery.com
No oak barrels used, to maintain freshness	$15–17	www.simiwinery.com
Widely available; crowd-pleasing style	$8–10	www.cavitcollection.com
Founded in 1848; located near slopes of Italian Alps	$13–15	www.tiefenbrunner.com
Complex white from classic Oregon winery	$15–17	www.adelsheim.com
Serve well chilled; blend of Procanico and Grechetto	$6–9	www.ruffino.com
Party-sized bottle—party price	$10–12 1 liter	www.skurnikwines.com (importer)
Albariño mostly with Loureiro and Treixadura	$17–18	www.bodegasantiagoruiz .com

SUMMER PINKS AND REDS

PRODUCER	WINE NAME	FROM	STYLE PROFILE
Marqués de Cáceres	Dry Rosé	Rioja, Spain	Light-bodied, light tannins, vibrant, fruity
Falesco	Vitiano Rosé	Umbria, Italy	Light-bodied, light tannins, vibrant, fruity
Paul Jaboulet Aîné	"Parallele 45" Rosé	Côtes du Rhône, France	Light-bodied, light tannins, vibrant, fruity
Red Bicyclette	Rosé	Vin de Pays d'Oc, France	Light-bodied, light tannins, vibrant, fruity
La Vieille Ferme	Rosé	Côtes du Ventoux, Rhône Valley, France	Light-bodied, light tannins, vibrant, fruity
Zaca Mesa	"Z Gris" Rosé	Santa Ynez Valley, California	Light-bodied, light tannins, vibrant, fruity
Etude	Pinot Noir Rosé	Carneros, California	Light-bodied, light tannins, vibrant, fruity
Couly-Dutheil	Chinon Rouge "Les Gravières"	Chinon, Loire Valley, France	Light-bodied, light tannins, bright, earthy
Black Opal	Shiraz	South Australia	Medium-bodied, supple tannins, smooth, juicy
Rosenblum	Zinfandel "Vintner's Cuvée"	California	Medium-bodied, supple tannins, smooth, juicy
Peachy Canyon	Incredible Red	California	Medium-bodied, supple tannins, smooth, juicy
High Altitude	Malbec/ Cabernet Sauvignon	Argentina	Medium-full-bodied, supple tannins, vibrant, juicy

SPECIAL BECAUSE	PRICE RANGE	MORE INFO . . .
Buy by the case—great-value sipper	$7–9	www.marquesdecaceres.com
Highly recommended, from star winemaker Riccardo Cotarella	$7–10	www.falesco.it or www.winebow.com (importer)
Made from grapes that go into the red Parallele 45	$9–11	www.jaboulet.com
Complex pink from Syrah, Grenache, and Pinot Noir	$9–11	www.redbicyclette.com
Perrin (Château de Beaucastel) family's value brand	$8–10	www.vineyardbrands.com (importer)
Grenache and Cinsault blend; classy, dry pink	$15–17	www.zacamesa.com
Pinot Noir star crafting, top dry pink	$19–22	www.etudewines.com
Classic producer; wine made from Cabernet Franc	$11–13	www.coulydutheil-chinon.com
From respected producer Wolf Blass	$7–9	www.beringerblass.com.au
One of California's best Zinfandel producers	$8–10	www.rosenblumcellars.com
Made mostly from Zinfandel	$10–12	www.peachycanyon.com
Name refers to vineyards planted in the Andes mountains	$8–10	www.pasternakwine.com (importer)

SUMMER BUBBLY

PRODUCER	WINE NAME	FROM	STYLE PROFILE
Michele Chiarlo	Moscato d'Asti	Moscato d'Asti, Italy	Light-bodied, crisp, lightly sweet
Marchesi di Gresy	Moscato "La Serra"	Moscato d'Asti, Italy	Light-bodied, crisp, lightly sweet
Vietti	Moscato d'Asti "Cascinetta"	Moscato d'Asti, Italy	Light-bodied, crisp, lightly sweet
Saracco	Moscato d'Asti	Moscato d'Asti, Italy	Light-bodied, crisp, lightly sweet
Fontanafredda	Moscato d'Asti	Moscato d'Asti, Italy	Light-bodied, crisp, lightly sweet
Mionetto	Prosecco di Valdobbiadene	Veneto, Italy	Light-bodied sparkler, crisp, refreshing
Canella	Prosecco di Conegliano	Veneto, Italy	Light-bodied sparkler, s lightly sweet
Martini and Rossi	Prosecco	Veneto, Italy	Light-bodied sparkler, crisp, refreshing

QUICK TIP
Lip-Smacking Lillet
* * *
Lillet, an aperitif wine from the Bordeaux region, is made
from white wine blended with exotic fruit liqueurs. Sip it in

SPECIAL BECAUSE	PRICE RANGE	MORE INFO . . .
One of Piedmont's top wineries	$9–12 half bottle	www.chiarlo.it
Personal favorite, very bright and fresh	$12–15	www.marchesidigresy.com
Barolo specialist making delicate Asti	$13–15	www.vietti.com
Stylish wines from classic producer	$14–16	www.dallaterra.com (importer)
Elegantly shaped bottle; great gift idea	$14–16	www.domaineselect.com (importer)
Widely available—top pick for summer parties	$10–12	www.mionettousa.com
Ideal mixer for mimosas and an alternative to Champagne	$11–13	www.empson.com (importer)
Known for vermouth, but try this juicy bubbly	$12–15	www.martiniprosecco.com

the summer over ice with a dash of tonic and slice of lemon or lime, or use it as a low-alcohol replacement for rum in Mojitos or tequila in Margaritas.

Fall Wines

CRISP YET RICH WINES TO TRANSITION FROM
HOT TO COOL WEATHER

∞

Fall is my favorite season. The leaves are turning and there is a compelling smell in the air that's unmistakable. The key words for fall are *earthy* and *warm*. Fall wines possess rich, spicy flavors and smooth textures but aren't overwhelmingly powerful. They're the elegant cashmere sweater of a wine wardrobe.

Look for . . .

- **Whites:** Nutty, yet crisp Sémillon-based wines from Australia and white Bordeaux from France, which is a blend of Sauvignon Blanc and Sémillon grape varieties, sport layers of flavor. How about Spanish whites made from Verdejo grapes in the Rueda region, Australian Verdelho, or Italian beauties like Vernaccia di San Gimigano, which is minerally yet full?
- **Reds:** Drink Carmènere from Chile or explore the depth and breadth of wines made from Grenache. Spicy, earthy, and intense, this grape variety produces wines from the southern Rhône region of France where it's blended with a host of other varieties from Syrah to Cinsault. Grenaches hail from gnarly, old vines in Australia and Spain, and new plantings in California produce sultry versions. You'll feel like building a pile of fallen leaves and jumping in like a kid after sipping these sumptuously rustic reds.

Want more picks? Check out these lists: Meat-Lover Wines, Spring Wines, Cheese-Friendly Wines, Hot Spots

FALL WHITES

PRODUCER	WINE NAME	FROM	STYLE PROFILE
Black Swan	Chardonnay/Semillon	South Eastern Australia	Medium-full-bodied, crisp, fruity
Peter Lehmann	Semillon	Barossa Valley, Australia	Medium-full-bodied, crisp, fruity
Château Bonnet	Entre-Deux-Mers Blanc	Bordeaux, France	Medium-full-bodied, crisp, fruity
Château Carbonnieux	Pessac-Léognan Blanc	Graves, Bordeaux, France	Medium-bodied, light oak, juicy
Clos Du Val	Sémillon/Sauvignon Blanc "Ariadne"	Napa Valley, California	Medium-bodied, light oak, juicy
Ferrari-Carano	Fumé Blanc	Sonoma County, California	Medium-bodied, light oak, juicy
Bonacchi	Vernaccia di San Gimignano	Tuscany, Italy	Medium-full-bodied, crisp, fruity
San Quirico	Vernaccia di San Gimignano	Tuscany, Italy	Medium-full-bodied, crisp, fruity
Teruzzi & Puthod	Vernaccia di San Gimignano	Italy	Light-bodied, crisp, refreshing
Hope Estate	Verdelho	Hunter Valley, Australia	Medium-bodied, crisp, minerally
Fox Creek	Verdelho	South Australia	Medium-bodied, crisp, minerally
Dos Victorias	"Jose Pariente"	Rueda, Spain	Medium-bodied, crisp, minerally

SPECIAL BECAUSE	PRICE RANGE	MORE INFO . . .
Traditional Aussie blend, good value	$7–9	www.blackswanwines.com
A top Barossa winery with labels showcasing the Queen of Hearts	$12–15	www.peterlehmannwines .com
Sémillon, Sauvignon Blanc, Muscadelle blend	$9–12	www.andrelurton.com
Must-try white Graves. Blend of Sauvignon Blanc/Sémillon	$28–32	www.carbonnieux.com
French winemaker living in Napa; elegant style	$26–30	www.closduval.com
Fuller style with subtle oak character	$15–18	www.ferrari-carano.com
Excellent value for quality	$8–10	www.bonacchi.it
Vernaccia grapes planted near hillside town of San Gimignano	$11–13	www.winebow.com (importer)
Famous as Italy's first DOC wine region	$13–15	www.empson.com (importer)
Available and affordable— good combination	$8–10	www.hopeestate.com.au
Mineral yet creamy	$12–14	www.foxcreekwines.com.au
Top-notch, limited production Verdejo	$13–15	www.dosvictorias.com

FALL REDS

PRODUCER	WINE NAME	FROM	STYLE PROFILE
Baron Philippe de Rothschild	Carmenère "Reserva"	Rapel Valley, Chile	Full-bodied, supple tannins spicy, ripe
Capçanes	Mas Donis "Barrica"	Montsant, Spain	Medium-bodied, supple tannins, vibrant, earthy
Scala Dei	"Negre"	Priorat, Spain	Medium-bodied, supple tannins, vibrant, earthy
Pasanau	"Ceps Nous"	Priorat, Spain	Medium-bodied, supple tannins, vibrant, earthy
Vall Llach	"Embruix"	Priorat, Spain	Full-bodied, supple tannins smooth, earthy
J. Vidal-Fleury	Côtes du Rhône	Côtes du Rhône, France	Medium-bodied, supple tannins, vibrant, earthy
Domaine de Sénéchaux	Châteauneuf-du-Pape Rouge	Châteauneuf-du-Pape, France	Full-bodied, supple tannins smooth, earthy
Domaine de Vieux Télégraphe	Châteauneuf-du-Pape	Châteauneuf-du-Pape, France	Full-bodied, supple tannins, smooth, earthy
Torbreck	Grenache "Les Amis"	Barossa Valley, Australia	Full-bodied, supple tannins smooth, earthy
D'Arenberg	Grenache "The Custodian"	McLaren Vale, South Australia	Full-bodied, supple tannins smooth, earthy
Grant Burge	Holy Trinity	Barossa Valley, Australia	Full-bodied, supple tannins smooth, earthy
Zaca Mesa	"Z" Cuvée	Santa Ynez Valley, California	Full-bodied, supple tannins smooth, earthy
Beckman	Grenache	Santa Ynez Valley, California	Full-bodied, supple tannins smooth, earthy

SPECIAL BECAUSE	PRICE RANGE	MORE INFO . . .
Excellent value; French Rothschild pedigree	$10–12	www.bpdr.com
Personal favorite, great value; buy by the case	$10–12	www.cellercapcanes.com
Captures distinctive character of Priorat at unbelievable price	$13–15	www.grupoCodorniu.com (importer)
Blend of Garnacha, Merlot, Mazuelo, and Syrah	$18–20	www.classicalwines.com (importer)
Garnacha, Cabernet Sauvignon; ageworthy and concentrated	$25–28	www.vallllach.com
Oldest wine firm in the Rhône Valley	$10–11	www.wjdeutsch.com (importer)
Sister winery of Château du Trignon in Gigondas	$38–42	www.chateauneuf.dk
Ageworthy red from one of the region's classic producers	$40–43	www.vignoblesbrunier.fr
Limited availability but worth the effort to find	$185–200	www.torbreck.com
An Aussie leader of Rhône-style wine production, highly recommended	$19–21	www.darenberg.com.au
Blend of Grenache, Shiraz, Mourvèdre; big big	$30–32	www.grantburgewines.com.au
Grenache, Mourvèdre, Syrah, Cinsaut blend from California Rhône star	$14–16	www.zacamesa.com
Flagship wine of this top Rhône-style producer	$22–24	www.beckmenvineyards.com

WINE ABCS
Grenache

* * *

One of the most widely planted red wine grapes in the world, Grenache makes earthy, spicy wines that, despite high levels of alcohol, don't pummel with power. Though widely known as the key variety in blends from France's southern Rhône appellations of Châteauneuf-du-Pape and Côtes-du-Rhône, the grape is indigenous to Spain, where it's called Garnacha. Planted primarily in the red-hot region of Priorat and often blended with native Cariñena (also called Carignane), Garnacha delivers intensity combined with elegance. Keep your eyes open for old-vine versions from Australia, too. Down Under the variety shines when combined with Shiraz and Mourvèdre in wines dubbed "GSM."

Rhône-style

* * *

The Rhône is a famous winegrowing region in France home to appellations such as Hermitage, Côte-Rôtie, and Condrieu in the northern Rhone, and Gigondas and Châteauneuf-du-Pape further south. White grape varieties planted in the Rhône include Viognier, Marsanne, and Roussanne. Red grapes are Syrah (the red grape used in the northern Rhône), Grenache, Carignane, Mourvèdre, and Cinsault to name a few. Reds coming from the famous region of Châteauneuf-du-Pape are a blend of up to thirteen different varieties. When these Rhône grapes are planted in other winegrowing regions around the world, the wines made from them are dubbed Rhône-style. For more information, check out http://rhonerangers.org/.

Winter Wines

THINK CASHMERE AND LEATHER,
HEARTY COMFORT WINES THAT WARM THE SOUL

∞

Baby, it's cold outside, but winter wines will keep you warm inside. These luscious sippers are unmistakable: plush, sexy, and powerful. Think of them as the vinous equivalent of velvet. You almost want to sink into a glass of voluptuous Viognier or wrap yourself with a shawl of chocolaty Vintage Port. Wines gracing my winter picks list are equally at home on the dinner table alongside hearty soups and stews as they are next to a roaring fire.

Look for . . .

- **Whites:** There's winter white for clothes so why not wine? Hunt down buttery Chardonnays, rich Rhône-style wines made from Viognier, Marsanne, and Roussanne grapes or aromatic varieties like Torrontes from Argentina. My favorite winter whites have to be fleshy Gewurztraminers, Pinot Blancs, and Pinot Gris from the Alsace region of France.
- **Reds:** It will be a winter wonderland if you seek out big, bold, brawny Cabernets Sauvignon and Syrahs, especially those from Washington State. Pick up powerhouse California Zinfandel, sun-drenched Australian Shiraz, and complex Amarone from Italy.
- **Sweets:** Port sales soar in winter because it's the perfect wine to warm your soul. Think of them as the pajamas of the wine world. Even if you don't think you like Port, give it a try. Start with a 10-Year-Old Tawny or Late-Bottled Vintage Port and explore from there.

Want more picks? Check out these lists: Sexy Wines, Dessert Wines, Cheese-Friendly Wines

WINTER WHITES

PRODUCER	WINE NAME	FROM	STYLE PROFILE
Sebastiani	Chardonnay	Sonoma County, California	Full-bodied, creamy, oaky, ripe
Villa Mt. Eden	Chardonnay "Grand Reserve-Bien Nacido Vineyard"	Santa Maria Valley, California	Full-bodied, creamy, oaky, ripe
Flora Springs	Chardonnay "Barrel Fermented"	Napa Valley, California	Full-bodied, creamy, oaky, ripe
Bouchard Père & Fils	Meursault "Les Clous" 1er Cru	Meursault, Burgundy, France	Full-bodied, crisp, spicy, elegant
Joseph Drouhin	Puligny-Montrachet	Puligny-Montrachet, Burgundy, France	Full-bodied, crisp, spicy, elegant
Santa Julia	Torrontes	Mendoza, Argentina	Full-bodied, soft, aromatic
Susana Balbo	Crios de Torrontes	Cafayete, Argentina	Full-bodied, soft, aromatic
Clay Station	Viognier	Lodi, California	Full-bodied, soft, aromatic
Arrowood	Viognier	Sonoma Valley, California	Full-bodied, soft, aromatic
Domaine Georges Vernay	Condríeu "Coteau de Vernon"	Condrieu, France	Full-bodied, soft, aromatic
D'Arenberg	Marsanne-Viognier "The Hermit Crab"	McLaren Vale, Australia	Full-bodied, soft, aromatic
Tablas Creek	Roussanne	Paso Robles, California	Full-bodied, soft, aromatic
Domaines Schlumberger	Gewurztraminer "Fleur"	Alsace, France	Full-bodied, soft, aromatic

SPECIAL BECAUSE	PRICE RANGE	MORE INFO . . .
Can't beat the price for a big, bold Chard	$10–13	www.sebastiani.com
Great quality for the price; overdelivers	$16–19	www.villamteden.com
Ageworthy and impressive for complexity	$22–25	www.florasprings.com
Classic producer of elegant Chardonnay	$27–30	www.bouchard-pereetfils.com
World-class Chardonnay at a reasonable price	$38–42	www.drouhin.com
Unique variety worth seeking out	$8–12	www.familiazuccardi.com
Vineyards among the world's highest; hard to find	$16–18	www.vineconnections.com (importer)
Great value brand from the Delicato family	$9–12	www.claystationwine.com
One of California's top Viognier bottlings	$28–30	www.arrowoodvineyards.com
Viognier benchmark; limited production	$70–75	www.georges-vernay.fr
Winemaker Chester Osborn is Down Under star	$16–18	www.darenberg.com.au
American outpost of French Perrin family	$27–30	www.vineyardbrands.com (importer)
Personal favorite; gorgeously floral	$20–22	www.domaines-schlumberger.com

(continued)

PRODUCER	WINE NAME	FROM	STYLE PROFILE
Josmeyer	Gewurztraminer "Les Folastries"	Alsace, France	Full-bodied, soft, aromatic
Marc Kreydenweiss	Kritt Pinot Blanc "les Charmes"	Alsace, France	Full-bodied, soft, aromatic
Elk Cove Vineyards	Pinot Blanc	Willamette Valley, Oregon	Full-bodied, soft, aromatic
Chalone Vineyard	Pinot Blanc	Monterey County, California	Full-bodied, soft, aromatic

MYTH-BUSTER
Serving Temperatures
* * *

We tend to serve whites too cold and reds too warm. Keep these points in mind:

- *The lighter the body and color of the wine, the cooler the serving temperature.*
- *Oak character seems even stronger when a wine is cold, so don't overchill oaky whites like Chardonnay.*
- *Sweetness tastes more pronounced when too warm, so serve sweeter wines colder.*
- *Alcohol seems more apparent when warm, so don't serve high-alcohol wines like Zinfandel too warm.*

TEMPERATURE RANGES

For: *Lighter sparkling wine, white dessert wine, sweeter Riesling, Pinot Grigio, Sauvignon Blanc, Blush wine*
Serve: *Cold to the touch (40 to 50 degrees)*
How: *An hour or two in a standard temperature refrigerator or 20 to 25 minutes in a half water, half ice bath.*

SPECIAL BECAUSE	PRICE RANGE	MORE INFO . . .
Classic producer dating to 1854	$28–32	www.josmeyer.com
Sexy wine, organically grown	$18–20	www.wilsondaniels.com
One of Oregon's oldest wineries	$15–18	www.elkcove.com
California's best Pinot Blanc	$22–24	www.chalonevineyard.com

For: *Full-bodied Champagne, Chardonnay, White Bordeaux, Viognier, dry Rosé*
Serve: *Cool to touch (50 to 55 degrees)*
How: *Half an hour to an hour in the refrigerator or 15 to 20 minutes in an ice bath.*

For: *Beaujolais, light-bodied Pinot Noir or Chianti*
Serve: *Slightly cool to the touch (55 to 60 degrees)*
How: *5 to 15 minutes in the refrigerator*

For: *Chianti Classico/Sangiovese–based wines, fuller-bodied Pinot Noir, Merlot, Cabernet Sauvignon, Zinfandel, Syrah, Port*
Serve: *Slightly lower than room temperature (60 to 68 degrees)*
How: *When the "room temperature" verbiage became popular many years ago, rooms were a lot colder than they are now. If stored somewhere fairly warm, it doesn't hurt to put even your biggest, boldest reds in the refrigerator for several minutes.*

WINTER REDS

PRODUCER	WINE NAME	FROM	STYLE PROFILE
Covey Run	"Quail Series" Syrah	Columbia Valley, Washington	Medium-full-bodied, supp tannins, vibrant, juicy
Grant Burge	Shiraz "Filsell"	Barossa Valley, Australia	Full-bodied, strong tannin lush, concentrated
Gordon Brothers	Cabernet Sauvignon	Columbia Valley, Washington	Medium-full-bodied, supp tannins, vibrant, juicy
Dunham Cellars	Cabernet Sauvignon	Columbia Valley, Washington	Full-bodied, strong tannin lush, concentrated
Dry Creek Vineyard	Zinfandel "Heritage"	Sonoma County, California	Full-bodied, supple tanni spicy, ripe
Carol Shelton	Zinfandel "Monga Zin"	Cucamonga Valley, California	Full-bodied, supple tanni spicy, ripe
Ravenswood	Zinfandel "Teldeschi Vineyard"	Dry Creek Valley, California	Full-bodied, supple tanni spicy, ripe
Elyse Winery	Zinfandel "Morisoli Vineyard"	Napa Valley, California	Full-bodied, supple tanni spicy, ripe
Feudo Monaci	Primitivo	Puglia, Italy	Medium-bodied, supple tannins, vibrant, earthy
Bolla	Valpolicella	Veneto, Italy	Medium-bodied, supple tannins, vibrant, earthy
Masi	"Campofiorin" Ripasso	Rosso del Veronese, Italy	Full-bodied, supple tanni smooth, earthy
Zenato	Valpolicella Superiore Ripasso	Veneto, Italy	Full-bodied, supple tanni smooth, earthy
Allegrini	Amarone della Valpolicella Classico	Veneto, Italy	Full-bodied, strong tannin lush, concentrated

SPECIAL BECAUSE	PRICE RANGE	MORE INFO . . .
Easy-drinking style; party wine	$8–10	www.coveyrun.com
Big Aussie style made from century-old vines	$30–35	www.grantburgewines.com .au
Good-value wine for level of quality	$16–19	www.gordonwines.com
Limited availability; Eric Dunham makes amazing wine	$45–47	www.dunhamcellars.com
Classic Dry Creek Zin with dash of Petite Sirah	$14–16	www.drycreekvineyard.com
Carol is the Queen of Zinfandel; limited production	$27–30	www.carolshelton.com
Winemaker Joel Peterson is King of California Zinfandel	$32	www.ravenswood-wine.com
Small, family-owned winery making huge Zin	$37–40	www.elysewinery.com
Earthier than Zin, but same grape variety	$7–9	www.frederickwildman.com (importer)
Widely available party pick	$6–8	www.bolla.com
Personal favorite; great deal for "baby" Amarone	$13–15	www.masi.it
Hot winery specializing in quality Valpolicella	$17–20	www.zenato.it or www.winebow.com (importer)
Legendary producer; amazing, ageworthy wine	$70–75	www.winebow.com (importer)

WINTER SWEETS

PRODUCER	WINE NAME	FROM	STYLE PROFILE
Croft	Late-Bottled Vintage	Portugal	Full-bodied, lightly sweet, smooth
Quinta do Noval	Late-Bottled Vintage (LBV)	Portugal	Full-bodied, lightly sweet, smooth
Warre's	Late-Bottled Vintage (LBV)	Portugal	Full-bodied, lightly sweet, smooth
Taylor Fladgate	Vintage Porto, "Quinta de Vargellas"	Portugal	Full-bodied, sweet, supple, rich
Fonseca	Vintage Porto	Portugal	Full-bodied, sweet, supple, rich
Delaforce	Tawny "Colheita"	Portugal	Medium-bodied, sweet, nutty

PORT CHEAT SHEET
Discovering the Beauty of Port
* * *

Port is a fortified wine made in Portugal. Grapes that go into making Port include Touriga Nacional, Tinta Roriz, Touriga Francesa, and Tinta Cão. The magic of Port starts in the hot and hilly upper Douro Valley where the vineyards are planted, but finishes in the coastal city of Oporto where the Douro river empties into the Atlantic Ocean. In each winery's headquarters—known as lodges—great Port is made and aged. There are two types of Port: wood-aged and bottle-aged. Tawnies are blends of wines from many different years and as they rest in wooden casks gain their telltale nutty qualities. Vintage and Late-Bottled Vintage Ports maintain their fruitiness while aging, protected in bottles.

SPECIAL BECAUSE	PRICE RANGE	MORE INFO . . .
Terrific price for high quality	$17–20	www.kobrandwine.com (importer)
Historic property making great Ports since 1715	$18–20	www.quintadonoval.com
Unique LBV style aged for nine years before release	$26–28	www.warre.com
Limited production from a single estate; ageworthy	$55–60	www.taylor.pt
House style is one of lushness and amazing smoothness	$85	www.fonseca.pt
Personal favorite; very rare wine made only in special vintages	$60–70	www.kobrandwine.com (importer)

Here is what you'll see on the bottle and what the wines taste like:

10-year-old Tawny Port: Not overly sweet with a nutty, citrusy quality

20-year-old Tawny Port: Sweet and caramely with rich apricot and dried fruit flavors

30-year-old Tawny Port: Expensive and utterly decadent, like drinking caramel

Colheita: Vintage tawny Port. Rare and pricey.

Vintage Port: Bottle-aged Port from exceptional vintages. It's meant to be aged for years before you drink it.

Late-Bottled Vintage: Usually half to quarter price of Vintage Port with similar character. Ready to drink upon release.

WINE ALPHABET
A to Z

* * *

AMARONE DELLA VALPOLICELLA

Made in Valpolicella in northern Italy from grape varieties such as Corvina, Rondinella, and Molinara, Amarone comes by its unique character because once the grapes are harvested, they are dried into what looks like raisins on either straw mats or small open crates. The process removes moisture and concentrates the flavors and sugars in the grape. This makes the wines high in alcohol (often around 15 percent) and imparts a rich complexity rarely surpassed in other full-bodied, dry reds.

ZINFANDEL

Zinfandel is a red grape variety that also produces rich and sometimes raisinlike wines. They're powerhouse reds serving up full-frontal fruit and alcohol followed by a piquant, peppery chaser. Zinfandel's brazen decadence is a result of the fact that it's an uneven ripener, which means the same cluster of grapes may contain unripe green berries mixed with ones that look like raisins. A bright hit of acidity is delivered by green grapes, while raisiny ones saturate the grape juice with sugar. This sugar is turned into high levels of alcohol during fermentation. Primitivo from southern Italy's Puglia region is essentially the same grape variety as Zinfandel, so if you like hearty Zins, try Primitivo.

Holiday Spirit
WINES TO SIP ON MAJOR CELEBRATIONS

∞

VALENTINE'S DAY ⬳

Since wine invites romance, how about picking up a bottle for your sweetie? All of these pair beautifully with chocolate, flowers, and lingerie.

Look for . . .

- **Sweet and sparkling:** Nearly all these bubblies are red, yes, deep red sparkling wine. Australian Sparkling Shiraz is a wine that sizzles. So is Brachetto d'Acqui, a northern Italian fizzy that is perfect with chocolate-covered strawberries.
- **Reds:** A roundup of high-quality, seductive reds that all have Valentine-themed names and splashes of red—from hearts to flowers—on the labels. These decorative wines are appealing to look at and sip.

Want more picks? Check out these lists: Winter Wines, Dessert Wines, Sexy Wines

---

QUICK TIP
Removing Wine Stains

* * *

According to a study conducted by the University of California at Davis, the most effective way to remove wine stains is with a mixture of equal parts hydrogen peroxide and Dawn liquid soap. It works best on fresh stains, but I've found it to be successful on older wine stains, too. I also recommend a product named Stain RX, which performed well in the Davis study.

VALENTINE'S DAY: BUBBLY AND SWEET

PRODUCER	WINE NAME	FROM	STYLE PROFILE
Segura Viudas	"Aria" Pinot Noir Cava	Spain	Medium-bodied sparkler, smooth, juicy
Vigne Regali/Banfi	"Rosa Regale" Brachetto d'Acqui	Piedmont, Italy	Light-bodied sparkler, soft, lightly sweet
Korbel	Rouge Sparkling Red Wine	Sonoma County, California	Full-bodied sparkler, creamy, lightly sweet
Lorikeet	Sparkling Shiraz	South Eastern Australia	Full-bodied sparkler, creamy, lightly sweet
Rumball	Sparkling Shiraz	Coonawarra, Australia	Full-bodied sparkler, creamy, lightly sweet
Hardys	Sparkling Shiraz	Australia	Full-bodied sparkler, creamy, lightly sweet
Shingleback	Sparkling Shiraz "Black Bubbles"	McLaren Vale, South Australia	Full-bodied sparkler, creamy, lightly sweet
Geyser Peak	Sparkling Shiraz	Sonoma County, California	Full-bodied sparkler, creamy, rich, toasty
Peter Lehmann	Sparkling Shiraz "The Black Queen"	Barossa, Australia	Full-bodied sparkler, creamy, rich, toasty
Bonny Doon	Framboise	California	Medium-bodied, sweet, juicy
Sonoma Valley PortWorks	Deco Port	California/South Australia	Full-bodied, sweet, supple, rich
Sanchez Romate	Pedro Ximénez Very Rare Sherry	Jerez, Spain	Full-bodied, sweet, supple, rich
Mayo Family Winery	"Ricci Vineyard" Old Vine Zinfandel Port	Russian River Valley, California	Full-bodied, sweet, supple, rich
Inniskillen	Cabernet Franc Icewine	Niagara Peninsula, Canada	Medium-bodied, sweet, juicy

SPECIAL BECAUSE	PRICE RANGE	MORE INFO . . .
Great value; sapphire pink bubbly in elegant package	$11–13	www.seguraviudas.com
Personal favorite; perfect pairing with chocolate-covered strawberries	$16–18	www.vigneregali.com or www.castellobanfi.com
Dry wine made with Pinot Noir and Cabernet Sauvignon	$12–14	www.korbel.com
Surprisingly delicious version for the price	$9–12	www.cwine.com (importer)
Goes with lamb as easily as chocolate	$26–28	www.scottst.com (importer)
Most available version from classic Aussie producer	$20–24	www.hardys.com.au
Try with dark chocolate truffles	$20–24	www.shingleback.com
Only 280 cases, but worth the effort to find	$32–35	www.geyserpeakwinery.com
Limited availability, from top Barossa winery; lush	$31–35	www.peterlehmann.com
Fortified raspberry wine—wow	$12–14 half bottle	www.bonnydoonvineyard .com
Port blended with the essence of chocolate	$17–19 500 ml	www.portworks.com
Intensely sweet from aging thirty-five years in casks	$35–37 500 ml	www.shaw-ross.com (importer)
High-quality, boutique producer; limited production	$30–32 half bottle	www.mayofamilywinery.com
Red ice wine; very limited production	$100–110 half bottle	www.inniskillin.com

VALENTINE'S DAY: HOT REDS

PRODUCER	WINE NAME	FROM	STYLE PROFILE
Montes	"Cherub" Rosé of Syrah	Colchagua, Chile	Light-bodied, light tanni bright, earthy
Davey Family Wines	"Red Knot" Shiraz	McLaren Vale, Australia	Medium-bodied, supple tannins, smooth, juicy
Elio Altare	Dolcetto d'Alba	Piedmont, Italy	Medium-bodied, light tannins, fresh, spicy
Michael & David Phillips	Zinfandel "7 Deadly Zins"	Lodi, California	Full-bodied, supple tann spicy, ripe
Spandina	Nero d'Avola	Sicily, Italy	Full-bodied, supple tann smooth, earthy
O'Brien Family Vineyard	"Seduction"	Napa Valley, California	Full-bodied, strong tann lush, concentrated
Swanson	"Alexis"	Napa Valley, California	Full-bodied, strong tanni lush, concentrated
Terra Valentine	Cabernet Sauvignon "Spring Mountain"	Napa Valley, California	Full-bodied, strong tann lush, concentrated

QUICK TIP
Sparkling Appetizer
* * *

*Bread Stick Flutes: Take three or four champagne flutes
and fill them halfway with sesame seeds, then stand thin*

SPECIAL BECAUSE	PRICE RANGE	MORE INFO . . .
Sports cherub on label	$14–16	www.monteswines.com
Great value for quality and visual appeal	$10–12	www.redknotwine.com
A dry red, though Dolcetto means "little sweet one"	$20–22	www.skurnikwines.com (importer)
Cutting-edge winery, creative wines	$17–20	www.lodivineyards.com
Roses adorn label of this hearty red	$8–10	www.spadinawines.com
Bordeaux-style blend from boutique Napa producer	$26–29	www.seductionwine.com
Cabernet, Syrah, Merlot blend with heart on label	$58–60	www.swansonvineyards.com
Perfect Valentine's wine; world-class Cabernet with ideal name	$35–37	www.terravalentine.com

breadsticks in each flute. Serve the flutes on a platter with a selection of olive oils, vinegars, and dipping sauces like spicy mustard and cranberry chutney.

THANKSGIVING 🐦

The cacophony of flavors on a traditional Thanksgiving table—from sweet candied yams to tart cranberry sauce and savory sausage stuffing—presents a wine-pairing challenge. Your best bet is to stay away from whites with too much oak and reds with strong tannins, and look for wines packed with fruity character.

Look for . . .

- **Whites:** Aromatic whites such as Riesling and Gewürztraminer are bird-friendly wines. Look for versions with a whisper of sweetness to complement the spicy, sweet dishes on the table. If you want drier styles, pick up versions from France's Alsace region or northern California's Anderson Valley.
- **Reds:** My favorite choice is elegant Pinot Noir because of its generally light oak treatment and balanced tannins. Beaujolais is also a winner due to a unique combination of fruitiness and earthiness.

Want more picks? Check out these lists: Bathtub Wines, Spring Wines, Girls' Night In, Sexy Wines

---

WINE ABCS
Gewürztraminer
* * *

When you pour Gewürztraminer, a mélange of floral, fruity, and spice aromas jump from the glass. Though Gewürztraminer reaches its pinnacle of expression in the French region of Alsace, it grows well in California, Washington, and New Zealand. The name comes from the German word for spiced, gewürz, and from a village named Tramin in northern Italy's Alto Adige region, where the grape is thought to have originated. Styles run the gamut from dry to sweet.

WINE ABCS
Beaujolais

* * *

Beaujolais is a wine region located in the south of Burgundy in France where wine is made not from Pinot Noir but from Gamay. The fun side of Beaujolais makes its annual appearance the third Thursday of November, when inexpensive Beaujolais Nouveau is released. Nouveau, or "new wine," is bottled mere months after the Gamay grapes are harvested.

But Beaujolais is far more than Nouveau. To take a step up the quality ladder search for wines called Beaujolais-Villages, or the Cru wines of Beaujolais. These bright, juicy, and spicy reds are complex yet quaffable. There are ten Crus named after the villages where the hillside vineyards are located.

Look for wines carrying place names such as Morgon, Fleurie, Chiroubles, Saint-Amour, Chénas, Juliénas, Brouilly, Côte de Brouilly, Régenié, and Moulin-à-Vent.

THANKSGIVING: BIRD-FRIENDLY WHITES

PRODUCER	WINE NAME	FROM	STYLE PROFILE
Blackstone	Riesling	Monterey County, California	Light-bodied, racy, off-dry
Chateau St. Jean	Johannisberg Riesling	Sonoma County, California	Light-bodied, racy, off-dry
Poet's Leap	Riesling	Columbia Valley, Washington	Light-bodied, racy, off-dry
Dr. Loosen	Riesling Spätlese "Wehlener Sonnenuhr"	Mosel-Saar-Ruwer, Germany	Medium-bodied, aromatic, off-dry
Müller-Catoir	Riesling Spätlese "Haardter Bugergarten"	Pfalz, Germany	Medium-bodied, aromatic, off-dry
A to Z Wineworks	Pinot Gris	Oregon	Medium-bodied, aromatic, off-dry
King Estate	Pinot Gris	Oregon	Medium-full-bodied, crisp, fruity
Brassfield Estate	"Serenity" White wine blend	Clear Lake, California	Medium-bodied, aromatic, off-dry
Chateau Ste. Michelle	Gewürztraminer	Columbia Valley, Washington	Medium-bodied, aromatic, off-dry
Chateau St. Jean	Gewürztraminer	Sonoma County, California	Medium-bodied, aromatic, off-dry
Husch Vineyards	Gewürztraminer	Anderson Valley, California	Full-bodied, soft, aromatic
Navarro Vineyards	Gewürztraminer "Dry"	Anderson Valley, California	Full-bodied, soft, aromatic

SPECIAL BECAUSE	PRICE RANGE	MORE INFO . . .
Popular for Merlot, but don't miss their Riesling	$10–14	www.blackstone-winery.com
Low production but delicious style	$14–16	www.chateaustjean.com
By renowned German winemaker Armin Diel, of Schlossgut Diel	$18–22	www.poetsleap.com
Personal favorite from famous vintner Ernst Loosen (pronounced Low-zen)	$35–40	www.drloosen.com
Limited availability; world-class and ageworthy	$40–45	www.muller-catoir.com
Top-value brand started by four friends	$10–14	www.atozwineworks.com
An Oregon classic known for quality	$12–15	www.kingestate.com
Sauvignon Blanc, Pinot Gris and Gewürztraminer blend	$14–16	www.brassfieldestate.com
Excellent deal; wide availability and crowd-pleasing style	$7–8	www.ste-michelle.com
Fall in love with this sumptuous sipper	$13–15	www.chateaustjean.com
Oldest winery in Anderson Valley	$14–16	www.huschvineyards.com
Similar richness as an Alsatian version	$18–20	www.navarrowine.com

THANKSGIVING: BIRD-FRIENDLY REDS

PRODUCER	WINE NAME	FROM	STYLE PROFILE
Georges Duboeuf	Beaujolais Nouveau	Beaujolais, France	Light-bodied, light tannins, vibrant, fruity
Louis Jadot	Beaujolais-Villages	Beaujolais, France	Light-bodied, light tannins, vibrant, fruity
Château de La Chaize	Brouilly Cru	Beaujolais, France	Medium-bodied, light tannins, fresh, spicy
Joseph Drouhin	Moulin-à-Vent Cru	Beaujolais, France	Medium-bodied, light tannins, fresh, spicy
Château des Jacques	Moulin-à-Vent Cru	Beaujolais, France	Medium-bodied, light tannins, fresh, spicy
Domaine Pierre Morey	Pinot Noir Bourgogne	Burgundy, France	Medium-bodied, supple tannins, vibrant, earthy
Willamette Valley Vineyards	Pinot Noir "Whole Cluster Fermented"	Oregon	Light-bodied, light tannin, vibrant, fruity
Chehalem	Pinot Noir "3 Vineyard"	Willamette Valley, Oregon	Medium-bodied, supple tannins, vibrant, earthy
Olssens	Pinot Noir "Jackson Barry"	Central Otago, New Zealand	Full-bodied, supple tannin, smooth, earthy
Sanford	Pinot Noir Estate	Santa Rita Hills, California	Full-bodied, supple tannin, smooth, earthy
Goldeneye	Pinot Noir	Anderson Valley, California	Full-bodied, supple tannin, smooth, earthy
Brick House	Gamay Noir	Willamette Valley, Oregon	Medium-bodied, light tannins, fresh, spicy

SPECIAL BECAUSE	PRICE RANGE	MORE INFO . . .
Region's leading producer with their benchmark Nouveau style	$8–10	www.duboeuf.com
Widely available; great quality—price ratio	$8–10	www.louisjadot.com
Gorgeous castle built in 1676	$13–17	www.chateaudelachaize.com
Complex Beaujolais from top Burgundian producer	$16–18	www.drouhin.com
Historic property owned by Louis Jadot in Burgundy	$22–25	www.louisjadot.com
Morey is one of Burgundy's highly regarded winemakers	$17–19	www.wilsondaniels.com (importer)
Made in fresh, Beaujolais style	$17–20	www.willamette valleyvineyards.com
Blend of three estate vineyards	$24–27	www.chehalemwines.com
Central Otago is hot spot for world-class Pinot	$32–35	www.olssens.co.nz
Santa Barbara's pioneer of Pinot	$22–25	www.sanfordwinery.com
Personal favorite; owned by Napa's Duckhorn Winery	$50–55	www.goldeneyewinery.com
Small production, best domestic Gamay	$22–24	www.brickhousewines.com

QUICK TIP
The Champagne Story
* * *

Contrary to popular belief, Dom Pérignon, the seventeenth-century monk who worked in France's Champagne region, didn't invent bubbly. He was responsible, though, for improvements in grape growing and winemaking that made modern Champagne possible.

At that time, no one really understood why the wine sparkled. Winemakers believed it was a flaw, because pressure caused by the bubbles made many bottles explode. When the British and others started to embrace this fizzy wonder in the early 1700s, the ever-crafty Champagne makers decided to go with the flow. Capitalizing on its popularity, they utilized stronger bottles and powerful corks, making bubbly the drink of the day.

Champagne houses hired flamboyant traveling salesmen who were legendary for getting their products in the hands of famous revelers from Russian czars to French kings and American presidents such as Thomas Jefferson. Champagne became synonymous with celebration, and in the span of a few hundred years it had become the most famous wine in the world.

NEW YEAR'S EVE ≈

The best New Year's Eve I ever spent was on Copacabana in Río de Janeiro, Brazil. My husband and I watched the fireworks from the beach, celebrating the new millennium with dear friends. We weren't drinking caipirinhas—Brazil's national cocktail—but Champagne. No matter where you are, sparkling wine is the only wine to pour on New Year's Eve.

Want more picks? Check out these lists: Wedding Wines, Bathtub Wines, Glamorous Gift Wines, Makeover Wines

---

QUICK TIP
How to Open a Bottle of Bubbly

* * *

To pop the cork on a bottle of bubbly,

1. *Before you open the bottle, make sure it's very cold. It will be less likely to overflow.*
2. *Remove the outer foil and the wire cage slowly.*
3. *Hold the bottle with your thumb in the punt (the indent in the bottom of the bottle).*
4. *Grasp the cork with the other hand and turn the bottle counterclockwise.*
5. *You should feel the cork move under all the pressure, so be prepared: the key to opening bubbly is to go slowly.*

NEW YEAR'S EVE: PARTY BUBBLES

PRODUCER	WINE NAME	FROM	STYLE PROFILE
Freixenet	Brut Cava "Cordon Negro"	Spain	Light-bodied sparkler, crisp, refreshing
Juvé y Camps	Cava Brut Natural "Reserva de la Familia"	Penedès, Spain	Medium-bodied sparkler, crisp, elegant
Domaine Ste. Michelle	Cuvée Brut	Washington State	Light-bodied sparkler, crisp, refreshing
Roederer Estate	Brut	Anderson Valley, California	Medium-bodied sparkler, smooth, juicy
Schramsberg	Blanc de Blancs	Napa Valley, California	Medium-bodied sparkler, crisp, elegant
Mumm Napa	Brut "Reserve"	Napa Valley, California	Medium-bodied sparkler, smooth, juicy
Lanson	Brut Black Label	Champagne, France	Full-bodied sparkler, creamy, rich, toasty
Comte Audoin de Dampierre	Brut "Cuvée des Ambassadeurs"	Champagne, France	Medium-bodied sparkler, crisp, elegant
Gosset	Brut "Excellance"	Champagne, France	Full-bodied sparkler, creamy, rich, toasty
Pol Roger	Brut	Champagne, France	Full-bodied sparkler, creamy, rich, toasty
Alfred Gratien	Brut	Champagne, France	Medium-bodied sparkler, crisp, elegant
Bellavista	Franciacorta Brut	Franciatorta, Italy	Medium-bodied sparkler, crisp, elegant

SPECIAL BECAUSE	PRICE RANGE	MORE INFO . . .
Popular, good-value wine in familiar black bottle	$8–10	www.freixenetusa.com
Champagne-like quality, highly recommended value	$16–18	www.winebow.com (importer)
Top party choice for price and packaging	$11–13	www.domaine-ste-michelle.com
Personal favorite; top-quality, affordable wine	$20–22	www.champagne-roederer.com
Original, Chardonnay-based bubbly from top California producer	$22–25	www.schramsberg.com
Must-visit Napa winery with art gallery	$24–27	www.mummnapa.com
Classicly rich style; historic producer since 1760	$33–36	www.lanson.fr
Limited production; sexy Chardonnay/Pinot Noir blend	$35–40	www.dampierre.com
Founded in 1584; Chardonnay, Pinot Noir, Pinot Meunier blend	$38–42	www.champagne-gosset.com
Family-owned, highly respected winery	$48–52	www.frederickwildman.com (importer)
Lean, citrusy style; try with salty nuts	$49–53	www.alfredgratien.com
Northern Italian sparkling wine; gorgeous bottle	$35–40	www.empson.com (importer)

Wines for a Reason

L ooking for kosher wines to serve for the holidays? How about world-class bottles made from organically grown grapes? Wondering which of the "critter-themed" labels—from penguins to wallabys—are worth sipping? You'll find the hottest picks right here. Scan the following pages for gift ideas that won't cost a fortune, as well as those carrying a price tag meant to impress. Did you know that famous sports figures and actors make wine? Don your star-gazing glasses to see which celebrities win wine gold.

QUICK GIFT TIP
Must-Have Wine Gadgets

* * *

Foil cutter: easily cuts the top foil section so a corkscrew can be inserted.

Sparkling wine stopper: (often called a clamshell) Shaped like a cork with metal wings that attach to the bottle to preserve sparkling wine.

Bottle collar: slip this circular metal or plastic ring around the neck of the bottle to prevent spills.

Fabulous Organics
ECO-FRIENDLY WINES FROM AROUND THE WORLD

Interest in organic wine is growing, but it can be a confusing subject. How do you know when a wine is made with organically grown grapes versus biodynamically grown fruit? What about certified vineyards? How do you find a wine that is completely organic? The following producers focus on respecting the environment while making the best wine possible. Here's the lowdown on what to look for:

Organically grown: This means that grapes are grown without the use of pesticides or chemicals. Pests and vine diseases are managed through natural measures such as cover crops. Vineyards can be certified organic through a number of organizations like the California Certified Organic Farmers, but don't have to be. Wineries large and small are focusing on converting to organic growing methods and sustainable agriculture.

Organic: While more and more vineyards are employing organic growing techniques, actually making an organic wine is less common. Not only do grapes need to be from organically grown sources, winemakers cannot add sulfites. It sounds good but added sulfites act as a preservative, so without them wine has a shorter shelf life.

Biodynamic: Think of biodynamics as über-organics based on principles developed by Austrian Rudolf Steiner in the early 1920s. As with organically grown wines, the use of synthetic and chemical fertilizers, pesticides, and herbicides are not allowed (though added sulfites are allowed during winemaking), but biodynamics is much more than that. *Biodynamic* is derived from the Greek words for life and energy. The biodynamic approach to growing grapes treats the soil as a living organism and focuses on balancing the entire vineyard and winery environment with the world at large. Wineries that adhere to the rigorous tenants of biodynamics can attain the gold standard of certification from an international organization called Demeter.

• • •

For more information, check out the following Web sites: www.organic wine.com, www.theorganicwinecompany.com, www.ccof.org, and www .demeter-usa.org.

MYTH-BUSTER
Sulfites Cause Wine Headaches
* * *

This is probably one of the biggest wine myths. First, what are sulfites? They are a preservative used to increase stability and shelf life not only in wine but also dried fruits, juices, and salad bars. Sulfites are also a naturally-occurring byproduct of fermentation, so technically it's almost impossible to have a wine without sulfites. And no, European wines do not contain fewer sulfites. It's just that American regulations require a warning label. Go figure. In terms of headaches, less than one percent of the population is actually allergic (meaning they lack the enzymes necessary to break down sulfites). If you don't react to other sources of sulfites, you're most likely not allergic. Sulfites are not usually the culprit of wine headaches. That would most likely be alcohol, which causes dehydration. My rule of thumb is one glass of water for every glass of wine. Your aching head will thank me in the morning.

FABULOUS ORGANICS: WHITES

PRODUCER	WINE NAME	FROM	STYLE PROFILE
Snoqualmie	Riesling "Naked"	Columbia Valley, Washington	Medium-bodied, aromatic, off-dry
Zind-Humbrecht	"One"	Alsace, France	Medium-bodied, aromatic, off-dry
Santa Julia	Chardonnay "Organica"	Mendoza, Argentina	Medium-full-bodied, crisp, fruity
Jeriko Estate	Chardonnay	Mendocino, California	Medium-full-bodied, crisp, fruity
Patianna Organic Vineyards	Sauvignon Blanc	Mendocino County, California	Medium-full-bodied, crisp, fruity
Handley Cellars	Gewürztraminer	Anderson Valley, California	Full-bodied, soft, aromatic
Bonterra	Viognier	Mendocino County, California	Medium-full-bodied, crisp, fruity
Grgich Hills	Fumé Blanc	Napa Valley, California	Medium-bodied, light oak, juicy
Marc Kreydenweiss	Gewurztraminer "Kritt"	Alsace, France	Full-bodied, soft, aromatic
Josmeyer	Pinot Blanc "Mise du Printemps"	Alsace, France	Medium-full-bodied, crisp, fruity
Mas de Daumas Gassac	Blanc	Languedoc-Roussillon, France	Full-bodied, crisp, spicy, elegant
Château de Beaucastel	Châteauneuf-du-Pape Blanc	Châteauneuf-du-Pape, France	Full-bodied, crisp, spicy, elegant
La Coulée de Serrant	Coulée de Serrant	Savennières, France	Medium-bodied, crisp, minerally

SPECIAL BECAUSE	PRICE RANGE	MORE INFO . . .
Organically grown grapes, from winemaker Joy Andersen	$11–12	www.snoqualmie.com
Biodynamic; Chardonnay, Pinot Auxerrois, and Pinot Blanc	$14–16	www.winebow.com (importer)
Organically grown grapes	$10–14	www.familiazuccardi.com
Made from biodynamically grown grapes	$18–21	www.jerikoestate.com
Started by Patti Fetzer-Burke of Fetzer family fame	$14–16	www.patianna.com
Certified organic vineyards; sumptuous wine by Milla Handley	$15–18	www.handleycellars.com
Certified organic vineyards; Bonterra means "good earth"	$17–21	www.bonterra.com
All their vineyards are biodynamically farmed	$20–23	www.grgich.com
Personal favorite; lush wine from biodynamic grower	$20–23	www.kreydenweiss.com
Organically grown grapes from Alsatian star	$22–24	www.josmeyer.com
Blend of Chardonnay and Viognier; legendary producer	$36–42	www.daumas-gassac.com/gb
Mostly Roussanne with Grenache Blanc	$57–60	www.beaucastel.com
Owner Nicolas Joly is the world's biodynamic leader	$75–80	www.coulee-de-serrant.com

FABULOUS ORGANICS: REDS

PRODUCER	WINE NAME	FROM	STYLE PROFILE
Lolonis Winery	"Ladybug" Red Blend	Redwood Valley, California	Medium-full-bodied, supp tannins, vibrant, juicy
Frey Vineyards	Sangiovese "Masut Vineyards"	Mendocino County, California	Medium-bodied, light tan fresh, spicy
Quivira	Zinfandel	Dry Creek Valley, California	Full-bodied, supple tannins, spicy, ripe
Frog's Leap	Zinfandel	Napa Valley, California	Medium-full-bodied, supp tannins, vibrant, juicy
Marcel Lapierre	Morgon	Beaujolais, France	Medium-bodied, light tan fresh, spicy
Robert Sinskey	Pinot Noir "Los Carneros"	Napa Valley, California	Full-bodied, supple tanni smooth, earthy
M. Chapoutier	"La Bernardine"	Châteauneuf-du-Pape, France	Medium-bodied, supple tannins, vibrant, earthy
Sokol Blosser	Pinot Noir "Old Vineyard Block"	Willamette Valley, Oregon	Full-bodied, supple tanni smooth, earthy
Domaine Leroy	Gevrey-Chambertin	Burgundy, France	Medium-bodied, supple tannins, vibrant, earthy
Spottswoode Vineyards	Cabernet Sauvignon	Napa Valley, California	Full-bodied, strong tanni lush, concentrated
Benziger Sonoma Mountain Estate	Bordeaux style blend "Tribute"	Sonoma Valley, California	Full-bodied, strong tanni lush, concentrated
J. L. Chave	Hermitage	Hermitage, France	Full-bodied, supple tanni smooth, earthy
Quintessa	Red wine blend	Napa Valley, California	Full-bodied, strong tanni lush, concentrated

SPECIAL BECAUSE	PRICE RANGE	MORE INFO . . .
Celebrates ladybugs' role in organic farming	$10–12	www.lolonis.com
Organic wine; no added sulfites; from biodynamically grown grapes	$13–15	www.freywine.com
Organically grown vineyards	$19–21	www.quivirawine.com
Owner John Williams is principal in Napa's organic movement	$21–24	www.frogsleap.com
Organically grown; one of the region's best wines	$22–25	www.marcel-lapierre.com
Sustainable organic techniques influenced by biodynamic methods	$30–35	www.robertsinskey.com
Personal favorite; Michel Chapoutier—passionate biodynamic advocate	$38–40	www.chapoutier.com
Leader in eco-friendly and organically grown movement in Oregon	$50–55	www.sokolblosser.com
Owner Lalou Bize-Leroy is famous biodynamic producer	$110	www.domaineleroy.com
Organically farmed and run by amazing lineup of women	$100–110	www.spottswoode.com
Demeter-certified biodynamic wine	$68–75	www.benziger.com
One of the greats of the Rhône; cellarworthy Syrah	$120	www.bacchus importersltd.com (importer)
Biodynamic; gorgeous blend of Cabernet Sauvignon and Merlot	$100–110	www.quintessa.com

Kosher and Beyond

TOP-QUALITY KOSHER BOTTLES

∽

Kosher wines were once limited to sugary beverages uncorked at Passover, but high-quality kosher wines are in demand and command respect. These wines are not only for those looking to keep kosher. The ones I've highlighted below are ones everyone should try.

KOSHER CHEAT SHEET
What Is It?

* * *

What is a kosher wine? It has nothing to do with the grape varieties, sweetness level, or type of wine, but rather with how the wine is made. Kosher wines must follow a set of guidelines, including:

- *the use of kosher products such as yeast for fermentation*
- *maintaining separate equipment dedicated to the production of kosher wines*
- *only allowing Sabbath-observant Jews to handle the grapes from the beginning of the winemaking process to the end*
- *if the crushed grape juice used to make the wine is flash-pasteurized for a few seconds, the wine is* mevushal. *This means non-Jewish people can deal with the wine (for example, a waiter serving it in a restaurant) and the wine still remains kosher.*

For more information and to buy, visit www.kosherwine.com

KOSHER WINES

PRODUCER	WINE NAME	FROM	STYLE PROFILE
Baron Herzog	Chenin Blanc	Clarksburg, California	Light-bodied, racy, off-dry
Golan Heights Winery	Chardonnay "Golan"	Golan Heights, Israel	Medium-full bodied, crisp, fruity
Yarden	"Mt. Hermon"	Galilee, Israel	Medium-bodied, supple tannins, smooth, juicy
Teal Lake	Shiraz/Cabernet	Australia	Medium-bodied, supple tannins, smooth, juicy
Recanati	Merlot	Galilee, Israel	Medium-bodied, supple tannins, smooth, juicy
Baron Philippe de Rothschild	Mouton Cadet	Bordeaux, France	Medium-bodied, light tannins, fresh, spicy
Baron Herzog	Syrah "Special Reserve"	Edna Valley, California	Full-bodied, supple tannins, smooth, earthy
Hagafen Cellars	Pinot Noir	Napa Valley, California	Medium-bodied, light tannins, fresh, spicy
Hagafen Cellars	Cabernet Sauvignon	Napa Valley, California	Full-bodied, strong tannins, lush, concentrated
Covenant	Cabernet Sauvignon	Napa Valley, California	Full-bodied, strong tannins, lush, concentrated
Yarden	Blanc de Blancs sparkling wine	Galilee, Israel	Medium-bodied sparkler, smooth, juicy
Carmel Winery	Moscato di Carmel	Samson, Israel	Light-bodied sparkler, soft, lightly sweet

SPECIAL BECAUSE	PRICE RANGE	MORE INFO . . .
Personal favorite; leader in quality kosher wines—family originated in Slovakia	$8–10	www.baronherzog.com
Top-notch producer, also owner of Yarden	$10–12	www.golanwines.co.il
Good-value blend of Cabernet Sauvignon, Merlot, and Cabernet Franc	$10–13	www.yardenwines.com
Limited availability; mevushal	$10–12	www.kosherwine.com
High-tech, new winery owned by banker Lenny Recanati	$10–13	www.recanati-winery.com or www.palmbayimports.com
Merlot/Cabernet blend; owned by Baron's daughter, Baroness Philippine	$13–15	www.bpdr.com
Herzog's ultra-premium line; no fining or filtration	$27–29	www.baronherzog.com
Family-owned, operated by Irit and Ernie Weir	$28–30	www.hagafen.com
This wine has been served to foreign dignitaries at the White House	$38–40	www.hagafen.com
Owner Jeff Morgan created the world's top kosher wine	$90–100	www.covenantwines.com
Delicious sparkler made from Chardonnay	$20–22	www.yardenwines.com
Dessert style; world's largest producer of kosher wines	$8–10	www.carmelwines.co.il

Impress-for-Less Gift Wines

MAKE THE GRADE WITHOUT BUSTING THE BUDGET

∾

You want to bring a gift of wine, but don't feel like spending a fortune. Don't worry, you don't have to. My picks for this category meet the following criteria:

- Brands that overdeliver in the quality department, but aren't over-exposed.
- Sport impressive packaging such as elegant or creative label design and/or weighty bottles.
- Range in price from $8 to $20.

Want more picks? Check out these lists: Wedding Wines, Twice-the-Price Wines

---

QUICK TIP
Creative Wine Gift Ideas
* * *

Party of One: Bubble bath, candles, relaxing CD, a bottle of bubbly.

Wine and Dine: Wine, a recipe, and the ingredients to make one of your favorite dishes.

Sweet Treats: Vintage Port and chocolate, tawny Port with nuts, or Vin Santo and biscotti.

Honeymoon Heaven: One of my favorite cocktails is a dash of Cognac at the bottom of a flute filled with Champagne. For wedding gifts I often give a bottle of Cognac, a bottle of Champagne, and two flutes.

IMPRESS-FOR-LESS GIFT WINES: TRADITIONAL

PRODUCER	WINE NAME	FROM	STYLE PROFILE
Mason	Sauvignon Blanc	Napa Valley	Medium-bodied, racy, herba
Drylands Estate Wines	Sauvignon Blanc	Marlborough, New Zealand	Medium-bodied, racy, herba
Silverado Vineyards	Sauvignon Blanc	Napa Valley, California	Medium-full bodied, crisp, fruity
Casa Lapostolle	Chardonnay	Casablanca Valley, Chile	Medium-bodied, light oak, juicy
Georges Duboeuf	Chardonnay "Réserve"	Vin de Pays d'Oc, France	Medium-bodied, light oak, juicy
Sterling Vineyards	Merlot "Vintner's Collection"	Central Coast, California	Medium-bodied, supple tannins, smooth, juicy
Chateau St. Jean	Merlot	California	Medium-bodied, supple tannins, smooth, juicy
Veramonte	Merlot	Casablanca Valley, Chile	Medium-bodied, supple tannins, vibrant, earthy
Feudo Arancio	Cabernet Sauvignon	Sicily, Italy	Medium-bodied, supple tannins, vibrant, earthy
Michael Pozzan	Cabernet Sauvigon	Alexander Valley, California	Medium-bodied, supple tannins, vibrant, earthy
Cousiño-Macul	Cabernet Sauvignon "Antiguas Reservas"	Maipo, Chile	Medium-bodied, supple tannins, vibrant, earthy
Louis M. Martini	Cabernet Sauvignon	Sonoma County, California	Medium-bodied, supple tannins, smooth, juicy
Los Vascos	Cabernet Sauvignon "Reserve"	Colchagua, Chile	Medium-bodied, supple tannins, vibrant, earthy
B. R. Cohn	Cabernet Sauvignon "Silver Label"	North Coast, Calfiornia	Medium-full bodied, supple tannins, vibrant, juicy

SPECIAL BECAUSE	PRICE RANGE	MORE INFO . . .
Boutique, family-owned producer; New Zealand–style version	$14–16	www.masoncellars.com
Well-known Nobilo winery's premium brand; impressive wine	$14–16	www.nobilo.co.nz
Elegant packaging; top producer	$13–16	www.silveradovineyards.com
Great value from cool-climate Casablanca	$8–10	www.casalapostolle.com
Wrapped in colorful floral sheath; fun gift	$8–10	www.duboeuf.com
Classic Napa Valley producer	$12–15	www.sterlingvineyards.com
Petite Sirah and Malbec add complexity	$18–20	www.chateaustjean.com
One of the highest-quality bargain brands on the market	$8–10	www.veramonte.com
Sicily is hot spot for intense, sexy reds	$10–12	www.feudoarancio.it
Hidden gem; boutique producer, value prices	$13–15	www.michaelpozzan winery.com
Top Chilean property with 150-year-old history	$15–17	www.cousinomacul.com
Winemaker Michael Martini is California Cabernet specialist	$15–17	www.louismartini.com
Personal favorite; owned by France's Barons de Rothschild	$18–21	www.lafite.com
Chic wine from former manager of the Doobie Brothers	$18–21	www.brcohn.com

PRODUCER	WINE NAME	FROM	STYLE PROFILE
Codorníu	Pinot Noir Cava	Spain	Medium-bodied sparkler, smooth, juicy
Segura Viudas	Brut Reserva "Heredad"	Cava	Medium-bodied sparkler, smooth, juicy
Franz Haas	Pinot Grigio "Kris"	Delle Venezie, Italy	Light-bodied, crisp, refreshing
Peter Lehmann	Riesling	Eden Valley, Australia	Light-bodied, crisp, refreshing
Marchesi di Barolo	Barbera "Maràia"	Monferrato, Italy	Medium-bodied, supple tannins, vibrant, earthy
Viña MontGras	"Quatro" Reserva	Colchagua Valley, Chile	Full-bodied, supple tanni smooth, earthy
Masi	Ripasso "Campofiorin"	Rosso del Veronese, Italy	Full-bodied, supple tanni smooth, earthy
DaVinci	Chianti Classico	Chianti Classico, Italy	Medium-bodied, light tannins, fresh, spicy
Luna Vineyards	Sangiovese	Napa Valley, California	Medium-full bodied, supp tannins, vibrant, juicy
Château Greysac	Bordeaux	Bordeaux, France	Medium-bodied, supple tannins, vibrant, earthy
Zuccardi	Malbec "Q"	Mendoza, Argentina	Medium-full-bodied, supp tannins, vibrant, juicy
Montevina	Zinfandel "Terra d'Oro"	Amador County, California	Full-bodied, supple tannir spicy, ripe
Grant Burge	Shiraz "Barossa Vines"	Barossa Valley, Australia	Full-bodied, supple tannir spicy, ripe
Two Brothers Winery	"Big Tattoo Red"	Colchagua, Chile	Medium-bodied, supple tannins, smooth, juicy

SPECIAL BECAUSE	PRICE RANGE	MORE INFO . . .
Great value; tastes like expensive dry pink Champagne	$14–16	www.codorniu.com
Gorgeously shaped bottle with top-quality bubbly inside	$17–20	www.seguraviudas.com
Family-run estate since 1880; playful packaging	$10–12	www.franz-haas.com
Classy dry style; queen of clubs adorns label	$17–19	www.peterlehmann wines.com.au
From historic Barolo producer; complex	$8–10	www.marchesibarolo.com
Cabernet Sauvignon, Merlot, Carmenère, and Malbec blend	$10–13	www.montgras.cl
"Baby" Amarone, from Corvina and Rondinella grapes	$13–15	www.masi.it
Sangiovese-based wine from Italian winemaking star Alberto Antonini	$18–20	www.gallofamily.com
One of California's best Sangioveses	$17–20	www.lunavineyards.com
Classic style at a bargain price; ageworthy	$15–18	www.greysac.com
For the steak-lover—big, lush red	$15–18	www.familiazuccardi.com
Gold-etched bottle with excellent-quality Zin	$15–18	www.montevina.com
Bargain brand of respected Barossa winery	$11–14	www.grantburgewines .com.au
Cabernet/Syrah blend; proceeds donated to breast cancer research	$12–15	www.bigtattoored.com

Glamorous Gift Wines
WHEN PRICE IS NO OBJECT

∽

Whether it's your boss's birthday, a holiday gift for a client who collects wine, or a present for the future in-laws, these extraordinary selections will impress at a price that's glamorous, not garish. They all meet the following criteria:

- Recognizable, much lauded wines that live up to their hype
- Cellarworthy bottles that can also be enjoyed immediately
- Not impossible to find, yet scarce enough to be special

Want more picks? Check out these lists: Gathering of the Greats, 25 to Try Before You Die, Wedding Wines, Girls' Night In

---

QUICK TIP
Birthyear in a Bottle
* * *

If you would like to buy a bottle for a newborn to celebrate their birthyear, you'll need a wine that will age at least twenty-one years. My top pick is Vintage Port from Portugal (vintage years aren't declared every year, however). Next would be an Italian Brunello di Montalcino or Barolo. French Bordeaux from a high-quality producer would also be a fine choice. Check out the Quick-Pick Guides for these suggested wine types.

CLASSIC CALIFORNIA CHARDONNAYS

For white wine lovers on your list, these wines deliver the goods.

PRODUCER	WINE NAME	FROM	STYLE PROFILE
Chateau Montelena	Chardonnay	Napa Valley, California	Full-bodied, crisp, spicy, elegant
Frank Family Vineyards	Chardonnay	Napa Valley, California	Full-bodied, crisp, spicy, elegant
Beringer	Chardonnay "Private Reserve"	Napa Valley, California	Full-bodied, creamy, oaky, ripe
Staglin Family Vineyards	Chardonnay "Salus"	Napa Valley, California	Full-bodied, creamy, oaky, ripe
Nickel & Nickel	Chardonnay "Truchard Vineyard"	Carneros, California	Full-bodied, crisp, spicy, elegant
Shafer Vineyards	Chardonnay "Red Shoulder Ranch"	Carneros, California	Full-bodied, crisp, spicy, elegant
Rochioli	Chardonnay	Russian River Valley, California	Full-bodied, crisp, spicy, elegant
Newton	Chardonnay "Unfiltered"	Napa Valley, California	Full-bodied, creamy, oaky, ripe
Patz & Hall	Chardonnay "Hyde Vineyard"	Carneros, California	Full-bodied, crisp, spicy, elegant
Far Niente	Chardonnay	Napa Valley, California	Full-bodied, creamy, oaky, ripe
Ramey	Chardonnay "Hudson Vineyard"	Carneros, California	Full-bodied, crisp, spicy, elegant

SPECIAL BECAUSE	PRICE RANGE	MORE INFO . . .
Classic producer whose Chardonnay won 1976 Paris tasting	$30–35	www.montelena.com
Made in the historic Larkmead Winery building	$33–36	www.frankfamily vineyards.com
Oldest continuously operating winery in Napa Valley	$35–38	www.beringer.com
Their Chardonnay was served to England's Queen Elizabeth	$35–40	www.staglinfamily.com
Winery's focus is on all vineyard-designate wines	$40–43	www.nickelandnickel.com
Established by John Shafer, publisher turned vintner	$42–46	www.shafervineyards.com
Legendary Russian River producer run by third generation	$44–46	www.paternowines.com
Su Hua Newton crafts complex, world-class wines	$45–50	www.newtonvineyard.com
Personal favorite; Burgundian-style from Donald Patz and team	$48–50	www.patzhall.com
Established by Gil Nickel, who also started Nickel & Nickel	$50–55	www.farniente.com
David Ramey is known for ageworthy Chardonnay	$55–60	www.rameywine.com

Famous "One Name" Red Blends from Napa 🍷

Classic Bordeaux-style blends, made primarily from Cabernet Sauvignon with other grapes such as Merlot, Cabernet Franc, Petite Verdot, and Malbec, which never fail to impress. Like Cher, these wines are so chic they need only one name.

PRODUCER	WINE NAME	FROM	STYLE PROFILE
Conn Creek	Anthology	Napa Valley, California	Full-bodied, strong tannin, lush, concentrated
St. Supéry	Élu	Napa Valley, California	Full-bodied, strong tannin, lush, concentrated
Flora Springs	Trilogy	Napa Valley, California	Full-bodied, strong tannin, lush, concentrated
Merryvale	Profile	Napa Valley, California	Full-bodied, strong tannin, lush, concentrated
Chimney Rock	Elevage	Napa Valley, California	Full-bodied, strong tannin, lush, concentrated
Quintessa	Quintessa	Napa Valley, California	Full-bodied, strong tannin, lush, concentrated
Rubicon Estate	Rubicon	Rutherford, Napa Valley, California	Full-bodied, strong tannin, lush, concentrated
Joseph Phelps	Insignia	Napa Valley, California	Full-bodied, strong tannin, lush, concentrated
Dominus Estate	Dominus	Napa Valley, California	Full-bodied, strong tannin, lush, concentrated
Opus One	Opus One	Napa Valley, California	Full-bodied, strong tannin, lush, concentrated

SPECIAL BECAUSE	PRICE RANGE	MORE INFO . . .
Excellent quality/price ratio from Napa hidden gem	$50–55	www.conncreekwinery.com
From hand-selected grapes; *Élu* literally means elected	$60–65	www.stsupery.com
Family-run winery named for mother, Flora	$60–65	www.florasprings.com
Historic property, must-stop on tour of Napa	$95–100	www.merryvale.com
Ultra-smooth style due to Merlot focus	$95–100	www.chimneyrock.com
Personal favorite—elegant; name alludes to the vineyard's hills	$100–110	www.quintessa.com
From organically grown vineyards; powerful style	$100–110	www.rubiconestate.com
First proprietary-named Bordeaux blend in California	$145–150	www.jpvwines.com
Owned by France's famed vintner Christian Moueix, of Château Petrus	$145–150	www.dominusestate.com
Technically two words, but it's a classic	$155–165	www.opusonewinery.com

QUICK TIP
Homemade Wine Vinegar
* * *

1. *Purchase a large glass or pottery container, preferably one with a spout on the bottom and fairly wide mouth so the wine can have contact with the air.*

2. *Decide whether you want to make red wine or white wine vinegar (don't mix the two) and gather up your half-empty wine bottles. Never use a corked or otherwise tainted wine to make your vinegar. It will spoil the entire batch.*

3. *The only other thing you'll need is a starter culture, called "the mother." What turns wine into vinegar is a bacteria,* mycoderma aceti, *and it is contained in the mother. You can buy them at home brew stores, but I've found the easiest way to get the ball rolling is to buy an unpasturized, unfiltered vinegar.*

4. *Pour in equal parts of the starter culture, or store-bought vinegar, and wine. Cover the opening of the jar with a piece of porous fabric, like cheesecloth, and secure it with a rubber band.*

5. *Store the jar in a dark place and in three to six months you'll have delicious vinegar. The best part is, the longer it ages the more intense the flavors become. Keep adding wine anytime you have some leftover.*

6. *Wash and refill old dessert wine bottles with your vinegar.*

7. *Wrap up a bottle of high-quality olive oil, your homemade vinegar, and a bottle of wine for a special gift.*

ITALY'S TUSCAN STARS 🐟

Brunello di Montalcino

These are the Italian stallions of Tuscany and some of the most coveted, ageworthy wines in the world. Made from a special clone of Sangiovese dubbed Sangiovese Grosso, whose local nickname is brunello or "little dark one," Brunello is planted on rugged hillsides surrounding the small, picturesque town of Montalcino, in central Italy. Brunellos aren't even released for up to five years after bottling in order to give them a chance to soften up and start showing their true potential. Though Brunello is not an everyday wine, its younger sibling should be. Called Rosso di Montalcino, these juicy reds are affordable and ready to drink upon release.

Super Tuscans

The category is not an official one, rather an amorphous group of wines with the common thread of quality. Their recognizable names—Sassicaia, Tignanello, Ornellaia—pepper restaurant wine lists and command prices befitting First-Growth Bordeaux and California cult Cabs. What sets Super Tuscans apart from other well-known Tuscan wines like Chianti Classico and Brunello di Montalcino is that they often contain grapes other than those officially allowed by Denominazione di Origine Controllata e Garantita (D.O.C.G.) regulations. Produced from Sangiovese (the recognized red grape variety of the region), Cabernet Sauvignon, Cabernet Franc, Merlot, and even Syrah, these wines opt for excellence over tradition. For more information, visit www.italianmade.com.

TUSCAN STARS

PRODUCER	WINE NAME	FROM	STYLE PROFILE
Fontodi	Flaccianello delle Pieve	Colli Toscana, Italy	Full-bodied, supple tannins, spicy, ripe
Antinori	Tignanello	Toscana, Italy	Full-bodied, supple tannins, spicy, ripe
Tenuta dell'Ornellaia	Ornellaia	Bolgheri, Italy	Full-bodied, supple tannins, spicy, ripe
Tenuta San Guido/ Marchese Incisa della Rocchetta	Sassicaia	Bolgheri, Italy	Full-bodied, supple tannins, spicy, ripe
Col d'Orcia	Brunello di Montalcino	Brunello di Montalcino, Italy	Full-bodied, strong tanni lush, concentrated
Banfi	Brunello di Montalcino	Brunello di Montalcino, Italy	Full-bodied, strong tanni lush, concentrated
Silvio Nardi	Brunello di Montalcino	Brunello di Montalcino, Italy	Full-bodied, strong tanni lush, concentrated
Tenuta Caparzo	Brunello di Montalcino "La Casa"	Brunello di Montalcino, Italy	Full-bodied, strong tanni lush, concentrated
Poggio Antico	Brunello di Montalcino	Brunello di Montalcino, Italy	Full-bodied, strong tanni lush, concentrated
Ruffino	Tenuta Greppone Mazzi	Brunello di Montalcino, Italy	Full-bodied, supple tann smooth, earthy

SPECIAL BECAUSE	PRICE RANGE	MORE INFO . . .
One of first Super Tuscans made solely of Sangiovese	$60–65	www.fontodi.com
Sangiovese-based with Cabernet Sauvignon and Cabernet Franc	$70–75	www.antinori.it
Mostly Cabernet Sauvignon with Merlot. Now owned by Frescobaldi	$120–125	www.ornellaia.it
Most famous Super Tuscan. Cabernet Sauvignon-based classic	$195–200	www.sassicaia.it or www.kobrandwine.com (importer)
Historic property making reasonably-priced Brunello	$46–50	www.coldorcia.it
Classy wine from world-class winery	$50–55	www.banfi.com
Traditional style from highly-regarded producer	$58–60	www.tenutenardi.com or www.kobrandwine.com (importer)
Modern-styled Brunellos with jammy fruit	$65–70	www.caparzo.com
From the highest vineyards in Montalcino	$70–75	www.empson.com (importer)
A single-estate wine from Tuscan landmark	$62–67	www.ruffino.com

Prestige Cuvées 🐟

The best of the best in bubbly never fails to delight.

PRODUCER	WINE NAME	FROM	STYLE PROFILE
Laurent-Perrier	"Grand Siècle"	Champagne, France	Full-bodied sparkler, creamy, rich, toasty
Charles Heidsieck	"Blanc des Millenaires"	Champagne, France	Full-bodied sparkler, creamy, rich, toasty
Pommery	"Cuvée Louise"	Champagne, France	Full-bodied sparkler, creamy, rich, toasty
Moët & Chandon	"Dom Pérignon"	Champagne, France	Full-bodied sparkler, creamy, rich, toasty
Taittinger	"Comtes de Champagne" Blanc de Blancs	Champagne, France	Full-bodied sparkler, creamy, rich, toasty
Veuve Clicquot	"La Grande Dame"	Champagne, France	Full-bodied sparkler, creamy, rich, toasty
Louis Roederer	"Cristal"	Champagne, France	Full-bodied sparkler, creamy, rich, toasty
Domaine Chandon	"Etoile"	Napa Valley, California	Full-bodied sparkler, creamy, rich, toasty
Roederer Estate	"L'Ermitage"	Alexander Valley, California	Full-bodied sparkler, creamy, rich, toasty
Domaine Carneros	"Le Rêve" Blanc de Blancs	Carneros, California	Full-bodied sparkler, creamy, rich, toasty
Gloria Ferrer	"Carneros Cuvée"	Carneros, California	Full-bodied sparkler, creamy, rich, toasty
Schramsberg	"J. Schram"	Napa Valley, California	Full-bodied sparkler, creamy, rich, toasty

SPECIAL BECAUSE	PRICE RANGE	MORE INFO . . .
Personal favorite; well priced considering amazing quality	$75–80	www.laurent-perrier.co.uk
Hidden gem among better known Champagnes—amazing wine	$95–100	www.charlesheidsieck.com
Primarily Chardonnay with Pinot Noir; elegant style	$100–110	www.pommery.com
Arguably the most famous Champagne; first produced in 1936	$115–120	www.moet.com
Made exclusively from Chardonnay grapes	$138–140	www.taittinger.com
Named for the widow Clicquot, who ran the company in the 1800s	$145–150	www.veuve-clicquot.com
Wine originally created for Russian Tsar Alexander II	$195–200	www.champagne-roederer.com
Etoile is French for star; Chardonnay/Pinot Noir blend	$32–36	www.chandon.com
Founded in 1982 by Louis Roederer, of Champagne	$38–42	www.rodererestate.net
Chardonnay-based bubbly from American outpost of Taittinger	$48–52	www.domainecarneros.com
Pinot Noir/Chardonnay blend in stunning black bottle	$50–55	www.gloriaferrer.com
Named for original founder Jacob Schram; Chardonnay-based	$80–85	www.schramsberg.com

Wild Wines

FUN WINES FROM CRITTER LABELS TO HUMOROUS STORIES

༄

You can't walk down a wine store aisle without feeling like you're in a zoo. With the record success of Yellow Tail, an Australian brand, critter labels have proliferated like rabbits. The good news is that because they're focused on fun and enjoyment, the crush of animal-themed brands has reinvigorated the wine category. But which ones are worth taking for a walk? The following wines are seriously fun to sip.

Want more picks? Check out these lists: Snack Food Wines, Take-out Favorites, Twice-the-Price Wines

STEMWARE CHEAT SHEET
Bigger Is Better

* * *

While I do believe that any glass with wine in it is a wine-glass, enjoyment is increased by using proper stemware. Look for a stemmed glass with a bowl that holds about 16 ounces. A bigger bowl allows plenty of room for swirling, which gives the wine space to release its aromas and flavors. If you want separate glasses for red and white, buy stemware with a larger bowl for reds and a slightly smaller bowl for whites.

SHAPE IT UP

Avoid glasses that curve out at the top of the bowl. Wine glasses should be narrower at the top and wider toward the bottom in order to focus the aromas and flavors of the wine.

THIN IS IN

Seek out slightly thinner crystal or glass. Make sure the glasses aren't too thin, though, or they'll have a tendency to break when washing them.

WILD WHITES

PRODUCER	WINE NAME	FROM	STYLE PROFILE
Jackaroo	Chardonnay	South Eastern Australia	Medium-bodied, light oak, juicy
Smoking Loon	Viognier	California	Medium-full-bodied, crisp, fruity
Mad Fish	Sauvignon Blanc	Western Australia	Medium-bodied, racy, herb
Monkey Bay	Sauvignon Blanc	Marlborough, New Zealand	Medium-bodied, racy, herbal
Yellow Tail	Chardonnay "Reserve"	South Eastern Australia	Medium-bodied, light oak, juicy
Fox Creek	Verdelho	South Australia	Medium-bodied, crisp, minerally
Frog's Leap Winery	"Leapfrogmilch"	Napa Valley, California	Medium-bodied, aromatic, off-dry

RAUCOUS REDS

PRODUCER	WINE NAME	FROM	STYLE PROFILE
The Little Penguin	White Syrah	South Eastern Australia	Light-bodied, light tannin off-dry, juicy
Rex Goliath	Pinot Noir	California	Light-bodied, light tannin bright, earthy
Four Emus	Shiraz	Western Australia	Medium-bodied, supple tannins, smooth, juicy
Fairview	"Goats do Roam" Red	South Africa	Medium-bodied, supple tannins, vibrant, earthy

SPECIAL BECAUSE	PRICE RANGE	MORE INFO . . .
"Jackaroo" is a nickname for Australian cowboys	$7–9	www.clickwinegroup.com (importer)
Good varietal character at great price	$7–9	www.smokingloon.com
Lean, grassy New World style	$12–14	www.madfishwines.com
Named for portion of Cloudy Bay where monkeys cavort	$8–10	www.monkeybaywine.com
This Reserve is quite complex	$9–11	www.yellowtailwine.com
Label adorned with a fox	$12–14	www.foxcreekwines.com
Personal favorite; Riesling-Chardonnay blend, organic	$13–14	www.frogsleap.com

SPECIAL BECAUSE	PRICE RANGE	MORE INFO . . .
If you like White Zin, try this	$7–8	www.thelittlepenguin.com
Label adorned with world's largest rooster, Rex	$7–10	www.rexgoliath.com
Emus are the rock stars of the Outback	$10–12	www.fouremus.com.au
Bestselling South African wine in the United States	$8–10	www.fairview.co.za

(*continued*)

PRODUCER	WINE NAME	FROM	STYLE PROFILE
Rancho Zabaco	Zinfandel "Dancing Bull"	California	Full-bodied, supple tann spicy, ripe
Dr. Konstantin Frank	Meritage "Salmon Run"	New York	Medium-bodied, light ta fresh, spicy
Wild Horse	Cabernet Sauvignon	Paso Robles, California	Medium-full-bodied, supple tannins, vibrant,

OTHER FUN BRANDS

PRODUCER	WINE NAME	FROM	STYLE PROFILE
Folie à Deux	"Menage à Trois" White	California	Medium-bodied, aromat off-dry
Cline Cellars	"Red Truck"	California	Medium-bodied, supple tannins, smooth, juicy
The Fat Bastard	Merlot	Vin de Pays d'Oc, France	Medium-bodied, supple tannins, smooth, juicy
Kenwood Vineyards	Merlot "Jack London Vineyard"	Sonoma Valley, California	Medium-bodied, supple tannins, smooth, juicy
Twin Fin	Shiraz	California	Medium-bodied, supple tannins, smooth, juicy
Concha y Toro	Carmenère "Casillero del Diablo"	Rapel Valley, Chile	Medium-bodied, light tannins, fresh, spicy
Norman Vineyards	Zinfandel "The Monster"	Paso Robles, California	Full-bodied, supple tann spicy, ripe
Nova Wines	Marilyn Merlot	Napa Valley, California	Medium-full-bodied, su tannins, vibrant, juicy

SPECIAL BECAUSE	PRICE RANGE	MORE INFO . . .
Great value, overdelivers in quality	$9–12	www.ranchozabaco.com
From upstate New York's best-known producer	$13–16	www.drfrankwines.com
A serious animal label; high quality	$18–20	www.wildhorsewinery.com

SPECIAL BECAUSE	PRICE RANGE	MORE INFO . . .
Moscato, Chardonnay, Chenin Blanc blend	$10–12	www.folieadeux.com
Fun combo of Syrah, Petite Sirah, Cabernet Franc	$10–12	www.clinecellars.com
Popular wine from Thierry Boudinaud and Guy Anderson	$8–10	www.fatbastardwine.com
Named for author Jack London's *Call of the Wild*	$20–23	www.kenwoodvineyards.com
Retro convertible and finned surfboard adorn the label	$8–10	www.twinfinwines.com
A devilishly good value, from top Chilean producer	$7–8	www.conchaytoro.com
Ultra-ripe, rustic wine from family-owned operation	$18–20	www.normanvineyards.com
Adorned with a picture of Marilyn Monroe	$22–24	www.marilynmerlot.com

STAR-STUDDED WINES—FAMOUS NAMES

PRODUCER	WINE NAME	FROM	STYLE PROFILE
Firestone	Gewürztraminer	Santa Ynez Valley, California	Medium-bodied, aromatic, off-dry
Andretti	Sauvignon Blanc	Napa Valley, California	Medium-full-bodied, crisp, fruity
Seresin Estate	Sauvignon Blanc	Marlborough, New Zealand	Medium-bodied, racy, herbal
Fleming-Jenkins	Chardonnay	Santa Cruz Mountains, California	Full-bodied, crisp, spicy, elegant
Koala Blue	Shiraz	South Australia	Medium-bodied, supple tannins, smooth, juicy
Virgin Vines	Shiraz	California	Medium-bodied, supple tannins, smooth, juicy
J. Garcia	Merlot	Sonoma County, California	Medium-bodied, supple tannins, smooth, juicy
Arnold Palmer	Cabernet Sauvignon	California	Medium-bodied, supple tannins, smooth, juicy
Greg Norman	Shiraz	Limestone Coast, Australia	Medium-full-bodied, supple tannins, vibrant, ju
Fess Parker	Syrah	Santa Barbara County, California	Full-bodied, supple tannir spicy, ripe
Chiarello Family Vineyards	"Giana" Zinfandel	Napa Valley, California	Full-bodied, supple tannir spicy, ripe
Frank Family Vineyards	Cabernet Sauvignon	Napa Valley, California	Full-bodied, strong tannir lush, concentrated
Rubicon Estate	Cabernet Franc	Rutherford, Napa Valley, California	Full-bodied, strong tannir lush, concentrated
Ernie Els Wines	"Ernie Els"	Stellenbosch, South Africa	Full-bodied, strong tannir lush, concentrated

SPECIAL BECAUSE	PRICE RANGE	MORE INFO . . .
Firestone tire family; son Andrew was "The Bachelor"	$10–12	www.firestonewine.com
Racecar driver Mario Andretti	$13–16	www.andrettiwinery.com
Michael Seresin, a world-famous cinematographer	$22–24	www.seresin.co.nz
Personal favorite, from Olympic skater Peggy Fleming's home vineyard	$35–36	www.flemingjenkins winery.com
Singer Olivia Newton-John is co-owner	$8–10	www.koalabluewines.com.au
Richard Branson, creator of the Virgin empire; fun wine	$8–10	www.virginvines.com
Named for Jerry Garcia of The Grateful Dead band	$13–15	www.jgarciawine.com
Made by Napa's Luna Vineyards for golf legend	$15–17	www.arnoldpalmerwines.com
Golfer with the nickname "The Shark"	$16–18	www.shark.com
A salute to the nostalgic days of Davy Crockett	$18–20	www.fessparker.com
Celebrity chef Michael Chiarello's wine; limited production	$26–28	www.chiarellovineyards.com
Rich Frank, former president of Walt Disney Studios; excellent	$40–45	www.frankfamilyvineyards .com
Unique red from movie director Francis Ford Coppola	$42–46	www.rubiconestate.com
Hole in one from golfer Els; ageworthy Bordeaux-style blend	$90–100	www.ernieelswines.com

Insider Wines

Want to increase your wine-savvy quotient quickly? Step up and sample these insider picks from wines you thought you might not like but will love (think dry Riesling, rosé and Sherry) to hidden treasures made by small producers. Take a tasting tour and discover some of the best wines in the world with roundups such as "25 to Try Before You Die" and "Gathering of the Greats." Have friends you want to introduce to the joys of the grape but aren't sure where to start? My "Secret Weapon" wines are just the answer. Wrapping up the section is a makeover medley taking expensive wines and offering a lesser-priced but similar-tasting alternative.

Hidden Treasures
THEY MAY BE HARD TO FIND BUT
ARE WORTH THE EFFORT

This is the spot to discover boutique producers crafting small lots of amazing Chardonnay and Pinot Noir, as well as uncovering unique finds you probably never heard of or tasted. Sampled wines made from grape varieties such as Sauvignon Gris, Xarel-lo, Sagrantino, or Colorino? How about an Australian Viognier or a regal red from Lebanon? While all of these selections are compelling and classy, their beauty lies in the fact that most won't cost a pirate's ransom to buy. Now that's a treasure.

Want more picks? Check out these lists: Hot Spots, Wines to Watch, Virtual Vacation Vino

HIDDEN TREASURES: WHITES

PRODUCER	WINE NAME	FROM	STYLE PROFILE
Cousiño-Macul	Sauvignon Gris	Maipo Valley, Chile	Medium-bodied, crisp, minerally
Millton	Chenin Blanc "Te Arai Vineyard"	Gisborne, New Zealand	Medium-bodied, crisp, minerally
Grosset	Riesling "Polish Hill"	Clare Valley, Australia	Medium-bodied, crisp, minerally
Craggy Range	Riesling "Rapaura Road Vineyard"	Marlborough, New Zealand	Medium-bodied, aromatic off-dry
Kangarilla Road	Viognier	McLaren Vale, Australia	Full-bodied, soft, aromatic
Cold Heaven	Viognier "Sanford & Benedict"	Santa Barbara County, California	Full-bodied, soft, aromatic
Segura Viudas	Xarel-lo	Penedes, Spain	Full-bodied, soft, aromatic
Peay Vineyards	Roussanne/Marsanne	Sonoma Coast, California	Full-bodied, soft, aromatic
Domaine des Comtes Lafon	Macon-Milly-Lamartine	Macon-Villages, France	Medium-bodied, light oak, juicy
Forgeron Cellars	Chardonnay	Columbia Valley, Washington	Full-bodied, crisp, spicy, elegant
Buty Winery	Chardonnay "Conner Lee Vineyard"	Columbia Valley, Washington	Full-bodied, crisp, spicy, elegant
LaTour Vineyards	Chardonnay	Napa Valley, California	Full-bodied, creamy, oaky, ripe
Pierre Gimonnet et Fils	"Fleuron" Blanc de Blancs	Champagne, France	Medium-bodied sparkler, crisp, elegant

SPECIAL BECAUSE	PRICE RANGE	MORE INFO . . .
Ancient variety that's rarely seen anymore	$12–14	www.cousinomacul.com
As complex as greats from France's Loire Valley	$18–20	www.millton.co.nz
One of the world's best dry Rieslings; ageworthy	$32–35	www.grosset.com.au
Oldest Riesling vineyard in New Zealand	$23–25	www.craggyrange.com
Family-owned, innovative producer	$28–30	www.kangarillaroad.com.au
Morgan Clendenen makes only Viognier	$33–35	www.coldheavencellars.com
Dry white from grape normally used in Cava blends	$18–20	www.seguraviudas.com
Very limited production, but worth the search	$35–40	www.peayvineyards.com
Classic producer; Chardonnay with nutty elegance	$28–30	www.comtes-lafon.fr
French winemaker Marie-Eve Gilla crafts stunning wines	$22–24	www.forgeroncellars.com
Young couple focused on single-vineyard bottlings	$28–30	www.butywinery.com
Lush style from businessman-turned-vintner Tom Latour	$30–35	www.latourvineyards.com
A grower Champagne with grip	$58–62	www.skurnickwines.com (importer)

HIDDEN TREASURES: REDS

PRODUCER	WINE NAME	FROM	STYLE PROFILE
Kosta-Browne	Pinot Noir "Kanzler Vineyard"	Sonoma Coast, California	Medium-bodied, supple tannins, vibrant, earthy
Brogan Cellars	Pinot Noir "Summa Vineyard"	Sonoma Coast, California	Medium-bodied, supple tannins, vibrant, earthy
Roar Wines	Pinot Noir "Rosella's Vineyard"	Santa Lucia Highlands, California	Medium-bodied, supple tannins, vibrant, earthy
Margerum Wines	"M5" red blend	Santa Ynez Valley, California	Medium-bodied, supple tannins, vibrant, earthy
Alban	Grenache	Edna Valley, California	Full-bodied, supple tannins, smooth, earthy
C. G. di Arie	Zinfandel	Shenandoah Valley, California	Full-bodied, supple tannins, spicy, ripe
Sineann	Zinfandel "The Pines Vineyard"	Columbia Valley, Oregon	Full-bodied, supple tannins, spicy, ripe
K Vintners	Syrah "Cougar Hills"	Walla Walla Valley, Washington	Full-bodied, strong tannins, lush, concentrated
Copain Wine Cellars	Syrah "Coccinelle and Cailloux"	Walla Walla Valley, Washington	Full-bodied, strong tannins, lush, concentrated
Chateau Musar	Rouge	Bekaa Valley, Lebanon	Full-bodied, supple tannins, smooth, earthy
Arnaldo Caprai	Sagrantino di Montefalco "Collepiano"	Umbria, Italy	Full-bodied, supple tannins, smooth, earthy
Ruffino	Romitorio di Santedame	Toscano, Italy	Full-bodied, strong tannins, lush, concentrated
Château Valandraud	Grand Cru	Saint-Emilion, Bordeaux, France	Full-bodied, strong tannins, lush, concentrated

SPECIAL BECAUSE	PRICE RANGE	MORE INFO . . .
Dan Kosta and Michael Browne's Pinots are hot	$45–50	www.kostabrowne.com
From Burt Williams's daughter Margi (of Williams-Selyem fame)	$55–60	www.brogancellars.com
Top winemaking team including Adam Lee, of Siduri	$70–75	www.roarwines.com
Rhône-style blend including Syrah and Grenache	$24–28	www. margerumwine company.com
The best New World Grenache	$68–75	www.albanvineyards.com
Stunning Zins from winemaker Chaim Gur-Arieh	$25–27	www.cgdiarie.com
Oregon Zin? Yes, from hundred-year-old vines	$30–33	www.sineann.com
Personal favorite; owner Charles Smith is a Syrah specialist	$45–48	www.kvintners.com
Wells Guthrie makes Northern Rhône–style Syrah; smoky	$55–60	www.copainwines.com
Cabernet Sauvignon, Carignan, Cinsault blend	$45–50	www.chateaumusar.com.lb
Amazing, ageworthy red made from Sagrantino	$35–40	www.arnaldocaprai.it
Inky purple wine made with rare grape variety, Colorino	$70–75	www.ruffino.com
Highly touted, tiny production "garagiste" or cult wine	$175–200	www.thunevin.com

Overlooked Surprises

WINES YOU THINK YOU WOULDN'T LIKE BUT WILL LOVE

∞

If you've avoided Riesling, rosé, or Sherry for fear that they're sweet sippers, get ready for a surprise. You can still drink dry while enjoying these classic wine styles.

Want more picks? Check out these lists: Snack Attack Party Food, Take-Out Favorites, Spring Wines, Summer Wines, Bathtub Wines

DRY-STYLE RIESLING 🐟

If I had to choose one wine type with which to be stranded on a deserted island, Riesling would be it. What other wine could go as easily with speared fish and wild boar as coconut cream pie?

Grown all over the world and made in styles from dry to sweet, Riesling ranks as one of the noblest grape varieties. It has such naturally high acidity that even if there is a hint of residual sugar in the wine, it usually doesn't taste sweet, just balanced and fruity. If you want to start exploring the beauty of Riesling, but don't like sweet wines, start with drier versions. Many of them hail from Australia's Clare and Eden valleys and Great Southern region, New Zealand, and New York State. Some wines from California or Washington even have the word *dry* written on the label. My favorites include dry-style Kabinett Rieslings from the Mosel-Saar-Ruwer region of Germany. Naturally low in alcohol (around 7 to 9 percent), they are ethereal, elegant, and affordable. Carl von Schubert, producer of the highly regarded Maximin Grünhäuser wines, calls his Riesling Kabinett a "No-regret wine. You can drink, enjoy, relax, and not feel overwhelmed with oak and alcohol. You can even head back to work after wine at lunch." Surprised?

OVERLOOKED SURPRISES: DRY-STYLE RIESLING

PRODUCER	WINE NAME	FROM	STYLE PROFILE
Jacob's Creek	Riesling	South Eastern Australia	Light-bodied, crisp, refreshing
McWilliams Hanwood Estate	Riesling	South Eastern Australia	Light-bodied, crisp, refreshing
Wolf Blass	Riesling "Gold Label"	Eden and Clare Valleys, Australia	Medium-bodied, crisp, minerally
Plantagenet Wines	Riesling	Mount Barker, Western Australia	Medium-bodied, crisp, minerally
Isabel Estate	Dry Riesling	Marlborough, New Zealand	Medium-bodied, crisp, minerally
Dr. Konstantin Frank	"Dry" Johannisberg Riesling	Finger Lakes, New York	Light-bodied, crisp, refreshing
Trefethen	Dry Riesling	Napa Valley, California	Medium-full-bodied, crisp, fruity
Selbach-Oster	Dry Riesling "Fish label"	Mosel-Saar-Ruwer, Germany	Medium-bodied, crisp, minerally
Leitz	"Dragonstone" Riesling	Rheingau, Germany	Medium-full-bodied, crisp, fruity
Schlossgut Diel	Riesling "Classic"	Nahe, Germany	Medium-bodied, crisp, minerally
Dr. Bürklin-Wolf	Estate Riesling	Pfalz, Germany	Medium-bodied, crisp, minerally
Von Schubert/ Maximin Grünhäuser	Riesling "Herrenberg" Kabinett	Mosel-Saar-Ruwer, Germany	Medium-bodied, crisp, minerally

SPECIAL BECAUSE	PRICE RANGE	MORE INFO . . .
Widely available. Ideal party pick	$9–11	www.jacobscreek.com
Great value for complexity	$10–12	www.mcwilliams.com.au
Leading Aussie producer started in 1966 by Wolf	$14–16	www.wolfblass.com.au
Stunningly dry, elegant white. Ageworthy	$17–19	www.plantagenetwines.com
Boutique winery, limited availability	$16–18	www.isabelestate.com
New York's Riesling leader	$14–16	www.drfrankwines.com
Classic Napa producer; unique, small production wine	$18–20	www.trefethen.com
One of Mosel's best wineries, with an affordable second label	$10–12	www.selbach-oster.de
Hot winemaker crafting modern-style Riesling	$15–17	www.leitz-wein.de or www.skurnikwines.com (importer)
Famed producer; "Classic" refers to dry style	$19–22	www.skurnikwines.com (importer)
Produced from vineyards more than twenty-five years old	$19–22	www.classicalwines.com (importer)
Historic property dating to Roman times; world-class	$25–27	www.vonschubert.de

GERMAN RIESLING CHEAT SHEET
Deciphering the Label
* * *

When wines are labeled Qualitätswein mit Prädikat (QmP), that indicates they are of the highest quality. They are then divided into categories that correspond to ripeness levels at harvest:

Kabinett: *The first grapes picked, producing wines that are lighter and drier in style. Generally affordable.*

Spätlese: *Means "late-picked." Grapes are riper than those for Kabinett wines. Tends to be off-dry to a touch sweet.*

Auslese: *Very ripe grapes that have often been affected by noble rot, or Botrytis cinerea, produce these opulent wines. Usually on the sweet side and fairly expensive.*

Beerenauslese, or BA, and Trockenbeerenauslese, or TBA: *Pickers select individual berries of incredibly ripe grapes affected by noble rot to make these honeyed, concentrated wines. Rare, expensive, and gloriously sweet.*

QUICK TIP
Make Mine Pink
* * *

To make rosé, red grapes are gently crushed and the juice has a brief rendezvous—from several hours to several days—with the skins. This short-lived interaction imparts the appealing pinkish hue. Sweeter wines contain various levels of residual sugar, while dry versions, or rosés, are fermented to dryness like a red wine. Pink wines can be made from different types of red grape varieties, including Syrah, Pinot Noir, Zinfandel, Cinsault, Sangiovese, and Tempranillo.

DRY ROSÉ 🐟

Contrary to popular belief, all pink wines aren't all sweet. Those dubbed rosé are generally dry while blush wines (or ones with the word white in front such as White Zinfandel or White Merlot) are sweeter in style. Light and refreshing dry rosé is the ultimate insider wine. It's what the pros drink. In fact, dry rosé has always been hugely popular in Europe, from sunny Provence in the south of France to Spain and Italy. Dry rosés are made worldwide, but be on the lookout for versions from the following regions: Côtes de Provence, Bandol, and Tavel in France; and Rioja or Navarra, in Spain. For more information visit www.rapwine.com.

SHERRY 🐟

Talk about misunderstood. No longer just something you cook with or pour for old Aunt Milly, Sherry is undergoing a renaissance. It's one of the wine world's best bargains, an ideal food wine, and something you must discover.

What is Sherry? A style of fortified wine made in Spain's Andalusia region, in a town named Jerez de la Frontera (Sherry is actually an anglicized name for the original name Xerez, or Shareesh in Persian). Sherry comes in bone-dry-to-immensely-sweet versions and is made from three grape varieties: Palomino, Pedro Ximénez, and Muscat. Fortified with brandy during the winemaking process, Fino Sherries develop a unique yeast covering called *flor*, which protects the wine from oxidation. These wines are fresh, light, and dry. Sweeter, darker, fortified styles such as Oloroso are allowed contact with air, which imparts a nutty richness. For more information, go to www.sherry.org.

OVERLOOKED SURPRISES: DRY ROSÉ

PRODUCER	WINE NAME	FROM	STYLE PROFILE
Regaleali	Rosé di Regaleali	Sicily, Italy	Light-bodied, light tannin, vibrant, fruity
Château Routas	"Rouvière" Rosé	Coteaux Varois, France	Light-bodied, light tannin, bright, earthy
Domaine de Curebéasse	Rosé "Angelico"	Côtes de Provence, France	Light-bodied, light tannin, bright, earthy
Jean-Luc Colombo	Rosé Côte Bleue "Pioche et Cabanon"	Coteaux d'Aix en Provence, France	Light-bodied, light tannin, bright, earthy
Domaine Ott	Rosé	Côtes de Provence, France	Light-bodied, light tannin, bright, earthy
Lawson's Dry Hills	Pinot Rosé	Marlborough, New Zealand	Light-bodied, light tannins, vibrant, fruity
Charles Melton	"Rosé of Virginia"	Barossa, Australia	Light-bodied, light tannins, vibrant, fruity
Iron Horse	Rosato Di Sangiovese	Alexander Valley, California	Light-bodied, light tannins, vibrant, fruity
Wölffer Estate	Rosé	The Hamptons, Long Island, New York	Light-bodied, light tannins, vibrant, fruity
Frog's Leap Winery	"La Grenouille Rouganté Rosé"	Napa Valley, California	Light-bodied, light tannins, vibrant, fruity
Miner Family	Rosato	Mendocino, California	Light-bodied, light tannins, vibrant, fruity
SoloRosa	Rosé	California	Light-bodied, light tannins, vibrant, fruity
Swanson	Rosato	Napa Valley, California	Light-bodied, light tannins, vibrant, fruity

SPECIAL BECAUSE	PRICE RANGE	MORE INFO . . .
Deep pink Nerello Mascalese and Nero d'Avola blend	$12–14	www.winebow.com (importer)
Grenache-based blend	$10–12	www.routas.com
Composed of Mourvèdre, Cinsault, Grenache, and Carignane	$10–12	www.curebeasse.com
Syrah/Mourvèdre blend from visionary Rhône winemaker	$12–14	www.palmbayimports.com (importer)
Famous rosé producer; amphora-shaped, highly recognizable bottle	$28–30	www.domaines-ott.com
Limited production from hot New Zealand property	$16–19	www.lawsonsdryhills.co.nz
Charlie is a Down Under star making Grenache-based rosé	$18–22	www.charlesmelton wines.com.au
Spicy pink from well-known sparkling wine house	$10–14	www.ironhorsevineyards.com
Former potato farm is now gorgeous, must-visit winery	$12–14	www.wolffer.com
Owner John Williams's playful take on Valdiguié rosé	$10–13	www.frogsleap.com
Sangiovese-based; limited production but worth the search	$12–15	www.minerwines.com
Makes only world-class rosé from Sangiovese and Merlot	$15–17	www.solorosawines.com
Complex, Syrah-based pink from top Napa winery	$16–18	www.swansonvineyards.com

OVERLOOKED SURPRISES: SHERRY

PRODUCER	WINE NAME	FROM	STYLE PROFILE
Osborne	Manzanilla Sherry	Sanlúcar de Barrameda, Spain	Light-bodied, crisp, refreshing
Sandeman	Fino Apitiv	Jerez de la Frontera, Spain	Light-bodied, crisp, refreshing
Domecq	Dry Fino "La Ina"	Jerez de la Frontera, Spain	Light-bodied, crisp, refreshing
Lustau	Dry Oloroso "Don Nuño"	Jerez de la Frontera, Spain	Full-bodied, creamy, oaky, ripe
Williams-Hymbert/Dry Sack	Amontillado	Jerez de la Frontera, Spain	Medium-bodied, lightly sweet, nutty

SHERRY CHEAT SHEET
Deciphering the Label

* * *

Fino: Driest, palest, and most crisp sherry. Use as appetizer wines with nuts, olives, and other finger foods.

Manzanilla: Dry style of fino with a unique salty tang as the result of maturing in bodegas (or wineries) in the seaside town of Sanlúcar de Barrameda. Serve this pale-colored sipper very cold with an appetizer plate of cold cuts and cheeses; almonds; or barbeque chicken wings.

Amontillado: Dry to slightly sweet, these medium-bodied wines go with appetizers or light dishes.

SPECIAL BECAUSE	PRICE RANGE	MORE INFO . . .
Great value; sports hint of salty tang	$9–10	www.osborne.es or www.wjdeutsch.com (importer)
Best enjoyed ice cold with nuts	$13–15	www.sandeman.com
Personal favorite, widely available from classic producer	$15–18	www.domecq-usa.com
Reminiscent of full-bodied dry white wine	$18–20	www.emilio-lustau.com
Just a touch of well-balanced sweetness	$12–14	www.williams-humbert.com

Oloroso: Can be dry or sweeter and sports a rich, nutty, full-bodied flavor that is ideal with soups, stews, and hearty foods.

Cream Sherry: A blended style of Sherry serving up sweetness and smoothness. Think dessert wine.

PX: Stands for Pedro Ximénez, which is a grape variety. These deep, chocolate-colored wines are the ultimate in sweetness and richness.

WINE LIST CHEAT SHEET
Tips for Finding Values in a Restaurant

* * *

GO FOR HALF

Half bottles (375 ml) contain about two to three glasses. If you're dining alone or on a romantic date, it's the perfect size. Have a group of people with diverse opinions and menu desires? Order a few half bottles.

FIND ALTERNATIVES

With the popularity of progressive wine lists, which organize wine by style, many establishments are offering sections on their list called "Other Interesting Wines" or "Alternative Wines." You may not recognize the names, but talk to the server about them. This is often where I see the best bargains.

CONSIDER THE MARKUP

Markups at restaurants cover overhead such as storage of wine, service, and stemware. But all markups aren't equal. Often, lower-priced wines are marked-up the most while the high-price beauties have lower price hikes.

ASK FOR HELP

I generally consult with the sommelier to compare notes and seek out the hidden gems or great value wines on their list. The sommelier, or wine director, is usually the person who puts a wine list together and wants nothing more than to help you find what you need.

Restaurant Darlings

FAVORITES ON WINE LISTS

∞

I'm often asked about wine in restaurants. Questions focus primarily on finding values, recommending classic bottlings, and discovering new wines while dining out. Due to the diversity of wine lists across the country, there are no standard answers. However, I've scanned hundreds of top lists from California to New York to select a lineup of omnipresent wines to mention. Obviously there's no telling what's on tap at your neighborhood spot, but if you remember a number of these winners you'll feel empowered ordering off a wine list. My choices meet the following criteria:

- Are wines I choose when dining out for excellent quality: cost ratio (notable names are missing; that's on purpose, because I don't think they're worth the price normally charged at restaurants).
- Generally well-priced wines, though it's impossible to predict the markup. I've listed the average retail price range.
- Fall into one of two categories: Familiar and Adventurous.

Want more picks? Check out these lists: Twice-the-Price Wines, Hot Spots, Wines to Watch

---

MYTH-BUSTER
You Must Sniff the Cork

* * *

There is really no need to pick up the cork and smell it. Simply eye it to make sure the cork is intact and moist. After the taste has been poured for you, feel free to swirl it and take a quick smell and taste. Unless the wine is flawed, say thanks and enjoy your meal.

RESTAURANT DARLINGS: FAMILIAR WHITES AND BUBBLY

PRODUCER	WINE NAME	FROM	STYLE PROFILE
Simi	Sauvignon Blanc	Sonoma County, California	Light-bodied, crisp, refreshing
Cloudy Bay	Sauvignon Blanc	Marlborough, New Zealand	Medium-bodied, racy, herbal
Chateau St. Jean	Johannisberg Riesling	Sonoma County, California	Light-bodied, racy, off-dry
Kendall-Jackson	Chardonnay "Grand Reserve"	California	Medium-full-bodied, crisp, fruity
Morgan	Chardonnay "Metallico"	Monterey County, California	Medium-full-bodied, crisp, fruity
Clos du Bois	Chardonnay "Calcaire"	Alexander Valley, California	Full-bodied, creamy, oaky, ripe
Gallo Family Vineyards	Chardonnay "Laguna Vineyard"	Russian River Valley, California	Full-bodied, creamy, oaky, ripe
Sonoma-Cutrer	Chardonnay "Russian River Ranches"	Russian River Valley, California	Medium-full-bodied, crisp, fruity
Nicolas Feuillatte	Brut Premier Cru	Champagne, France	Full-bodied sparkler, creamy, rich, toasty
Billecart-Salmon	Brut Rosé	Champagne, France	Medium-bodied sparkler, crisp, elegant
Piper-Heidsieck	Brut Vintage	Champagne, France	Full-bodied sparkler, creamy, rich, toasty

SPECIAL BECAUSE	PRICE RANGE	MORE INFO . . .
Blended with a dash of Sémillon; crowd-pleasing style	$15–17	www.simiwinery.com
Benchmark bottling that raised awareness of New Zealand	$28–30	www.cloudybay.co.nz
Excellent option with Chinese or spicy fare	$14–16	www.chateaustjean.com
Complex bottling from Chardonnay specialists	$20–22	www.kj.com
No oak character, making it tops for seafood	$20–22	www.morganwinery.com
Hand-selected from premium vineyards in Alexander Valley	$21–23	www.closdubois.com
Personal favorite; rich style with impeccable balance	$22–25	www.gallofamily.com
Upscale pick with elegance	$23–26	www.sonomacutrer.com
Well-known, widely available Champagne	$30–33	www.feuillatte.com
Impressive bubbly—light pink, dry; drink throughout the meal	$65–75	www.champagne-billecart.fr
Famous firm dating to 1785; ideal for dinner	$60–65	www.piper-heidsieck.com

RESTAURANT DARLINGS: FAMILIAR REDS

PRODUCER	WINE NAME	FROM	STYLE PROFILE
Hess Collection	Syrah "Hess Select"	California	Medium-bodied, supple tannins, smooth, juicy
Kenwood	Pinot Noir	Russian River Valley, California	Medium-bodied, supple tannins, vibrant, earthy
Hartley Ostini/ Hitching Post	Pinot Noir "Highliner"	Santa Barbara County, California	Medium-bodied, supple tannins, vibrant, earthy
Markham Vineyards	Merlot	Napa Valley, California	Medium-bodied, supple tannins, smooth, juicy
Duckhorn Vineyards	Merlot	Napa Valley, California	Full-bodied, strong tannins, lush, concentrated
Lambert Bridge	Merlot	Sonoma County, California	Medium-bodied, supple tannins, smooth, juicy
Beaulieu Vineyard	Cabernet Sauvignon "Rutherford"	Napa Valley, California	Full-bodied, strong tannins, lush, concentrated
Trefethen	Cabernet Sauvignon	Napa Valley, California	Full-bodied, strong tannins, lush, concentrated
Ferrari-Carano	"Siena"	Sonoma County, California	Medium-bodied, supple tannins, vibrant, earthy
Antinori	Chianti Classico "Pèppoli"	Chianti Classico, Italy	Medium-bodied, supple tannins, vibrant, earthy
Ruffino	Ducale "Gold Label" Chianti Classico Riserva	Chianti Classico, Italy	Medium-bodied, supple tannins, vibrant, earthy
Merry Edwards	Pinot Noir "Meredith Estate"	Sonoma Coast, California	Full-bodied, supple tannins, smooth, earthy

SPECIAL BECAUSE	PRICE RANGE	MORE INFO . . .
Blend of Syrah and Petite Sirah	$12–15	www.hesscollection.com
Good-value pick for chicken, fish, or meat	$15–17	www.kenwoodvineyards.com
Their restaurant was featured in the movie *Sideways*	$28–33	www.hitchingpost2.com
Merlot is this winery's specialty	$20–25	www.markhamvineyards.com
Impressive for its depth and complexity	$50–55	www.duckhorn.com
Producer's signature wine	$25–28	www.lambertbridge.com
Less-expensive alternative to BV's famed Georges de Latour Cabernet	$24–26	www.bvwines.com
Stylish wine delicious with chicken or steak	$42–44	www.trefethen.com
Mostly Sangiovese with dash of Malbec and Cabernet	$18–21	www.ferraricarano.com
Ideal pasta wine from Sangiovese, Merlot, and Syrah	$22–25	www.antinori.it
Gorgeously silky, Sangiovese-based wine	$35–40	www.ruffino.com
Stunner; exclusively in restaurants and from the winery	$47-50	www.merryedwards.com

RESTAURANT DARLINGS: ADVENTUROUS WHITES AND BUBBLY

PRODUCER	WINE NAME	FROM	STYLE PROFILE
Bründlmayer	Grüner Veltliner "Alte Reben"	Kamptal, Austria	Medium-bodied, crisp, minerally
Selbach-Oster	Riesling Kabinett	Mosel-Saar-Ruwer, Germany	Light-bodied, racy, off-dry
Trimbach	Riesling "Cuvée Frédéric Émile"	Alsace, France	Full-bodied, soft, aromatic
Von Schubert/ Maximin Grünhäuser	Riesling "Abtsberg" Kabinett	Mosel-Saar-Ruwer, Germany	Medium-bodied, crisp, minerally
Robert Sinskey	Pinot Blanc	Los Carneros, California	Full-bodied, crisp, spicy, elegant
Pascal Jolivet	Sancerre	Sancerre, France	Medium-bodied, crisp, minerally
Domaine Laroche	Saint Martin	Chablis, France	Medium-bodied, crisp, minerally
Ca'del Bosco	Franciacorta Brut	Franciacorta, Italy	Medium-bodied sparkler, crisp, elegant

CHEAT SHEET
When to Send Back a Bottle
* * *

MUSTY

Smells like Aunt Ida's basement, which means the wine is "corked." Most likely the culprit is the cork, which can be affected by something called TCA. It won't hurt you but it will dull the wine and cause it to smell like wet cardboard.

SPECIAL BECAUSE	PRICE RANGE	MORE INFO . . .
Ideal choice with fish or spicy fare	$40–44	www.bruendlmayer.com
Great value from leading Mosel winery	$12–14	www.selbach-oster.de
Classic Alsatian producer; wine named after family ancestor	$40–45	www.maison-trimbach.fr
Limited production, so if you see it, order it fast	$30–35	www.vonschubert.de
Foodie wine—vintner's wife is chef Maria Helm Sinskey	$18–20 half bottle	www.robertsinskey.com
Think oysters, scallops, or goat cheese salad	$28–30	www.pascal-jolivet.com
Family-run operation making modern-style Chablis	$22–25	www.larochewines.com
Elegant blend of Chardonnay, Pinot Blanc, and Pinot Noir	$37–42	www.paternowines.com (importer)

VINEGARY

A flawed wine with overtly high levels of acetic acid.

OXIDIZED

Caused by too much exposure to air. The wine might look brownish and smell like Sherry, which is bad unless it's Sherry.

RESTAURANT DARLINGS: ADVENTUROUS REDS

PRODUCER	WINE NAME	FROM	STYLE PROFILE
Domaine Tempier	Rosé	Bandol, France	Light-bodied, light tan bright, earthy
Qupé	Syrah	Central Coast, California	Medium-bodied, suppl tannins, vibrant, earth
Elio Altare	Dolcetto d'Alba	Piedmont, Italy	Medium-bodied, light t fresh, spicy
Allegrini	"La Grola"	Valpolicella Superiore, Italy	Medium-bodied, light t fresh, spicy
Quinta de Roriz	"Reserva"	Douro, Portugal	Full-bodied, supple tan smooth, earthy
Luce della Vite	"Lucente"	Toscana, Italy	Full-bodied, supple tannins, smooth, earth
Whitehaven	Pinot Noir	Marlborough, New Zealand	Medium-bodied, suppl tannins, vibrant, earth
A. Raffanelli	Zinfandel	Dry Creek Valley, California	Full-bodied, supple tan spicy, ripe
Rosenthal, The Malibu Estate	Cabernet Sauvignon	Malibu-Newton Canyon, California	Full-bodied, strong tannins, lush, concentr
Condado de Haza	Ribera del Duero Reserva	Ribera del Duero, Spain	Full-bodied, supple tan smooth, earthy
Seña	Red blend	Aconcagua Valley, Chile	Full-bodied, supple tan smooth, earthy

SPECIAL BECAUSE	PRICE RANGE	MORE INFO . . .
Leading French pink wine made from mostly Mourvèdre	$28–30	www.domainetempier.com
Mostly Syrah with mixture of other Rhône varieties	$20–22	www.qupe.com
Though a dry red, dolcetto means "little sweet one"	$20–23	www.skurnikwines.com (importer)
Blend of Corvina, Rondinella, and Sangiovese	$20–23	www.winebow.com (importer)
Personal favorite; dry red from famous Symington clan	$24–27	www.quintaderoriz.com
Sangiovese/Merlot blend	$24–27	www.foliowine.com (importer)
Decade-old winery on track to become a classic	$25–28	www.whitehaven.co.nz
Limited availability—only in restaurants and at the winery	$30–38	www.arafanelliwinery.com
Unique, sleek red from Los Angeles	$35–38	www.rosenthalestate wines.com
Having steak? Reach for this Tempranillo-based beauty	$38–42	www.condadodehaza.com or www.classicalwines.com (importer)
One of Chile's best; Cabernet Sauvignon, Merlot, Carmenère blend	$72–75	www.sena.cl

Gathering of the Greats
CLASSIC NAMES WORTHY OF THE HYPE

⌒

There are many amazing wines in the world. Only a sliver of those rise to be spoken of as the greatest. I'm fortunate enough to taste many of them, but only rarely. The wines I've listed below rank as my world-class favorites. They're among the most cellarworthy and will improve for decades. You may never get a chance to sample them and are living vicariously through reading this roundup, but consider splurging on a few bottles to share with friends. If you do, please give me a ring.

Want more picks? Check out these lists: Makeover Wines, 25 to Try Before You Die, Glamorous Gift Wines

---

MYTH-BUSTER
French Wines Age Better Than California Wines

* * *

In 1976 British wine retailer and writer Steven Spurrier arranged a blind tasting in Paris for a panel of esteemed French judges. Hailed as a turning point in wine history, the tasting (now known as the Judgment of Paris) pitted top French wines against young California unknowns. Chardonnay from Napa Valley's Chateau Montelena bested the top French white Burgundies. The 1973 Cabernet Sauvignon from Napa's Stag's Leap Wine Cellars beat out top red Bordeaux. The event was so pivotal to the growth of California wine that a bottle of each of the winning wines now rests in the Smithsonian Institution. But the story doesn't end there. In 2006 California again had the gall to defeat Gaul. During a thirty-year anniversary tasting of the original wines, the older French reds were expected to shine. Surprisingly, the decades-old vintages from California took top honors. "Mon dieu!" as the French might say.

GATHERING OF THE GREATS:
WHITE, BUBBLY, AND SWEET

PRODUCER	WINE NAME	FROM	STYLE PROFILE
Joh. Jos. Prüm	Riesling "Wehlener Sonnenuhr" Auslese	Mosel-Saar-Ruwer, Germany	Medium-bodied, aromat off-dry
Château Smith-Haut-Lafitte	Blanc	Pessac-Léognan, Graves, France	Medium-bodied, crisp, minerally
Château Margaux	"Pavillon" Blanc	Margaux, Bordeaux, France	Medium-bodied, crisp, minerally
Didier Dagueneau	Pouilly-Fumé "Pur Sang"	Pouilly-Fumé, Loire Valley, France	Medium-bodied, crisp, minerally
Kistler	Chardonnay "Kistler Vineyard"	Sonoma Valley, California	Full-bodied, crisp, spicy elegant
Peter Michael Winery	Chardonnay "Ma Belle-Fille"	Alexander Valley, California	Full-bodied, crisp, spicy elegant
François Raveneau	Chablis "Blanchot" Grand Cru	Chablis, Burgundy, France	Full-bodied, crisp, spicy elegant
Louis Latour	Bâtard-Montrachet Grand Cru	Bâtard-Montrachet, Burgundy, France	Full-bodied, crisp, spicy elegant
Leeuwin Estate	Chardonnay "Art Series"	Margaret River, Western Australia	Full-bodied. crisp, spicy elegant
Krug	Blanc de Blancs "Clos de Mesnil"	Champagne, France	Full-bodied sparkler, cr rich, toasty
Chateau d'Yquem	Sauternes	Sauternes, Bordeaux, France	Full-bodied, sweet, supple, rich
Dönnhoff	Riesling "Oberhauser Brucke" Eiswein	Nahe, Germany	Full-bodied, sweet, supple, rich

SPECIAL BECAUSE	PRICE RANGE	MORE INFO . . .
Known simply as J.J., this winery is Mosel mastery	$48–54	www.valckenberg.com (importer)
Property has must-visit spa with Merlot facials	$45–50	www.smith-haut-lafitte.com
Sauvignon Blanc–based wines from legendary producer	$45–50	www.chateau-margaux.com/fr
One of the world's best Sauvignon Blanc winemakers	$80–85	www.polanerselections.com (importer)
Limited production but worth the search	$65–70	www.kistlerwine.com
Named for the owner's daughter-in-law; elegant	$90–100	www.petermichael winery.com
Hard to find; improves with minimum five years' cellaring	$125–180	www.rarewineco.com
Vineyard lies between villages of Puligny-Montrachet and Chassagne-Montrachet	$200–250	www.louislatour.com
Stunning Chardonnay from Aussie leader	$65–75	www.leeuwinestate.com.au
My favorite bubbly in the world; limited production	$350–400	www.krug.com
Say "ee-kem" and it means sweet liquid gold	$175–200	www.yquem.fr
Decadent dessert wine that can age for decades	$200–220 half bottle	www.skurnikwines.com (importer)

GATHERING OF THE GREATS: REDS

PRODUCER	WINE NAME	FROM	STYLE PROFILE
Hanzell	Pinot Noir	Sonoma Valley, California	Medium-bodied, supple tannins, vibrant, earthy
Domaine Bouchard Père & Fils	"Le Corton" Grand Cru	Côte de Beaune, France	Medium-bodied, supple tannins, vibrant, earthy
Domaine de la Romanée-Conti	"La Tâche" Grand Cru	Vosne-Romanee, Burgundy, France	Medium-bodied, supple tannins, vibrant, earthy
Paul Jaboulet Aîné	Hermitage "La Chapelle"	Hermitage, France	Full-bodied, supple tannin smooth, earthy
Penfolds	Shiraz "Grange"	South Australia	Full-bodied, supple tannin spicy, ripe
Henschke	Shiraz "Hill of Grace"	Eden Valley, South Australia	Full-bodied, supple tannin spicy, ripe
Stag's Leap Wine Cellars	Cabernet Sauvignon "Cask 23"	Stags Leap District, Napa Valley, California	Full-bodied, strong tannin lush, concentrated
Château Haut-Brion	Grand Cru	Pessac-Léognan, Bordeaux, France	Full-bodied, strong tannin lush, concentrated
Château Cheval-Blanc	Grand Cru	Saint-Emilion, Bordeaux, France	Full-bodied, strong tannin lush, concentrated
Biondi-Santi	Brunello di Montalcino "Il Greppo"	Brunello di Montalcino, Italy	Full-bodied, strong tannin lush, concentrated
Gaja	Cru Barbaresco "Sorì San Lorenzo"	Langhe, Italy	Full-bodied, strong tannin lush, concentrated
Vega Sicilia	"Unico"	Ribera del Duero, Spain	Full-bodied, supple tannin smooth, earthy

SPECIAL BECAUSE	PRICE RANGE	MORE INFO . . .
Hidden gem; Burgundian-style Pinot that needs to age	$85–95	www.hanzell.com
Rare Pinot Noir–based red from top negociant	$100–120	www.bouchard-pereetfils.com
World's most-recognized Pinot producer; just say DRC	$500–525	www.wilsondaniels.com (importer)
Named for small chapel overlooking the vineyards	$130–150	www.jaboulet.com
Classic wine of Australia created by the legendary Max Schubert	$200–225	www.penfolds.com
Cult wine, extremely limited production	$290–320	www.henschke.com.au
Classic Napa Cabernet famous for winning the Paris Tasting	$140–165	www.cask23.com
Personal favorite—was Thomas Jefferson's favorite First-Growth	$190–230	www.haut-brion.com
Velvety texture; world's best Cabernet Franc–based wine	$290–300	www.chateau-cheval-blanc.com
Originator of Brunello style and still at the top	$150–170	www.biondisanti.it
Founded in 1859 and continuously ranks as Barbaresco's best	$275–300	www.paternowines.com (importer)
Tempranillo-based red from Spain's most historic and celebrated producer	$250–300	www.vega-sicilia.com

Twenty-Five to Try Before You Die

PERSONAL FAVORITES YOU MUST TRY

∞

Before the great beyond calls what does your to-do list look like? Learn a foreign language, trek the Himalayas, see the Great Pyramids? Think about adding a roundup of wines to try. My selections offer immense pleasure and cost a lot less than a trip to Egypt. These wines meet the following criteria:

- Are great, but not necessarily famous.
- Are not over-the-top expensive in most cases.
- Mostly can be found with a small amount of effort.

Want more picks? Check out these lists: Makeover Wines, Gathering of the Greats, Glamorous Gift Wines, Girls' Night In

WINE ABCS
Phylloxera

* * *

In the mid-to-late 1800s most European vineyards were devastated by a louse named phylloxera. This tiny aphid-like insect eats grape vines and slowly kills them. In order to save the wine business, European vines were essentially cut-and-pasted (called grafting) onto rootstocks from phylloxera-resistant native American vines. California and other domestic vineyards fared no better than those in Europe. By the early 1900s, this little bug had crippled the world's wine industry, which took decades to recover. However, vineyards in remote Chile, Spain, and parts of Australia escaped the onslaught of the disease, and today boast some of the only pre-phylloxera vines in the world.

RED BORDEAUX CHEAT SHEET
Deciphering the Label to Get
What You Want

* * *

Bordeaux is essentially split by rivers into two regions popularly known as the Left Bank and the Right Bank. The primary red grape varieties planted include Merlot, Cabernet Sauvignon, Cabernet Franc, Petite Verdot, and Malbec.

LEFT BANK

Cabernet Sauvignon is the Lord of the Left Bank because of the gravelly soils and temperate weather. These wines tend to be very structured, tannic, and age-worthy yet elegant. Recognizable appellations on the Left Bank include the larger Médoc and Haut-Médoc regions and sub-appellations such as Saint-Estèphe, Pauillac, Saint-Julien, and Margaux. Graves, a smaller winegrowing area located on the outskirts of the city of Bordeaux, is famous for its intense reds.

Classification of 1855: *The Bordeaux trade "classified" producers in the Médoc region (and one in Graves) by quality level. They were organized into five categories, from First Growths to Fifth Growths.*

Cru Bourgeois: *Best values of all Bordeaux. This is a group of high-quality producers in the Médoc that weren't included in the 1855 classification, but make delicious, affordable wine. Look for the words* Cru Bourgeois *on the label.*

RIGHT BANK

The Right Bank's slightly cooler climate and clay soils are the reason Merlot and Cabernet Franc reign supreme. If you crave plush, floral reds, search for wines from Right Bank spots such as Saint-Emilion, Pomerol, Côtes de Castillon, and Fronsac.

BURGUNDY CHEAT SHEET
Deciphering the Label to Get What You Want

* * *

Burgundy is broken down into five main regions going from north to south:

Chablis: *A small region at the northern tip of Burgundy that produces some of the most distinctive Chardonnays in the world: crisp, minerally, and complex.*

Côte d'Or: *This Golden Slope is what most people refer to when they talk about the source of Burgundy's top wines. A mere thirty miles in length, this little strip of land is broken into two distinctive regions roughly separated by the city of Beaune. The Côte de Nuits is located to the north of Beaune and is focused on world-class reds. The Côte de Beaune lies to the south of Beaune, and although reds are grown there, it is home to the majority of great whites of Burgundy. Within its boundaries lie Meursault, Puligny-Montrachet, and Chassagne-Montrachet.*

Côte Chalonnaise: *South of the Côte de Beaune, it produces good wines in places such as Rully and Montagny.*

Côte Maconnais: *The place for value Chardonnays such as those labeled Saint-Veran and Macon-Villages, but it's recognized as the home of Pouilly-Fuissé wines.*

Beaujolais: *A familiar name that's not often associated with Burgundy, but it's the largest growing area of the whole region and lies the farthest south. Reds coming from Beaujolais are made from the Gamay grape.*

TWENTY-FIVE TO TRY BEFORE YOU DIE

PRODUCER	WINE NAME	FROM	STYLE PROFILE
Dr. Loosen / Chateau Ste. Michelle	Riesling "Eroica"	Columbia Valley, Washington	Medium-bodied, aromatic, off-dry
Fritz Haag	Riesling Spätlese "Brauenberger Juffer-Sonnenhur"	Mosel-Saar-Ruwer, Germany	Medium-bodied, aromatic, off-dry
Pegasus Bay	Riesling	Waipara, New Zealand	Full-bodied, crisp, spicy, elegant
Franciscan Oakville Estate	Chardonnay "Cuvée Sauvage"	Napa Valley, California	Full-bodied, creamy, oaky, ripe
Testarossa	Chardonnay "Sleepy Hollow Vineyard"	Santa Lucia Highlands, California	Full-bodied, crisp, spicy, elegant
Domaine Leflaive	Puligny-Montrachet "Clavoillon" 1er Cru	Puligny-Montrachet, Burgundy, France	Full-bodied, crisp, spicy, elegant
Craggy Range	Pinot Noir "Te Muna Road Vineyard"	Martinborough, New Zealand	Medium-bodied, supple tannins, vibrant, earthy
Siduri Wines	Pinot Noir "Pisoni Vineyard"	Santa Lucia Highlands, California	Medium-bodied, supple tannins, vibrant, earthy
Domaine Drouhin	Pinot Noir "Laurène"	Willamette Valley, Oregon	Medium-bodied, supple tannins, vibrant, earthy
Thibault Liger-Belair	Clos-Vougeot	Clos-Vougeot, Burgundy, France	Full-bodied, supple tannins, smooth, earthy
Pepper Bridge Winery	Merlot	Walla Walla, Washington	Full-bodied, strong tannins, lush, concentrated
Bodega Numanthia	Numanthia	Toro, Spain	Full-bodied, strong tannins, lush, concentrated
Achaval Ferrer	Malbec "Finca Altamira"	Mendoza, Argentina	Full-bodied, strong tannins, lush, concentrated

SPECIAL BECAUSE	PRICE RANGE	MORE INFO . . .
Joint venture of German star and Washington's founding winery	$20–22	www.ste-michelle.com
Haag's stunner from nearly-vertical, slate-soiled vineyard	$30–34	www.weingut-fritz-haag.de or www.germanwine.net (importer)
Ageworthy Alsatian-styled dry Riesling	$27–32	www.pegasusbay.com
Named for wild yeasts used to make the wine	$34–38	www.franciscan.com
Personal favorite; complex, vineyard-designated wine	$38–42	www.testarossa.com
Cellar-worthy Chardonnay from classic producer	$110–115	www.wilsondaniels.com (importer)
Stunning wines; one of the world's most beautiful properties	$35–39	www.craggyrange.com
Adam and Diana Lee craft top-notch Pinots; limited production	$45–50	www.siduri.com
Named for winemaker Véronique Drouhin's daughter	$55–60	www.domainedrouhin.com
Limited production, silky Pinot Noir from historic vineyard	$125–135	www.vineyardbrands.com (importer)
Dense, rich Merlot from winemaker Jean-Francois Pellet	$48–52	www.pepperbridge.com
Made from old-vine Tempranillo that's like velvet; must buy	$40–45	www.jorgeordonez.com (importer)
Limited availability; cultlike status	$60–65	www.achaval-ferrer.com

(continued)

TWENTY-FIVE TO TRY BEFORE YOU DIE

PRODUCER	WINE NAME	FROM	STYLE PROFILE
Château Palmer	"Alter Ego de Palmer"	Margaux, Bordeaux, France	Full-bodied, supple tannins, smooth, earthy
Château Lynch-Bages	Grand Cru Classe	Pauillac, Bordeaux, France	Full-bodied, supple tannins, smooth, earthy
Château Monbousquet	Grand Cru	Saint-Emilion, Bordeaux, France	Full-bodied, strong tannins, lush, concentrated
Lokoya	Cabernet Sauvignon "Mount Veeder"	Napa Valley, California	Full-bodied, strong tannins, lush, concentrated
Katnook Estate	"Odyssey"	Coonawarra, Australia	Full-bodied, strong tannins, lush, concentrated
Antinori	Guado Al Tasso	Bolgheri, Italy	Full-bodied, supple tannins, spicy, ripe
C.V.N.E.	Pagos de Viña Real	Rioja, Spain	Full-bodied, supple tannins, smooth, earthy
Alvaro Palacios	"Finca Dofí"	Priorat, Spain	Full-bodied, supple tannins, smooth, earthy
Paolo Scavino	Barolo "Cannubi"	Barolo, Piedmont, Italy	Full-bodied, supple tannins, smooth, earthy
D'Arenberg	Shiraz/Viognier "Laughing Magpie"	McLaren Vale, South Australia	Full-bodied, supple tannins, spicy, ripe
Château de Beaucastel	Châteauneuf-du-Pape Rouge	Châteauneuf-du-Pape, France	Full-bodied, supple tannins, smooth, earthy
M. Chapoutier	Hermitage "La Sizeranne"	Hermitage, France	Full-bodied, supple tannins, smooth, earthy

SPECIAL BECAUSE	PRICE RANGE	MORE INFO . . .
Great-value second label; Cabernet/ Merlot/Petite Verdot blend	$40–45	www.chateau-palmer.com
Amazing and elegant, just like owner Jean-Michel Cazes	$50–55	www.lynchbages.com
Like drinking velvet; plush, Merlot-based red	$135–150	www.chateaupavie.com
California Cabernet that can age decades; limited production	$200–225	www.lokoya.com
Shows minty complexity of Cabernet Sauvignon from Coonawarra	$52–60	www.katnookestate.com.au
Famous Super Tuscan blend: Cabernet Sauvignon, Merlot, and Syrah	$80–85	www.antinori.it
Silky Tempranillo-based red from classic Rioja producer	$120–125	www.cvne.com
Age-worthy red from Spain's hottest winemaker	$65–70	www.jorgeordonez.com (importer)
Modern-style Barolo from celebrated Cannubi vineyard	$100–115	www.marcdegrazia.com (importer)
Styled after France's Côte-Rôtie; sexy sipper	$35–40	www.darenberg.com.au
Layered, ageworthy red from highly regarded Perrin family	$59–64	www.beaucastel.com
Braille labels adorn this organically grown, Syrah-based stunner	$90–110	www.chapoutier.com or www.paternoimports.com (importer)

Secret Weapon Wines

WINNING CHOICES FOR NOVICE WINE DRINKERS

∞

Some people, like my sister and my neighbor, don't drink much because they haven't found wines they like. I consider it my duty to introduce them to the joys of wine, so this is the list that I recommend. Armed with a case of my "secret weapon" winners, just about anyone can find a wine to love. They meet the following criteria:

- Are lightly sweet, or if not sweet, fruit-forward.
- Sport balanced levels of acidity, deft use of oak, and light tannins (my sister hates wines with "back-talking tannins")
- Carry easy-on-the-wallet price tags

Want more picks? Check out these lists: Picnic Picks, Overlooked Surprises, Spring Wines, Summer Wines, Take-Out Favorites

---

WINE ABCS
White Zinfandel

* * *

Sutter Home Winery in Napa Valley, California, created and named the popular wine made from red Zinfandel grapes. How does it get its pink hue? Once crushed, the grape juice is quickly drained away from the fruit's red skins, leaving a hint of color. The pink juice is then made into an off-dry style of blush wine.

SECRET WEAPON WINES:
A CASE OF SUREFIRE WINNERS

PRODUCER	WINE NAME	FROM	STYLE PROFILE
Michele Chiarlo	Moscato d'Asti	Moscato d'Asti, Italy	Light-bodied, crisp, lightly sweet
Dr. Loosen	Riesling "Dr. L."	Mosel-Saar-Ruwer, Germany	Light-bodied, racy, off-dry
Columbia Winery	"Cellarmaster's Riesling"	Columbia Valley, Washington	Light-bodied, crisp, lightly sweet
Trimbach	Pinot Gris "Reserve"	Alsace, France	Medium-bodied, aromatic, off-dry
Kim Crawford	Sauvignon Blanc	Marlborough, New Zealand	Medium-bodied, racy, herbal
Clay Station	Viognier	Lodi, California	Full-bodied, soft, aromat
Montevina	White Zinfandel	Amador County, California	Light-bodied, light tanni off-dry, juicy
Marqués de Cáceres	Dry Rosé	Rioja, Spain	Light-bodied, light tanni vibrant, fruity
Georges Duboeuf	Beaujolais-Villages	Beaujolais, France	Medium-bodied, light ta fresh, spicy
Meridian	Pinot Noir	California	Medium-bodied, light tar fresh, spicy
Vigne Regali/Banfi	"Rosa Regale" Brachetto d'Acqui	Piedmont, Italy	Light-bodied sparkler, so lightly sweet
Hardys	Sparkling Shiraz	Australia	Full-bodied sparkler, cre lightly sweet

SPECIAL BECAUSE	PRICE RANGE	MORE INFO . . .
Lightly fizzy and only 7 percent alcohol	$9–12 half bottle	www.chiarlo.it
Smells like freshly cut peaches, low alcohol	$10–12	www.drloosen.com
Drink with take-out; serve well chilled	$10–15	www.columbiawinery.com
Easy-drinking, creamy style	$13–15	www.maison-trimbach.fr
Dry white but tastes like pink grapefruit	$15–18	www.kimcrawfordwines.co.nz
Floral aromas and smooth texture	$10–12	www.claystationwine.com
A touch of sweetness graces this pink quaffer	$6–8	www.montevina.com
Great value, ideal all-around food wine	$6–8	www.marquesdecaceres.com
Juicy Gamay-based red to serve chilled	$8–11	www.duboeuf.com
Silky, cherry-scented red that goes with fish or meat	$10–12	www.meridianvineyards.com
Pale red bubbly, perfect pairing with fruit	$16–18	www.vigneregali.com or www.castellobanfi.com
Deep-purple sparkler that works with burritos or chocolate	$20–24	www.hardys.com.au

Twice-the-Price Wines
BARGAIN BOTTLES THAT OVERDELIVER IN QUALITY
∞

When you sample at least a thousand bargain wines each year as I do, you develop an appreciation for producers that overdeliver. The following wines all are priced under $15 though taste better than many bottles costing twice the price. What sets them apart is not only a high-quaffability quotient, but the fact that they showcase a unique character and reflect their origins.

Want more picks? Check out these lists: Wedding Wines, Party Wines, Wines to Watch, Hot Spots, Overlooked Surprises

MYTH BUSTER
More Expensive Wine Is Always Better
* * *

Catch me laughing out loud here. What is "better"? Better with pizza or for putting in the wine cellar? It all depends upon your perspective and your pocketbook. While it is true that some of the world's most-lauded wines are extremely expensive, that doesn't make them better in every situation. Bottle price is related to a combination of overhead costs such as vineyard land and cellar equipment, as well as supply and demand. Simply because the price tag is higher doesn't mean one wine is always better than another. Case in point: When I judge wine competitions, inexpensive wines often take the highest medals, beating out pricier bottles. Why? They tend to be softer, more approachable, and show well in their youth.

TWICE-THE-PRICE WHITES

PRODUCER	WINE NAME	FROM	STYLE PROFILE
S.A. Prüm	Riesling "Essence"	Mosel-Saar-Ruwer, Germany	Light-bodied, racy, off-dry
Annie's Lane	Riesling	Clare Valley, Australia	Medium-bodied, crisp, minerally
Dry Creek Vineyard	Dry Chenin Blanc	Clarksburg, California	Medium-bodied, crisp, minerally
Wildhurst	Sauvignon Blanc "Reserve"	Lake County, California	Medium-bodied, racy, herbal
RedCliffe	Sauvignon Blanc	Marlborough, New Zealand	Medium-bodied, racy, herbal
Veramonte	Sauvignon Blanc	Casablanca Valley, Chile	Medium-bodied, racy, herbal
Rancho Zabaco	Sauvignon Blanc "Reserve"	Sonoma County, California	Medium-full-bodied, crisp, fruity
Cousiño-Macul	Chardonnay	Maipo Valley, Chile	Medium-bodied, light oak, juicy
Raimat	Chardonnay	Costers del Segre, Spain	Medium-full-bodied, crisp, fruity
Concannon	Chardonnay "Selected Vineyards"	Central Coast, California	Medium-full-bodied, crisp, fruity
Bonterra	Chardonnay	Mendocino County, California	Medium-full bodied, crisp, fruity
Pepperwood Grove	Viognier	California	Full-bodied, soft, aromatic
Jewel	Viognier	Lodi, California	Full-bodied, soft, aromat

SPECIAL BECAUSE	PRICE RANGE	MORE INFO . . .
Highly regarded producer captures essence of the Mosel	$8–10	www.sapruem.com or www.palmbayimports.com
Personal favorite; dry style loaded with lemon/lime fruitiness	$12–14	www.annieslane.com.au
Unique white from Zinfandel specialist	$10–12	www.drycreekvineyards.com
Sauvignon Blanc with a splash of Sémillon	$10–12	www.wildhurst.com
Embodies signature Marlborough style	$10–12	www.palmbayimports.com (importer)
Casablanca is a hot spot for cool wines	$7–10	www.veramonte.com
Like drinking bottled sunshine	$12–15	www.ranchozabaco.com
Classic Chilean producer; family-owned	$7–9	www.cousinomacul.cl
Creamy style but no oak barrels used	$7–9	www.raimat.com
Burgundian-style elegance but with lush fruitiness	$9–11	www.concannonvineyard.com
Terrific value for wine from certified organic vineyards	$11–13	www.bonterra.com
Brand from Sonoma's Don Sebastiani and sons	$8–10	www.donandsons.com
Great brand for bargain hunters	$10–11	www.jewelwine.com

TWICE-THE-PRICE REDS

PRODUCER	WINE NAME	FROM	STYLE PROFILE
Capçanes	Mas Donis "Barrica"	Montsant, Spain	Medium-bodied, supple tannins, vibrant, earthy
Falesco	Vitiano Rosso	Umbria, Italy	Medium-bodied, light tan fresh, spicy
Los Vascos	Cabernet Sauvignon	Colchagua Valley, Chile	Medium-bodied, supple tannins, vibrant, earthy
Altano	Dry red wine	Douro, Portugal	Medium-bodied, supple tannins, vibrant, earthy
Osborne	Tempranillo/Shiraz "Solaz"	Tierra de Castilla, Spain	Medium-bodied, supple tannins, smooth, juicy
Laurel Glen	REDS	Lodi, California	Medium-bodied, supple tannins, smooth, juicy
Telmo Rodriguez	Dehesa Gago	Toro, Spain	Full-bodied, supple tanni smooth, earthy
A-Mano	Primitivo	Puglia, Italy	Medium-full-bodied, supp tannins, vibrant, juicy
Rosemount Estate	Shiraz "Diamond Label"	South Eastern Australia	Full-bodied, supple tanni spicy, ripe
Cameron Hughes	Pinot Noir "Lot Series"	Monterey County, California	Medium-bodied, light tan fresh, spicy
Columbia Crest	Cabernet Sauvignon "Grand Estates"	Columbia Valley, Washington	Medium-full-bodied, supp tannins, vibrant, juicy
Catena	Malbec "Alamos"	Mendoza, Argentina	Medium-full-bodied, supp tannins, vibrant, juicy
Bogle Vineyards	Petite Sirah	Clarksburg, California	Full-bodied, supple tannir spicy, ripe

SPECIAL BECAUSE	PRICE RANGE	MORE INFO . . .
Personal favorite; buy by the case	$10–12	www.cellercapcanes.com
From winemaker Riccardo Cotarella; remarkable value for Sangiovese blend	$8–10	www.falesco.it or www.winebow.com (importer)
French pedigree as part of Domaines Barons de Rothschild	$9–11	www.lafite.com
Dry red wine; Tinta Roriz and Touriga Francesa blend	$7–9	www.symington.com
Spain is the source for red wine value	$8–10	www.osbornesolaz.com
Mostly Zinfandel with dash of Petite Sirah	$8–10	www.laurelglen.com
Seductive Tempranillo from hot winemaker Telmo Rodriguez	$12–14	www.jorgeordonez.com (importer)
A-mano means handmade; Primitivo is Italian Zinfandel	$8–10	www.empson.com (importer)
High-volume, popular wine but packs quality punch	$9–10	www.rosemountestate.com
Hughes, a negociant, blends surplus juice into complex wines	$10–13	www.chwine.com
Washington's value leader; superior quality	$10–12	www.columbia-crest.com
Flagship producer in Argentina whose Alamos brand rocks	$7–9	www.nicolascatena.com
Widely available sipper from underappreciated area of Clarksburg	$10–12	www.boglewinery.com

Makeover Wines

EXPENSIVE WINES WITH SIMILAR-TASTING, LESS
EXPENSIVE ALTERNATIVES

Like television shows focusing on home remodeling or magazines showcasing an expensive designer suit with a less-expensive option, my wine makeovers highlight pricey bottles with lower-cost alternatives. The similarity can be remarkable. How do you get the same character in wines with steep variability in prices? Play mix and match with the following elements:

- **Region:** You can find similar styles across regions.
- **Wine Type/Variety:** Hunt out the same wine type from different producers and places.
- **Classification/Style:** Sample varying levels of quality within wine types. For example, compare a Grand Cru Burgundy with a less expensive Village wine or Vintage Port with a similarly-styled Late-Bottled Vintage. The cheaper wine might not be as ageworthy or intense, but offer more immediate pleasure for half the price.
- **Producer:** Many wineries have tiers of quality. Sometimes you'd be surprised how close they are because grapes that didn't make the cut for the most expensive wine go straight into bottle for the "second" label or wine.

Want more picks? Check out these lists: Gathering of the Greats, Twice-the-Price Wines, Holiday Spirit

START WITH	MAKEOVER WINE	WHY IT WORKS . . .
Georges Roumier, **Chambolle Musigny** "Les Amoureuses," Burgundy, France ($100–120) www.roumier.com	Simon Bize & Fils, "Aux Grands Liards" **Savigny-les-Beaune**, Burgundy, France ($40–45) www.vineyardbrands .com Or Kim Crawford, Pinot Noir, Marlborough, New Zealand ($16–18) www.kimcrawford wines.co.nz	**Region:** Though all three of these wines are made from the same grape variety, Pinot Noir, they come from different places. The pricey wine is from a top producer in Chambolle Musigny, which is my favorite appellation in Burgundy. The Pinots are elegant and earthy but with a silky texture. I find the same is true of those coming from a nearby but lesser-known appellation, Savigny-les-Beaune. In terms of finding the same character outside of Burgundy, look to Marlborough, New Zealand. These Pinots share similar touches of earthy complexity and vibrant acidity coupled with silkiness.
Alvaro Palacios, "L'Ermita," **Priorat,** Spain ($300–350) www.jorgeordonez.com	Capçanes, Mas Donis "Barrica," **Montsant,** Spain ($10) www.cellercapcanes.com	**Region:** Priorat is one of the most respected wine regions in Spain and home to expensive bottles. But forming a ring around Priorat is the new appellation of Montsant. Both areas are planted to grape varieties such as Garnacha, Tempranillo, Cariñena, and newcomers Syrah and Cabernet Sauvignon, but wines from Montsant are some of the best deals you can find in Spanish wine.
Ladoucette "Comte Lafond," **Sancerre,** Loire Valley, France ($34–38) www.mmdusa.net (importer)	Henri Pelle, "Morogues," **Menetou-Salon,** Loire Valley, France ($11–13) www.henry-pelle.com	**Region:** Sancerre is a famous spot in France's Loire Valley and is home to some of the world's best Sauvignon Blanc. The neighboring appellation of Menetou-Salon shares

START WITH	MAKEOVER WINE	WHY IT WORKS . . .
		similar limestone soil, which imparts the telltale minerality to the wines. Wines from this little-known spot offer great value for lovers of Sauvignon Blanc.
Silvio Nardi, **Brunello di Montalcino,** Italy ($58) www.tenutenardi.com Or Altesino, **Brunello di Montalcino,** Italy ($50–55) www.altesino.it	Silvio Nardi, **Rosso di Montalcino,** Italy ($27) www.tenutenardi.com Or Altesino, **Rosso di Montalcino,** Italy ($19–24) www.altesino.it	**Class/Style:** Rosso is what I call "Baby Brunello." Both Brunello di Montalcino and Rosso di Montalcino come from the Tuscany region of Italy surrounding the hill-side village of Montalcino. Both are made with Sangiovese Grosso (otherwise known as Brunello) grapes, but Rosso is younger, less tannic, and ready to drink upon release. Brunello is more structured and ageworthy. Usually top producers produce both wines.
Masi **Amarone della Valpolicella** "Campolongo di Torbe" Veneto, Italy ($100) www.masi.it	Masi, "Campofiorin" **Ripasso,** Veneto, Italy ($15) www.masi.it	**Class/Style:** Valpolicella is a spot in northern Italy's Veneto region planted to Italian grapes such as Corvina, Molinara, and Rondinella. When processed normally, the resulting wine is simply called Valpolicella. To make rare, pricey Amarone, the grapes are dried on mats or bins to concentrate the flavors. Essentially raisins when they're pressed, the grapes produce an intense, chewy, dry red wine called Amarone (*Recioto della Valpolicella* is a sweet version). To make a Ripasso-style wine, the dried grapes that make Amarone are used like a coffee

START WITH	MAKEOVER WINE	WHY IT WORKS . . .
		filter and Valpolicella wine is poured over them, or *repassed*, to seep in more complexity and flavor. Ripasso wines are great deals.
Taylor Fladgate, **Vintage Porto,** Oporto, Portual ($ 90–100) www.taylor.pt	Taylor Fladgate, **Late-Bottled Vintage "LBV,"** Oporto, Portual ($22–25) www.taylor.pt	**Class/Style:** One of the best makeovers you can find is to pour a Late-Bottled Vintage (LBV) Port alongside a Vintage Port. Both are bottle-aged Ports that share chocolaty richness, but LBV is already aged and ready to drink, while Vintage Port should be cellared. Top producers often make both styles, and LBV versions can be uncanny in their likeness to Vintage Port.
E. Guigal, **"La Mouline,"** Côte-Rôtie, Rhone Valley, France ($200) www.guigal.com	McCrea Cellars, **Syrah "Cuvée Orleans,"** Yakima Valley, Washington ($50) www.mccreacellars.com Or d'Arenberg, **Shiraz/Viognier** "Laughing Magpie," McLaren Vale, Australia ($34) www.darenberg.com.au	**Wine Type:** Côte-Rôtie is a small hillside appellation in the northern Rhône region of France. Syrah grapes form the basis of the wine, but Côte-Rôtie's unique signature is that it's cofermented with a dash of the white grape Viognier. This combination makes the red wine more floral and elegant with smoky overtones. Outside of Côte-Rôtie, other producers are now copying the unique technique and making Shiraz (or Syrah)/Viognier blends.
Paul Jaboulet Aîné, **Hermitage Blanc** "Le Chevalier de Stérimberg,"	Torbreck, **"VMR,"** Barossa Valley, Australia ($29–33) www.torbreck.com	**Wine Type:** White Hermitage wines are rare and beautiful. The Jaboulet is a blend of white grapes Marsanne and

START WITH	MAKEOVER WINE	WHY IT WORKS . . .
Hermitage, France ($60–65) www.jaboulet.com		Roussanne. It's spicy, plush, and stylish. For similar character, try the Aussie Rhône specialist, Torbreck. Their VMR (stands for Viognier, Marsanne, Roussanne) adds the northern Rhône variety Viognier to the mix, but still captures the nutty richness of the Hermitage blanc.
Dominio de Pingus, "Flor de Pingus," **Ribera del Duero,** Spain ($70–75)	Artesa, **Tempranillo,** Alexander Valley, California ($22–25) www.artesawinery.com	**Wine Type:** Pingus is Spain's hottest cult winery so making over their less expensive "Flor" bottling was a tough one. The wine, made primarily with the Tempranillo grape, is intensely fruity and oaky, yet sleek. It's very New World in style, so I looked outside Spain for inspiration. I found it in the beautifully built Tempranillo from California's Artesa Winery. Artesa is owned by a Spanish company, Codorníu, so it makes sense there's a Spanish sensibility to the wine. You'll be amazed at the similarity of these two bottles.
Penfolds "Grange" Shiraz, South Australia ($200–225) www.penfolds.com	**Penfolds,** "Magill Estate" Shiraz, South Australia ($50) www.penfolds.com	**Producer:** Penfolds is the classic South Australia producer and Grange is Australia's most celebrated wine. Recognized as one of the world's top versions of Shiraz, I adore the plush, decadent wine. My favorite Shiraz from Penfolds, however, is the Magill Estate, which is supple and sexy.

START WITH	MAKEOVER WINE	WHY IT WORKS . . .
Yalumba, Viognier "Virgilius" Eden Valley, South Australia ($38–42) www.yalumba.com	**Yalumba,** "Y Series" Viognier, South Australia ($9–11) www.yalumba.com	**Producer:** Yalumba is another top-notch Australian brand known for their stylish bottlings of not only red wine, but white. They produce a world-class Viognier named "Virgilius" yet serve up a delicious version under the affordable Y Series label.
Louis Roederer, "Cristal" Champagne, France ($200–225) www.champagne roederer.com	**Roederer Estate**, "L'Ermitage," Anderson Valley, California ($40–45) Or **Roederer Estate**, Brut NV Mendocino County, California ($17–20) www.roedererestate.net	**Producer:** When I think of Champagne, Cristal comes to mind. This iconic wine—made by the famed house of Louis Roederer—is one of France's best-known exports. Roederer has set up shop in California, too, and their Roederer Estate bottlings rival Champagne. The "L'Ermitage" is layered and lush but because it's more fruit-driven than Cristal, in some ways it's more pleasing. Roederer Estate's regular Brut is simply the best deal you can find in sparkling wine. I poured this wine alongside Cristal during an appearance on NBC's *Today* show and the host chose this as the preferred wine!

Quick-Pick Guides

Style/Profile Index

Medium-bodied, supple tannins, smooth, juicy

Region/Producer Index

Wine Type/Price Index

WHITES

Chardonnay/White Burgundy

BARGAIN WINES (LESS THAN $15)

Alice White, 34
Beringer Vineyards, "Founders' Estate," 102
Black Swan, Chardonnay/Semillon, 124, 182
Bonterra, 296
Canyon Road, 62
Carmel Road, 22
Casa Lapostolle, 226
Castillo de Monjardin, "El Cerezo," 22
Columbia Crest, "Grand Estates," 102
Concannon, "Selected Vineyards," 296
Cousiño-Macul, 296
Dtour Wines, 28
Fetzer, "Valley Oaks," 34
French Rabbit, 28
Gallo Family Vineyards, 40, 102
Georges Duboeuf, "Réserve," 226
Golan Heights Winery, "Golan," 222
J. Lohr, "Riverstone," 116
Jackaroo, 244
Jacob's Creek, 22
Lagaria, 168
Lindemans, "Bin 65," 34
Meridian Vineyards, 40
Murphy-Goode, "Tin Roof," 168
Penfolds, "Thomas Hyland," 22
Raimat, 296
Raymond Estates, 148
Red Bicyclette, 148
Ruffino, "Libaio," 22
Santa Julia, "Organica," 216
Sebastiani, 188
Stag's Leap Wine Cellars, "Hawk Crest," 148
Toasted Head Vineyards, 102
Vasse Felix, "Adams Road," 82
Virgin Vines, 48
Wine Cube, 28
Woodbridge Winery, "Ghost Oak Select
   Vineyard Series," 102
Yellow Tail, "Reserve," 244

CLASSIC WINES ($15–$30)

Argyle, "Nuthouse," 124
Beaulieu Vineyards, "Carneros," 148

Bouchard Pere & Fils, Meursault "Les Clous"
   1er Cru, 188
Buty Winery, "Conner Lee Vineyard," 252
Cambria, "Katherine's Vineyard," 40
Ceja, 40
Chateau St. Jean, "Belle Terre Vineyard," 116
Clos du Bois, "Calcaire," 268
Domaine des Comtes Lafon, Macon-Milly-
   Lamartine, 252
Domaine Laroche, "Saint Martin" Chablis,
   272
Domaine Louis Moreau, Chablis, 168
Evans & Tate, 82
Flora Springs, "Barrel Fermented," 188
Forgeron Cellars, 252
Gallo Family Vineyards, "Laguna," 268
Hamilton Russell Vineyards, 124
The Hess Collection, 148
J. Lynne, 40
Jeriko Estates, 216
Joseph Drouhin, "Véro," 64
Kendall-Jackson, "Grand Reserve," 268
Kumeu River, "Village," 124
Louis Jadot, Pouilly-Fuissé, 148
Morgan Winery, "Metallico," 268
Sonoma-Cutrer, "Russian River Ranches,"
   268
Sterling, 116
Villa Mt. Eden, "Grand Reserve-Bien Nacido
   Vineyard," 188
Voyager Estate, 82

LUXURY WINES (MORE THAN $30)

Antinori/Cervaro della Sala, 48
Beringer, "Private Reserve," 232
Chateau Montelena, 232
Domaine Leflaive, Puligny-Montrachet
   "Clavoillon" 1er Cru, 286
Domaine Louis Moreau, Chablis "1er Cru
   Vaillons," 148
Far Niente, 232
Fleming-Jenkins, 248
Franciscan Oakville Estate, "Cuvée Sauvage,"
   286
François Raveneau, Chablis "Blanchot"
   Grand Cru, 278
Frank Family Vineyards, 232
Joseph Drouhin, Puligny-Montrachet, 188

Tarapaca, Carmenère, 92
Tenuta Rapitalà, "Nu har" Nero d'Avola Blend, 74
Two Brothers Winery, "Big Tattoo Red," 228
Viña Chocalán, Carmenère, 92
Viña MontGras, "Quatro" Reserva, 228
Wrongo Dongo, Monastrell, 70

CLASSIC WINES ($15–$30)

Allegrini, "La Grola," 274
Becker Vineyards, Claret, 76
Bodegas Estefania, "Tilenus" Mencía Crianza, 70
Bodegas Pittacum, Mencía "Aurea," 70
Brick House, Gamay Noir, 206
Château des Jacques, Moulin-à-Vent Cru, 206
Dr. Konstantin Frank, Cabernet Franc, 76
Dominio de Tares, Mencía "Baltos," 70
Elio Altare, Dolcetto d'Alba, 200, 274
Joseph Drouhin, Moulin-à-Vent Cru, 206
Marc Bredif, Chinon Rouge, 56
Marcel Lapierre, Morgon, 218
Palivou Vineyards, Agiorgitiko, 80
Pio Cesare, Barbera, 108
Quinta de Crasto, 152
Quinta do Carmo, 126
Quinta de Roriz, "Reserva," 274
Sokol Blosser, "Meditrina," 42
Spiropoulos, Agiorgitiko "Red Stag," 80
Stone Hill, Norton, 76
Zenato, Valpolicella Ripasso, 192

LUXURY WINES (MORE THAN $30)

Allegrini, Amarone della Valpolicella Classico, 192
Antinori, Guado Al Tasso, 288
Arnaldo Caprai, Sagrantino di Montefalco "Collepiano," 254
Château Musar, Rouge, 254
Fontanafredda, Barolo, 112
Fratelli Revello, Barolo, 112
Gaia Estate, "Gaia Estate" Agiorgitiko, 80
Gaja, Cru Barbaresco "Sorì San Lorenzo," 280
Marchesi di Barolo, Barolo, 112
Masi Amarone della Valpolicella "Campolongo di Torbe," 302
Paolo Scavino, Barolo "Cannubi," 288
Planeta, "Santa Cecilia" Nero d'Avola, 74
Rubicon Estate, Cabernet Franc, 248
Ruffino, Romitorio di Santedame, 254
Seña, Red Blend, 274
Swanson, "Alexis," 200

SWEETIES AND SPARKLERS

Desserts

BARGAIN WINES (LESS THAN $15)

Broadbent, Madeira "Rainwater," 160
Carmel Winery, Moscato di Carmel, 222
Covey Run, Late-Harvest Riesling, 52

Martin and Weyrich, Allegro Moscato, 158
Washington Hills, Late-Harvest Riesling, 158
Williams Hymbert/Dry Sack Amontillado, 264

CLASSIC WINES ($15–$30)

Beaulieu Vineyards, Muscat de Beaulieu, 160
Blandy's, Madeira "Alvada," 162
Bonny Doon, Framboise, 198
Bonny Doon Vineyards, Muscat "Vin de Glacière," 52, 158
Campbells, Muscat, 162
Castoro Cellars, Late-Harvest Zinfandel, 162
M. Chapoutier, Banyuls, 149
Osborne, Pedro Ximenez "1827" Sweet Sherry, 162
Pillitteri Estates, Riesling Icewine, 78
Quady Winery, "Essensia" Orange Muscat, 62, 158
Ste. Chapelle, Riesling Icewine "Reserve," 76
Yalumba, Muscat "Museum Reserve" NV, 52

LUXURY WINES (MORE THAN $30)

Argiolas, "Angiali," 162
Château Coutet, Sauternes, 162
Château Rieussec, Sauternes, 162
Château Suduiraut, Sauternes, 52
Château d'Yquem, Sauternes, 278
Dönnhoff , Riesling "Oberhauser Brucke" Eiswein, 278
Far Niente, "Dolce," 52
Fèlsina, Vin Santo "Berardenga," 160
Grgich Hills, "Violetta," 44
Inniskillen, Cabernet Franc Icewine, 198
Inniskillin, Icewine "Vidal" Oak-aged, 78
King Estate, "Vin Glacé," 160
Kracher, Cuvée Auslese, 160
Peter Lehmann, Botrytis Semillon, 160
Royal Tokaji Wine Company, Aszu 5 Puttonyos "Red Label," 52
Sanchez Romate, Pedro Ximenez Very Rare Sherry, 198

Ports and Port-Style Wines

BARGAIN WINES (LESS THAN $15)

Cockburn's, Fine Tawny, 152
Dow's, Vintage Porto, 160

CLASSIC WINES ($15–$30)

Croft, LBV, 194
Dow's, Reserve, 154
Offley, LBV, 154
Quinta do Noval, 194
Ramos Pinto, Tawny, 152
Sonoma Valley Port Works, Deco Port, 198
Taylor Fladgate, LBV, 64, 154, 303
W. & J. Graham's, "Six Grapes," Reserve, 154

Warre's, LBV, 194
Warre's, "Otima," 10-year Tawny, 52

Sparklers